RENEWALS 458-4574

DATE DUE

MAY 1

Taiwan's Security
in the Changing
International System

Taiwan's Security in the Changing International System

Dennis Van Vranken Hickey

LYNNE
RIENNER
PUBLISHERS

BOULDER
LONDON

*This book is respectfully dedicated
to the memory of Frank C. C. Kwei
1952–1996*

Published in the United States of America in 1997 by
Lynne Rienner Publishers, Inc.
1800 30th Street, Boulder, Colorado 80301

and in the United Kingdom by
Lynne Rienner Publishers, Inc.
3 Henrietta Street, Covent Garden, London WC2E 8LU

© 1997 by Lynne Rienner Publishers, Inc. All rights reserved

Library of Congress Cataloging-in-Publication Data
Hickey, Dennis Van Vranken.
    Taiwan's security in the changing international system / by Dennis
Van Vranken Hickey.
      p. cm.
    Includes bibliographical references and index.
    ISBN 1-55587-627-7 (hc : alk. paper)
    1. National security—Taiwan. 2. Taiwan—Defenses. 3. Taiwan—
Foreign relations—1945– I. Title.
DS799.847.H53   1997
355'.033051249—dc20   96-34628
                                                                                                                    CIP

British Cataloguing in Publication Data
A Cataloguing in Publication record for this book
is available from the British Library.

Printed and bound in the United States of America

        The paper used in this publication meets the requirements
        of the American National Standard for Permanence of
∞   Paper for Printed Library Materials Z39.48-1984.

CONTENTS

List of Tables   vii
Acknowledgments   ix

Introduction   1

PART 1   TAIWAN'S SECURITY ENVIRONMENT

1   Taiwan and National Security   7
2   Taiwan's Military: Structure, Composition, and Issues   15
3   Taiwan's Security Strategy: Policies, Options, and Prospects   37

PART 2   ENHANCEMENTS TO TAIWAN'S SECURITY

4   U.S.-PRC Relations   59
5   Taiwan's Recent Arms Purchases   77
6   Taiwan's Democratization and Economic Clout   93
7   Pragmatic Diplomacy and Taiwan's National Security   113

PART 3   CHALLENGES TO TAIWAN'S SECURITY

8   The Taiwanese Independence Movement   135
9   The PRC Military Buildup and the East Asian Arms Race   153
10   U.S. Foreign Policy in the 1990s   171
11   Conclusions   183

Select Bibliography   203
Index   223
About the Book   233

TABLES

1.1	ROC and PRC Estimates of Taiwan's Indirect Investment in China	10
1.2	Applications for Taiwanese Compatriots Cards Required to Visit Mainland China, 1988–1994	10
2.1	Reservists Classified by Military Service	21
2.2	Comparison of ROC and PRC Military Forces	21
2.3	Parameters for Taiwan's Jet Fighters	24
2.4	Comparison of ROC Ground, Naval, and Air Forces	29
3.1	U.S. Foreign Military Sales Agreements with Taiwan and Commercial Arms Exports to Taiwan: Fiscal Years 1984–1993	40
3.2	Support for Taiwanese Independence	44
4.1	U.S. Foreign Military Sales Agreements with the PRC and Deliveries to the PRC: Fiscal Years 1984–1989	63
4.2	How the U.S. Public Views China	64
4.3	Top Ten U.S. Negative Trade Balances, 1994	64
4.4	Chinese Arms Transfer Agreements and Deliveries to the World, 1986–1993	68
5.1	U.S. Foreign Military Sales Agreements with Taiwan and Commercial Arms Exports to Taiwan: Fiscal Years 1983–1989	84
6.1	Results of Taiwan's 1996 Presidential Election	94
6.2	Taiwanese Poll Ranking ROC Presidents by Contributions to Taiwan's Democracy	96
6.3	Taiwanese Poll Ranking Political Parties by Contributions to the Development of Democracy in Taiwan	97
6.4	Gross National Product of the ROC, 1952–1994	100
6.5	Per Capita National Income in the ROC, 1955–1994	101

6.6	Taiwan's Exports and Imports in World Merchandise Trade, 1994	102
6.7	U.S. Economic Aid to Taiwan, 1951–1968	103
7.1	Nations Having Diplomatic Relations with Taiwan	116
7.2	Taiwan's Unofficial Representative Offices in North and South America	118
7.3	Taiwan's Unofficial Representative Offices in the Asia Pacific Region	118
7.4	Taiwan's Unofficial Representative Offices in the Middle East and Africa	119
7.5	Taiwan's Unofficial Representative Offices in Europe (including Russia)	119
7.6	Taiwan's Membership in International Nongovernmental Organizations	121
9.1	U.S. Estimates of China's 1995 Defense Budget	154
10.1	Trend Toward Isolationism	172
10.2	U.S. Troop Strength	175
10.3	U.S. Department of Defense Budget: Fiscal Years 1990–1997	176
10.4	U.S. Trade Deficit with Taiwan, 1988–1994	177
10.5	Top Ten Deficit Countries in U.S. Trade, 1994	177
11.1	How the U.S. Public Views Taiwan	184
11.2	Public Opinion on the Future Development of Cross-Strait Relations	188

ACKNOWLEDGMENTS

My debts to those who helped me acquire the knowledge and form the opinions expressed in this study are far too numerous to list here. However, I would like to thank Byron Stewart, Tammy Stewart, Willa Garrett, Lynn Cline, and the entire staff at Southwest Missouri State University's Duane Meyer Library for their help in obtaining numerous materials relevant to this study. I would also like to thank Moses Lu, Jeff Yao, Eric Chiang, and the Republic of China's Government Information Office for providing resource materials and arranging interviews with officials in Taipei. Southwest Missouri State University provided financial support that helped me to complete this and numerous other scholarly endeavors, and I am grateful for their assistance. I would also like to express my appreciation to both my father and my father-in-law for their support and encouragement. Finally, I would like to thank my wife, Cheng-May, for her patience, endurance, and suggestions while I completed this project. She always will be "the brains in the family."

This book benefited from the astute observations and insights of colleagues at several professional meetings. The original idea for this study was generated by comments on my paper, "Taiwan's Security in the Post–Cold War Era," delivered at the 1994 annual meeting of the American Political Science Association in New York City. Chapter 3 is a revised and updated version of a paper, "Taiwan's Security Strategy in the Post–Cold War World: Policies, Options and Prospects," commissioned by the Los Alamos National Laboratory's Center for National Security Studies and presented at a Center for Strategic and International Studies workshop in Washington, D.C., on June 20, 1994. The concluding chapter includes some of my thoughts expressed in the study, "Taiwan's Security During the Short- to Medium-Term Future." This paper was delivered at the Atlantic Council of the United States conference, Developments in Taiwan to 2020: Implications for Cross-Strait Relations and for U.S. Policy, in Washington, D.C., on November 17, 1994.

Despite the best efforts and advice of numerous friends and colleagues, errors undoubtedly remain in the text. In appreciation for their advice and assistance, I do not mean to suggest that any of the above individuals or institutions agree with the ideas in this book. I assume sole responsibility.

—Dennis Van Vranken Hickey

INTRODUCTION

Things are changing in Taiwan. Martial law has been lifted, opposition parties have formed, free and popular elections have been held, and the government has ended its ban on economic and cultural exchanges with the People's Republic of China (PRC). On the international front, Taipei is seeking to join (or rejoin) international financial organizations, strengthen its substantive ties with other states, and return to the United Nations.

The extraordinary political, economic, and social changes occurring within Taiwan are beginning to attract increased interest among policymakers, members of the academic community, and the media. Prior to the "missile crises" of 1995 and 1996, however, surprisingly little attention focused on Taiwan's defenses.[1] This undertaking has been energized by the conviction that one of the most critical tasks facing a government today is the need to reassess its security now that the Cold War has come to an end. It represents the first comprehensive effort to analyze how recent transformations in the international system—changes that cannot be overstated—are affecting Taiwan's security.

This book examines Taiwan's security environment in the post–Cold War era. It is concerned primarily with questions about the impact of changes that have occurred at what is often described as the global or systemic level in international relations. This book demonstrates how recent transformations in the international system are generating *both* opportunities and challenges for Taipei.

On balance, this study suggests that the end of the Cold War and a conjunction of several long-term trends are combining to enhance Taiwan's security. In this respect, the recent modifications in the global system augur well for the island's security. However, changes occurring at another level of analysis—namely, domestic political developments within mainland China—may offset some of the gains generated by systemic changes. Indeed, these domestic considerations played a paramount role in the perilous deterioration in cross-Strait relations during 1995 and 1996.

This study covers the period from 1989, a watershed year in international relations, to 1996. Before 1989, the international system continued to be steered primarily by Cold War calculations, but afterward that structure crumbled. The recent transformations in global politics—changes that began in Eastern Europe during 1989 and culminated in the collapse of the Soviet Union in 1991—have opened a whole new range of problems. Those who make and execute policy are now forced to reexamine the entire nature of challenges facing their respective countries.

This volume is divided into several parts. The first three chapters provide readers with an introduction to Taiwan's security environment. Chapter 1 briefly explores the various meanings of the phrase "national security," and shows how officials in Taipei take a broad view of the island's security concerns. Chapter 2 outlines the structure and composition of Taiwan's armed services. It also provides an overview of key issues affecting Taiwan's military establishment. Chapter 3 examines Taiwan's current defensive strategy and explores several options that the island might consider to augment its security.

The next four chapters show how recent transformations in the international system are generating opportunities for Taipei. Chapter 4 explains why strains in U.S.-PRC relations—tensions elevated in part by the end of the Cold War and the accompanying demise of the so-called strategic triangle—are helping Taipei strengthen its ties with Washington. Chapter 5 examines Taiwan's recent arms purchases and suggests that Western governments increasingly view arms sales to Taiwan as a means by which key corporations can make it through the painful transition period away from a Cold War economy. These weapons boost the island's defensive capabilities and thereby deter PRC aggression. Chapter 6 analyzes Taiwan's democratization and growing economic clout. It contends that these considerations have led some governments to upgrade relations with Taiwan—several have elevated contacts with Taipei to a level just short of official recognition. These diplomatic successes, in turn, enhance the international standing of the Republic of China (ROC), bolster the position that it is a political entity, and undermine the People's Republic of China's claims of sovereignty over the island. Chapter 7 analyzes Taipei's new approach to foreign policy: pragmatic diplomacy. It explains that pragmatic diplomacy is finding a receptive audience in the post–Cold War world and shows how Taiwan's diplomatic breakthroughs reinforce the island's security.

Chapters 8, 9, and 10 suggest that even though some developments seem to contribute to Taiwan's security, the end of the Cold War also represents challenges for Taipei. Chapter 8 examines the drive for Taiwanese independence—a movement emboldened by what it perceives to be a global trend toward "self-determination" and "separatism." Chapter 9 discusses Beijing's acquisition of sophisticated Soviet weaponry and military technology and the accompanying dangers for Taiwan. The chapter also analyzes the East Asian arms race and its likely consequences. Chapter 10 examines the retreat of the United States from its leadership role in international affairs and explains why Washington's new emphasis on economic matters could complicate the U.S.-ROC security dyad.

Chapter 11, the concluding chapter, suggests that even though the end of the Cold War and a conjunction of several long-term trends are combining to enhance Taiwan's security, real threats to Taiwan remain. Especially worrisome are domestic political developments occurring within mainland China. These could offset some of the advantages engendered by systemic changes, and they hold important implications for U.S. policy.

Note

1. Notable exceptions to this observation include studies completed by a small number of dedicated security analysts including Martin L. Lasater, Cheng-yi Lin, Andrew Yang, and Peter Kienhong Yu.

Part 1

TAIWAN'S SECURITY ENVIRONMENT

1

Taiwan and National Security

The end of the era of superpower rivalry leaves a notable void that affects both decisionmakers and analysts. Many national security issues—concerns that seemed focused and clear during the Cold War—have become blurred. Is there a new meaning for the phrase "national security"? Have Taiwan's security interests changed? What new threats to Taiwan's security are being generated by systemic transformations, and how important are they? These are some of the questions addressed in this book.

The Concept of National Security

Like many other concepts and phrases employed in the field of international relations, national security is a term that means widely differing things to different people. Some contend that it signifies only the "protection of the nation's people and territories against physical assault and, in that narrow sense, is roughly equivalent to the traditionally used term, *defense*."[1] Others, however, believe that it has a more extensive meaning. The various definitions provided below underscore the ambiguity of the concept:

- Arnold Wolfers (1962): "Security, in an objective sense, measures the absence of threats to acquired values, in a subjective sense, the absence of fear that such values will be attacked."[2]
- Amos Jordan and William Taylor (1989): "National security has a more extensive meaning than protection from physical harm; it also implies protection, through a variety of means, of vital economic and political interests, the loss of which could threaten fundamental values and the vitality of the state."[3]
- Joseph Romm (1993): "The objective of national security is to sustain freedom from foreign dictation and improvement of living standards in an environmentally sustainable fashion."[4]
- Douglas Murray and Paul Viotti (1994): "The protection of a nation from all types of external aggression, espionage, hostile reconnais-

sance, sabotage, subversion, annoyance, and other inimical influences."[5]

The term "national security" remains a "weakly conceptualized, ambiguously defined, but politically powerful concept."[6] As one U.S. lawmaker lamented, the term is "such an ill-defined phrase that no one can give you a definition."[7] Perhaps, as Barry Buzan observed, "the nature of security defies pursuit of an agreed general definition."[8]

With the world shifting away from an age of superpower rivalry and strategic confrontation to an era of fierce economic competition, those definitions that identify *both* military and nonmilitary problems as serious threats to a nation's security are gaining widespread acceptance.[9] Taiwanese authorities have embraced this broadly based concept of national security.

Taiwan's National Security

Officials in Taipei take a broad view of the island's security concerns. According to Taiwan's *1992 National Defense Report,* "the main objective of national security is to protect the national interests from being violated and threatened."[10] These interests include the following:

- Under the stipulation of the ROC constitution, to safeguard all rights and interests to reach the goal of national unification
- To ensure territorial integrity and sovereignty
- To protect people's rights of security from invasion
- To maintain economic prosperity and social stability[11]

It is clear that Taiwan's security concerns are much broader than those relating to the immediate danger of an attack from the People's Republic of China. For example, the economic dimensions of Taiwan's security are critically important to the island's survival. But Taiwanese authorities emphasize that "the most serious threat to our national security at present is still the Chicom's [PRC's] use of force against Taiwan."[12] Therefore, much of the discussion in this book shows how the end of the Cold War affects China's threat to Taiwan's security.

China's Threat to Taiwan

For roughly three decades, the PRC threatened to "liberate" Taiwan. In fact, on two separate occasions (1954 and 1958), Beijing attempted to seize territory under Taipei's control. In the late 1970s, however, the PRC dropped this policy.

Beijing now pushes its "one country, two systems" formula for the "peaceful unification" of China. Under this arrangement, Taiwan would become a special administrative region of China. Jiang Zemin, general secretary of the Chinese Communist Party, explains:

> As a special administrative region, Taiwan will exercise a high degree of autonomy and enjoy legislative and independent judicial power, including that of final adjudication. It may also retain its armed forces and administer its party, governmental and military systems by itself. The Central Government will not station troops or send administration personnel there. What is more, a number of posts in the Central Government will be made available to Taiwan.[13]

Believing that this formula would jeopardize the security and welfare of the 21 million people on Taiwan, the ROC rejects these terms—a policy that enjoys widespread support in Taiwan. Public opinion polls reveal that almost 80 percent of Taiwan's residents oppose the PRC's "one-country, two systems" proposal.[14]

Taipei has advanced its own formula for national unification. In 1991, Taiwan declared an end to the war with the PRC and adopted the *Guidelines for National Unification*. The *Guidelines* state that China's unification should be achieved in three stages: (1) a short-term phase of exchanges and reciprocity; (2) a medium-term phase of mutual trust and cooperation; and (3) a long-term phase of consultation and unification.[15] Presently, Taipei is attempting to persuade the PRC to respond positively to specific elements in the first phase:

> During the first stage, both sides should not deny the other's existence as a political entity; they should expand people-to-people exchanges; they should push for active economic reform, freedom of expression, and adoption of a democratic rule of law on the Chinese mainland; and they should resolve differences through peaceful means (i.e. renounce the use of force against each other).[16]

ROC officials warn that

> if the Chinese Communists refuse to acknowledge us as a political entity, or refuse continuously to renounce the use of force against us, or refuse to stop interfering with our conduct of external relations under the principle of "one China," then we will not go on to the second stage [of the *Guidelines*], but *remain in the first stage indefinitely* [emphasis added].[17]

Some contend that Taipei's real policy is "a wait-and-see position or a policy of maintaining the status quo."[18]

Adjustments in other areas have accompanied changes in each Chinese government's approach to unification. Economic, cultural, and political exchanges between the two Chinas—contacts unthinkable only several years ago—have become common. Taiwanese trade and investment in the PRC has soared (Table 1.1).[19] Moreover, since travel restrictions were eased in 1987, several million Taiwanese "compatriots" have traveled to the mainland (Table 1.2). Finally, the two governments have established a formal channel for government-to-government communication, albeit an indirect one. The series of "Koo-Wang talks," informal talks named after the leader of each government's unofficial negotiation team, have marked a breakthrough in cross-Strait relations.

Table 1.1 ROC and PRC Estimates of Taiwan's Indirect Investment in China (U.S.$ in millions)

	1991	1992	1993	1994	Estimated total
ROC estimates	174.16	246.99	3,168.41	962.21	4,551.78
PRC estimates	—	5,540	9,970	5,397	24,357

Source: Economic Statistic Monthly Report of the Two Sides of the Taiwan Strait, Number 39 (Taipei: Mainland Affairs Council, November 1995), p. 28. Document provided courtesy of Su Chi, vice chairman, Mainland Affairs Council, Republic of China. Document translated courtesy of Kwei Cheng-May.

Table 1.2 Applications for Taiwanese Compatriots Cards Required to Visit Mainland China, 1988–1994

	Number of applications by Taiwanese compatriots
1988	430,766
1989	530,534
1990	925,768
1991	995,714
1992	1,511,990
1993	1,541,628
1994	1,150,000

Source: People's Republic of China, as reported in *Economic Statistic Monthly Report of the Two Sides of the Taiwan Strait, Number 39* (Taipei: Mainland Affairs Council, November 1995), p. 37. Document provided courtesy of Su Chi, vice chairman, Mainland Affairs Council, Republic of China. Document translated courtesy of Kwei Cheng-May.

Note: Figures reflect only the number of applications for permits, not the number of actual travelers, which could differ substantially.

These transformations in ROC-PRC relations are significant. But they should not be exaggerated. China still refuses to rule out the use of force to take Taiwan. Beijing's 1995 and 1996 military maneuvers and missile tests off Taiwan's coast served to underscore the Communist regime's continued threat to Taipei.

During the mid-1980s, Deng Xiaoping outlined the circumstances under which Beijing would employ coercion to unify China:

> If Taipei leans toward Moscow instead of Washington; if Taipei decided to build nuclear weapons; if Taipei claimed to be an independent state; if Taipei lost internal control as a result of the succession process; or if Taipei continued to reject reunification talks for a long period of time.[20]

With the easing of tensions across the Taiwan Strait and the end of the Cold War, the PRC appears to have dropped some of these conditions.[21]

On March 31, 1993, Premier Li Peng stated that the PRC would use force to take Taiwan only under two conditions:

> China would take resolute measures against Taiwan only under very special circumstances. And I do not hope to see that occur. If the forces of Taiwan independence run rampant, or if there is complete social chaos in Taiwan . . . resolute measures might be taken.[22]

In May 1993, Chen Guoqing, press counselor of the PRC embassy in Washington, D.C., implied that Beijing would use force against Taiwan *only* if the island declared itself independent: "So long as the Taiwan authorities stick to the 'one-China' policy, they should not worry about the process leading to the ultimate unification of the country."[23]

Taiwanese authorities also have identified various situations that might lead Beijing to resort to military action. According to ROC military officials, the PRC would employ force to unify the country under the following circumstances:

- If and when the ROC on Taiwan declares itself independent
- If and when an internal upheaval occurs on the island
- If and when the ROC's armed forces on Taiwan become comparatively weak
- If and when any foreign power interferes in the ROC's internal affairs
- If and when the ROC on Taiwan protractedly refuses to talk with the PRC about the issue of unification
- If and when the ROC on Taiwan develops nuclear weapons[24]

Taiwanese officials also are keenly aware that a power struggle among the PRC's leaders following the death of Deng Xiaoping could undermine the island's security. Indeed, authorities claim that the heightened cross-Strait tensions that followed President Lee Teng-hui's 1995 visit to Cornell University may be traced to China's domestic politics. As Rock Leng, the ROC's foreign affairs spokesman explained, "with uncertainty surrounding the power structure, it is likely that more attention will be drawn to Taiwan's affairs, with a hard line on Taiwan to serve as a bargaining chip."[25]

In sum, Taiwanese authorities believe that there are several circumstances under which Beijing might employ coercion to resolve the unification issue. But they emphasize that, among the considerations that might lead the PRC to attack the island, "the most likely one under which the PRC would invade is if and when the ROC on Taiwan declares itself independent."[26] Consequently, Taiwanese officials contend that "the most important thing for us to do is not to provide them with the excuse . . . independence."[27]

Should Beijing opt to use force against Taiwan, most military analysts believe that an outright assault on the island is unlikely. Taiwanese officials have identified several other military options available to China:

- Deploy operational aircraft to bases along the southeast coast of mainland China, west of Taiwan, with the aim of affecting social stability, industrial production, and harassing the morale of the people of the ROC on Taiwan
- Launch their intermediate-range missiles (with a range of 185–370 miles) against the west coast of Taiwan
- Create fishing disputes in the Taiwan Strait or seize Taiwan's fishing areas; then send naval vessels under the excuse of protecting their fishing boats to repulse Taiwan's fishing boats so as to gain control of the Taiwan Strait
- Raid Taiwan's supply ships by motored fishing boasts, naval vessels, or aircraft to cause and expand trouble
- Occupy the Pratas, Wuchiu, Matsu, and Kinmen islands through assault warfare under the principle of not employing large amounts of troops[28]

In early 1996, reports surfaced that China might consider attacking Taiwan using one missile per day for thirty days following the island's presidential election. But Fredrick Chien, Taiwan's foreign minister, claims that these reports were an exaggeration:

> The truth of the matter is . . . that Chas Freeman [a former U.S. Defense Department official] heard this from several senior military officers in the PLA [People's Liberation Army]. And the senior military officials told Chas Freeman that they have a lot of options that are open to them. One of those options is one missile a day. Chas Freeman just picked that up and stated it in the White House . . . and that was headlines.[29]

Considered most likely is a naval blockade.[30] As Andrew Yang, an analyst at Taiwan's prestigious Council for Advanced Policy Studies, observed, "the number one concern for us is a naval blockade, and it is a highly likely threat as far as we are concerned."[31] But a blockade would prove to be a difficult and expensive undertaking—some U.S. military specialists believe that it would escalate quickly into a "full-fledged war that could spread throughout the entire area."[32]

Summary

The touchstone for Taiwan's national security—the PRC threat—remains. The primary danger cited for more than forty-five years in justification for Taiwan's enormous military budget, universal conscription, and massive arms purchases remains. The principal prism through which Taiwan views most of its worldwide diplomatic activities and relationships remains. But the end of the Cold War is generating new opportunities and challenges for Taiwan. As Taiwan's *1993–1994 National Defense Report* observed, "the international system in the post–Cold War era is full of contradictions among its elements."[33]

Notes

1. Amos A. Jordan, William J. Taylor, Jr., and Lawrence J. Korb, *American National Security: Policy and Process* (Baltimore, Maryland: Johns Hopkins University Press, 1989), p. 3.
2. Arnold Wolfers, *Discord and Collaboration* (Baltimore, Maryland: Johns Hopkins University Press, 1962), p. 150.
3. Jordan, Taylor, and Korb, *American National Security*, p. 3.
4. Joseph J. Romm, *Defining National Security: The Nonmilitary Aspects* (New York: Council on Foreign Relations Press, 1993), p. 85.
5. Douglas J. Murray and Paul R. Viotti, *The Defense Policies of Nations: A Comparative Study*, 3d ed. (Baltimore, Maryland: Johns Hopkins University Press, 1994), p. 593.
6. See Barry Buzan, *People, States and Fear: The National Security Problem in International Relations* (Chapel Hill: University of North Carolina Press, 1983), p. 4.
7. Quoted from Romm, *Defining National Security*, pp. 4–5.
8. Barry Buzan, *People, States and Fear: An Agenda for International Security Studies in the Post–Cold War Era*, 2d ed. (Boulder, Colorado: Lynne Rienner Publishers, 1991), p. 16.
9. For more information, see Graham Allison and Gregory F. Treverton (eds.), *Rethinking America's Security: Beyond Cold War to New World Order* (New York: W. W. Norton and Company, 1992).
10. ROC Ministry of National Defense, *1992 National Defense Report: Republic of China* (Taipei: Li Ming Cultural Enterprise Co., 1992), p. 53. Translated from the Chinese by Ma Kainan. The same argument may be found in ROC Ministry of National Defense, *1993–1994 National Defense Report: Republic of China* (Taipei: Li Ming Cultural Enterprise Co., 1994), pp. 83–85. Translated from the Chinese by Yang Lien-chung, Li Chang-hao, and Hsieh Yung-t'ien.
11. Republic of China, Ministry of National Defense, *1992 National Defense Report*, p. 52.
12. Ibid., p. 49.
13. "Text of Jiang Speech," Xinhua (Beijing), January 30, 1995, in *Foreign Broadcast Information System, China*, January 30, 1995, p. 84.
14. See Sofia Wu, "Beijing's Intentions Toward Taiwan Doubted: Poll," *Central News Agency* (hereafter *CNA*) (Taipei), November 29, 1993, in *Lexis/Nexis*.
15. ROC Government Information Office, *The Republic of China Yearbook, 1993* (Taipei: Government Information Office, 1993), p. 149.

16. Ibid.

17. "Bilateral Action Needed to Terminate 'State of War,' MAC Spokesman Declares," *Free China Journal*, May 7, 1991, p. 2.

18. John F. Copper, *Taiwan: Nation-State or Province*, 2d ed. (Boulder, Colorado: Westview Press, 1995), p. 147.

19. According to unofficial estimates, Taiwan's investment in the PRC now stands at more than U.S.$15 billion. For more information, see "Investment in Mainland Declines 20%," *China News*, May 27, 1994, p. 12.

20. Guo-cang Huan, "Taiwan: A View from Beijing," *Foreign Affairs* 63, No. 5, 1985, p. 1068.

21. For more information, see Dennis Van Vranken Hickey, "China's Threat to Taiwan," *Pacific Review* 5, No. 3, 1992, pp. 250–258.

22. "Li Peng Offers Hope for Koo-Wang Talks," *China Post* (International Airmail Edition), April 1, 1993, p. 1.

23. See Chen Guoqing, "'China Threat' Rings Hollow," *Defense News* 8, No. 19, May 17–23, 1993, p. 20.

24. ROC Ministry of National Defense, *1993–1994 National Defense Report*, pp. 86–87.

25. Christopher Bodeen, "Diplomacy Suffers Setback in Canada," *China Post* (International Airmail Edition), July 22, 1995, p. 1.

26. ROC Ministry of National Defense, *1993–1994 National Defense Report*, p. 87.

27. Author's interview with Fredrick Chien, foreign minister of the Republic of China, February 7, 1996, Taipei, Taiwan, Republic of China.

28. See ROC Ministry of National Defense, *1993–1994 National Defense Report*, pp. 88–89.

29. Author's interview with Fredrick Chien, February 7, 1996.

30. See Shu-Ming Chang, "Taiwan Urged to Beef-up Air, Naval Forces," *China Post* (International Airmail Edition), September 28, 1993, p. 4.

31. Paul Lewis, "Taiwan May Create Special Budget for New Arms Buys," *Defense News*, October 12–18, 1992, p. 56.

32. See statement of Admiral (ret.) Thomas H. Moorer in Martin L. Lasater, *Beijing's Blockade Threat to Taiwan* (Washington, D.C.: Heritage Foundation, 1985), p. 6. Also see Paul Godwin, "The Use of Military Force Against Taiwan," in Parris H. Chang and Martin L. Lasater (eds.), *If China Crosses the Taiwan Strait: The International Response* (Lanham, Maryland: University Press of America, Inc., 1993).

33. ROC Ministry of National Defense, *1993–1994 National Defense Report*, p. 27.

2

Taiwan's Military: Structure, Composition, and Issues

Two principal objectives form the basis of this chapter. The first is to examine the changing composition and structure of the ROC's armed services and explain how day-to-day administration of the military is carried out in Taiwan. The second objective is to provide an analysis of the major security issues relating to Taiwan's armed forces. These concerns—which have many facets that are not widely understood—may well have real effects on the credibility of Taiwan's security policy.

Taiwan's Military

According to the ROC constitution, the president of the ROC serves as commander-in-chief of the armed forces. But day-to-day administration of the military is carried out by the Ministry of National Defense under the Executive Yuan. Within the Defense Ministry is the minister of national defense (who must be a civilian by law), and the General Staff Headquarters (GSH) and its Office of the General Staff, which was expanded with the consolidation of the ROC Army, Navy, and Air Force General Headquarters in 1993.[1] Under the GSH are these three services as well as a logistical command known as the Combined Services Force. The GSH also houses the Armed Forces Reserve Command, the Coast Guard Command, and the Military Police Command. Although intended primarily to serve as a fighting force, Taiwan's military also serves other functions, such as helping farmers harvest their crops and providing relief during natural disasters.

At one time, the ultimate goal of the ROC military was to take back by force the mainland lost to the Chinese Communists in 1949. Military planners concentrated on building an army capable of fielding forty or more divisions on the Chinese mainland. The structure of the armed forces reflected this mission: The ROC maintained a gigantic land army for offensive operations in mainland China. But this policy has changed. This chapter examines the new look of Taiwan's military.

ROC Ground Forces

Taiwan's ground forces consist of the ROC Army (268,000 troops) and 21,000 Armed Forces Police (Military Police, or MPs). These forces are no longer trained to retake mainland China. The army's current mission is to *defend* the territory of the ROC. The role of the Armed Forces Police is to guard governmental installations, maintain military discipline, support combat troops, and assist police when necessary to maintain public security.

During peacetime, the ground forces are stationed at strategic positions around the island. They also are positioned on the offshore islands (Penghu, Kinmen, and Matsu) and on several islets scattered throughout the South China Sea. The ground forces "are commissioned with the duties of alerting, training, battlefield planning, protecting the bases of [the] Navy and Air Force, civil defense as well as mountain and coastal defense."[2]

If attacked, the army "will conduct joint attacks against anchoring areas, beachhead combat, counter-airborne and continuous counter-attack to destroy the invading enemy."[3] According to more detailed accounts, however, the army is not expected to drive an enemy from the beaches. Rather, it is to "make its principal stand with its tanks and best troops along the highways, making use of these communications lines to concentrate forces against the invading army's main attack axis."[4]

Taiwan's army is organized into combat, combat support, and service support troops. It is subdivided into the following units:

- Three armies
- Quemoy, Matsu, Penghu, and Hualien-Taitung headquarters, and Airborne and Special Operations Command
- Tungyin Island Command and Chukuang Island Command
- Two mechanized infantry divisions
- Thirteen heavy infantry divisions
- Seven light infantry divisions
- Six armored brigades
- Two tank groups
- Two airborne brigades
- Two aviation commands
- One air defense missile group[5]

The Armed Forces Police has five subcommands and one training center.[6]

In keeping with efforts to restructure the island's forces to act as an effective deterrent against a mainland attack, Taiwan's Defense Ministry asserts that "to build an armored, automated and 3-dimensional Army is still the goal of development for the ground forces."[7] Weapons systems include tanks, self-propelled artillery, armored personnel carriers, helicopters, rocket systems, antitank missiles, and surface-to-air missiles. Recent moves to bolster ground-force capabilities include:

- Agreeing to buy 160 M-60A3 tanks from the United States. Taiwan began to take delivery of the tanks in 1995.[8]
- Agreeing to buy 120 Mistral shoulder-fired missiles from France[9]
- Acquiring forty-two AH1W Super Cobra attack helicopters and twenty-six OH-58D Kiowa Warrior Scout helicopters from the United States[10]
- Upgrading the nearly obsolete M48A1 main battle tank (MBT). More than 300 are now believed to have attained the much-improved M48A5 standards.[11]
- Developing a new and lighter version of the U.S. M60 MBT—the M48H or "Brave Tiger"[12]
- Developing a second generation of Sky Bow surface-to-air missiles. The Sky Bow II reportedly will have twice the range of the Sky Bow I.[13]
- Agreeing to buy 200 fourth-generation Patriot missiles from the United States. The missiles will be incorporated into a sophisticated air-defense system.[14]
- Agreeing to purchase Stinger missiles from the United States. These will replace the Chaparral missiles deployed on the ROC's offshore islands.[15]

There also are unconfirmed reports that Taiwan has resumed production of medium-range surface-to-surface missiles after mainland China conducted a series of provocative missile tests in 1995. These missiles—which could be armed with nuclear warheads—would be capable of striking targets in southern and southeastern China. Taiwan's Defense Ministry, however, has pledged not to develop nuclear weapons and denies that it is producing medium-range missiles.[16]

Since 1949, the ROC has reduced the size of its armed forces on several occasions. Current plans call for downsizing the military into a defensive force of roughly 400,000 troops. A majority of these cuts will affect the army, which will be downsized from 268,000 to 200,000 troops in ten years. But at these levels, the army will continue to make up approximately 50 percent of Taiwan's total armed services (the navy and air force will each comprise 25 percent). Military officials justify these force levels by arguing that the "decisive ground battle remains the last resort to win the war."[17]

ROC Naval Forces

The ROC Navy has roughly 68,000 officers and men (including 30,000 marines). During peacetime, the navy's primary mission is to retain control of territorial waters and ensure that vital sea lanes are kept open. The navy also provides aid to Taiwanese fishing boats requiring assistance and patrols the waters in the Taiwan Strait and, more recently, the South China Sea.[18]

If attacked, the ROC Navy will play a critical role in the island's defensive strategy. According to Taiwan's *1993–1994 National Defense Report,* "the Navy would, under air force support, employ surface vessels, submarines and mines to carry out their missions of anti-blockade and navigation protection."[19] If required, the navy will take the war to mainland China. The *Defense Report* states that "the Navy may have to take such offensive actions as intercepting enemy ships and attacking/destroying the enemy's harbor facilities."[20]

Taiwan's navy is divided into both operational and ground forces. The operational forces include:

- Destroyers (two destroyer fleets and one frigate fleet)
- Amphibious forces (one landing fleet and one landing vessel fleet)
- Submarines (one submarine group)
- Mine forces (one mine vessel fleet and one mine-sweeper/layer fleet)
- Logistic forces (one service fleet and one rescue fleet)
- Speedboats (one Hai-chiao group)
- Aviation forces (one antisubmarine helicopter group)
- Shore-based missiles (one Hai-feng group)
- Marine corps (two marine divisions, one landing tank regiment and one operational service regiment)[21]

As an island state, the ROC is especially sensitive to naval developments in the region. Officials are particularly concerned about mainland China's recent acquisition of Russian Kilo-class submarines, which are capable of laying twenty-two mines each. They also are worried about Beijing's much-publicized efforts to project its power in the East China, South China, and Yellow seas and its drive to transform its South Sea Fleet into a blue water navy. In 1994, Sun Chen, then Taiwan's defense minister, warned that these developments will "put Taiwan under easier control than before."[22]

In order to cope with the growing PRC threat, Taiwan is seeking to put more muscle into its naval forces. The ROC Navy is acquiring technology and equipment designed to enhance its naval warfare and antiblockade capabilities. It also has formed an antisubmarine command to study ways to counter a possible PRC blockade.[23] Recent moves to enhance naval forces include:

- Deploying Hsiung-feng II surface-to-surface ("blockade buster") missiles on naval vessels, Taiwan's coastline, and the offshore islands[24]
- Purchasing up to sixteen LaFayette-class frigates from France
- Constructing eight Perry-class missile frigates

- Purchasing four U.S.-made minesweepers
- Manufacturing several varieties of missile-equipped fast-attack craft
- Refurbishing its World War II era destroyers
- Purchasing twelve SH-2F Light Airborne Multipurpose System (LAMPS) antisubmarine helicopters from the United States
- Leasing six Knox-class destroyers from the United States
- Purchasing 150 Mk-46 torpedoes from the United States
- Actively attempting to purchase up to ten more submarines

In addition to these activities, the ROC Navy is conducting a growing number of antiblockade and antisubmarine exercises.

As Admiral Liu Ho-chien, Taiwan's chief of the general staff, observed, "the development and survival of our country is dependent on maintaining shipping links with other countries."[25] Officials hope that the navy's ambitious modernization program will deter, or at least discourage, a PRC blockade or some other form of interference in Taiwan's key shipping routes—an action Beijing might well attempt in the event of hostilities.

ROC Air Force

The ROC Air Force has approximately 68,000 officers and men. During peacetime, the air force's mission is "to protect the security of [Taiwan's] air space as well as the integrity and sovereignty of Taiwan areas."[26] In the event of hostilities, "the Air Force will conduct a coordinated air-defense, utilizing combat aircraft, air-defense missiles and artillery to carry out air attacks and overlapping interception to annihilate enemy aircraft one by one."[27] To accomplish this mission, Taiwan has deployed an integrated air-defense system, known as Tien Wuang, or Sky Net. It will be replaced by an even more sophisticated system—the Chang Wang (Strengthened Net) system—in the late 1990s.[28] Current battle plans may also call for "knocking out all radar stations along the mainland's southeast coast, as well as the 13 Communist airbases within 250 nautical miles of Taiwan."[29]

The ROC Air Force is divided into two systems: the operational system and logistic support system. The operational system includes:

- Six tactical combat aircraft wings
- One transport/antisubmarine wing
- One tactical control wing
- One communication and air traffic control (ATC) wing
- One weather wing
- Five separate teams
- One air-defense artillery guards command, which contains four commands, fourteen air-defense battalions, and eleven guards battalions[30]

Units in the logistics support system include three logistical support divisions, one fuel group, and logistical support sections and teams assigned to combat units.[31]

Taiwanese officials are nervous about the PRC's drive to upgrade its air force, especially Beijing's efforts to obtain sophisticated Russian warplanes and technology. The PRC has purchased a squadron of advanced Su-27 "Flanker" jet fighters and a handful of military transport planes, and there are reports that it is prepared to buy MiG-29s and Su-24s.[32] Perhaps more significant, in late 1995 Beijing successfully negotiated a U.S.$2 billion deal to manufacture the Su-27.[33] In order to cope with the growing threat, Taiwan is attempting to beef up its air defenses. Recent activities include:

- Agreeing to purchase 150 F-16/A and F-16/B aircraft from the United States (the deal also includes forty spare engines, 900 Sidewinder missiles, 600 Sparrow missiles, and 500,000 rounds of 20-mm cannon shells)
- Agreeing to purchase four E-2T early-warning aircraft from the United States
- Agreeing to lease T-38 training aircraft from the United States (used to train pilots picked to fly the F-16s)
- Agreeing to purchase sixty Mirage 2000-5 warplanes from France
- Developing the Indigenous Defense Fighter (IDF), also known as the Chiang Ching-kuo fighter

Defense officials acknowledge that the PLA Air Force enjoys a numerical advantage over the ROC Air Force in terms of force levels. They also caution that Taiwan's air defense could confront "real difficulties" while it waits for the delivery of U.S. and French warplanes.[34] At the same time, however, defense analysts stress that the ROC Air Force could handle a PRC attack:

> The ROC Air Force has a defensive strategy, and Taiwan's airspace is too small for the Chinese Communists to send all their aircraft over at once; each attack would be limited to 200 aircraft at the outside, attacking in a maximum of three waves a day.[35]

Military authorities claim that "we could easily deal with that [level of attack] at our current strength."[36]

Other ROC Forces

In addition to those forces outlined above, Taiwan maintains a coast guard force and a massive reservist force. The ROC Coast Guard was created after the dissolution of Taiwan's Garrison Command in 1992. With roughly 26,000 troops, the coast guard is "charged with securing and protecting the coastline from intrusion and smuggling and coordinates and integrates the responsible units in the execution of coastal patrol and defense missions."[37]

Taiwan's registered reservists number about 3,750,000 persons—more than 10 percent of the island's population. Table 2.1 classifies reservists by military service. Taiwan's reservists play a pivotal role in the ROC's defensive strategy. During peacetime, they serve as a powerful deterrent. If deterrence fails, however, they may be mobilized rapidly to augment the island's other defensive forces.

Table 2.1   Reservists Classified by Military Service

Army	Navy	Marine Corps	Air Force
3,010,000	194,000	233,000	332,000

Source: ROC Ministry of National Defense, *1993–1994 National Defense Report: Republic of China* (Taipei: Li Ming Cultural Enterprise Co., 1994), p. 217. Translated from Chinese by Yang Lien-chung, Li Chang-hao, and Hsieh Yung-t'ien.

Summary

Taiwan's military is relatively well trained and well equipped, and it possesses high morale. Its military strength is impressive. But the ROC Defense Ministry concedes that the PRC's combat capability is far superior to their own.[38] As outlined in Table 2.2, Beijing is superior to Taipei in combat aircraft, warships, and submarines. Given such figures, is Taiwan's military capacity sufficient to deter an attack?

Table 2.2   Comparison of ROC and PRC Military Forces

Military assets	Taiwan	PRC
Troops	425,000	2,930,000
Warships	33	55
Submarines	4	50
Combat aircraft	459	4,970

Source: International Institute for Strategic Studies, *The Military Balance: 1994–1995* (London: Brassey's, 1994).

Most Taiwanese military officials believe that the island's military capacity is sufficient to *deter* an attack. With its active duty forces numbering roughly 425,000 and with more than 3,000,000 reservists, the island's military poses a significant challenge to any potential invasion force. At the same time, however, some defense analysts claim that the PRC does possess the capability to invade Taiwan.

Security Issues in Taiwan

For more than four decades, questions and issues pertaining to Taiwan's military remained shrouded in mystery. Indeed, as a study commissioned by the Democratic Progressive Party (DPP)—the island's chief opposition party—observed, "the questions and affairs of Taiwan's defense have long been a mysterious forbidden zone."[39] Citizens as well as government agencies had "no way of learning of and exercising supervision over the operation of the armed forces."[40] As one legislator complained, "what we saw on the budget books was a name [of an arms deal] and a number, anything more than that, the Defense Ministry said was secret."[41] Even Taiwan's president has conceded that "many of us are not clear what kind of sophisticated weapons we have."[42] But this situation is changing.

With the lifting of martial law in 1987, questions began to be raised about Taiwan's security. Defense issues, sometimes described as the government's "final black box," are now subject to widespread debate. The following discussion examines some current issues relating to Taiwan's defense.

Indigenous Defense Fighter

Development of Taiwan's Indigenous Defense Fighter, also known as the Chiang Ching-kuo fighter, began in 1982 at the instruction of President Chiang Ching-kuo because of the government's difficulty in purchasing fighter aircraft from abroad.[43] The plane was developed by the Aero Industry Development Center (AIDC), a subsidiary of Taiwan's primary defense-related research and development facility, the Chung Shan Institute of Science and Technology (CSIST). It was unveiled officially on December 12, 1988, and military officials announced that it would eventually replace Taiwan's aging stock of more than eighty Lockheed F-104G and 300-plus Northrop F-5E/F aircraft.

In 1988, sources in Taipei estimated that "the budget for development and production of the fighter runs up to U.S.$1 billion."[44] By 1995, however, the cost to develop the warplane had soared to more than U.S.$4 billion.[45] Defense analysts now describe the plane as "the world's most expensive jet fighter."[46]

Taiwanese officials acknowledge that there have been "some problems" in the development of the IDF.[47] But critics claim that the program has been plagued by glitches. The plane's underpowered engine and overweight airframe contributed to the fatal crash of a prototype during testing in 1991. In

1995, another fighter crashed after suddenly experiencing a generator failure.[48] This accident led to the recall of all IDF fighters in service and the suspension of production "for six months due to design problems."[49] Other problems reportedly include fuel leakage, an unstable computer system, a substandard avionics system, a defective radar system, and a tendency for various components and parts found inside most IDF aircraft to differ in exact size.[50] Even the ROC Air Force has expressed concern about the fighter's performance.[51]

The IDF has become a contentious issue in Taiwanese politics. Skeptics have satirized the plane's initials to mean "It Don't Fly" or "I Dive Frequently." Lin Meng-kuei, a member of Taiwan's Control Yuan, has blasted the plane as "a lie [and] a rot that has been wasting the people's tax money."[52] When addressing AIDC officials, Lin charged that the complex intentionally misled both the government and the public about the program's prospects:

> You don't have the ability as you claimed to develop fighter jets. You merely purchased some crucial parts from the U.S. and stuffed them into fighters to muddle the attention from the Congress and the people.[53]

Some contend that there no longer is a need to manufacture the controversial warplane.[54] They argue that the new F-16 and Mirage 2000-5 warplanes will satisfy Taiwan's defensive requirements.

Defense Ministry officials dispute these charges. They claim that "the IDF is like a baby who needs encouragement to become fully grown."[55] Although the ROC Air Force has drastically cut its order for IDFs (from 250 down to 135), authorities still insist that the warplane plays an important role in Taiwan's defensive strategy. According to Koo Chung-lian, Taiwan's defense vice minister, the F-16, Mirage 2000-5, and IDF "each has its own capability, and together they will complete the ROC's air defense capability" (see Table 2.3).[56] Authorities also believe that the plane has export potential.[57] Finally, officials argue that the plane's production will help Taiwan develop the technological base required to establish an indigenous defense industry. Critics, however, remain unconvinced.

Problems Associated with Foreign Military Equipment

Now that Taiwan is acquiring sophisticated foreign military equipment—ranging from French frigates to U.S. warplanes—some question the need for the controversial IDF aircraft. But the foreign acquisitions also pose problems for Taiwan's military.

In addition to domestically manufactured vessels, Taiwan's navy includes U.S., French, German, and Dutch ships. The air force will soon fly U.S., French, and Taiwanese warplanes. The diversity of manufacturers is

Table 2.3 Parameters for Taiwan's Jet Fighters

	F-104	F-5E	F-16A/B	Mirage	IDF
Thrust (pounds)	17,500	5,000x2	23,450	21,385	9,460x2
Ratio (engine power/ aircraft weight)	0.84	0.63	1.6	1	1
G strength	5.8	5.85	9	9–13.5	6.5–9
Maximum speed (Mach)	2.1	1.62	2	2.2	1.7
Practical maximum altitude (ft)	58,000	53,500	50,000	59,000	55,000
Rate of climb (ft/min)	—	34,300	—	56,000	50,000
Maximum payload (kg)	—	—	16,000	17,000	9,000

Source: "Parameters for IDF and Other Jet Fighters," *Free China Journal,* December 30, 1994, p. 1.

contributing to both a complicated logistics problem and a personnel problem. The procurement of foreign military equipment also has led directly to what the Central News Agency, Taiwan's semiofficial news agency, described as "the worst military scandal in Taiwan's history."[58]

Taiwan's new foreign equipment requires different sets of technicians for maintenance and repair. For example, a technician trained to repair a Mirage fighter cannot necessarily service a U.S. warplane. This is going to put even more strain on the military's already scarce human resources.

Taiwanese military planners also have discovered that the armed forces lack the required data links and sensitive software required to mold the different air and sea systems into an integrated and cohesive force. Officials have turned to the United States for assistance and complain that Washington is unwilling to provide Taiwan with the necessary technology. But U.S. authorities claim that the Taiwanese are asking for a system that doesn't exist: "With the E-2T, they want to upgrade their [data links] to talk to 20 [different kinds of] aircraft. The system doesn't exist."[59] The United States also points out that "Taiwan created its own command, control and communication dilemmas through purchases of systems that can never be truly integrated into joint force packages."[60] The United States had warned Taiwan that certain purchases—particularly the purchase of Mirage 2000-5 jet fighters—could prove to be an "operational liability."[61]

U.S. military authorities have suggested that Taiwan work with some U.S.-based companies to develop its own indigenous data links. They point out that Taipei's troubles are neither unique nor insurmountable. Dan Goure, deputy director for political and military studies at Washington's prestigious Center for Strategic and International Studies, explains:

> This is a classic command and control problem. The Israelis had this problem, linking their surveillance aircraft with the fighters. However, the

Israelis had the capability to develop their own communications links and did so. The Koreans are having this problem now and the Japanese have these problems.[62]

Taiwan is acting on Washington's advice. Military officials now claim that "Taiwan has the ability to develop data links and computer software that can integrate the complex weapons systems it has acquired and ordered from different countries."[63]

Finally, the acquisition of foreign military equipment has led to embarrassing military procurement scandals. One European arms dealer claims that Taiwan is becoming as corrupt as Shanghai in the 1940s: "It's so easy [to sell arms to Taiwan] now. And sometimes it doesn't even take money. All it takes is some girls in Paris."[64] The biggest scandal broke in late 1993 after the murder of Yin Ching-feng, an ROC Navy captain. Captain Yin had intended to expose a pattern of bribery and corruption in which active duty officers received bribes from foreign arms dealers and retired ROC military officers representing foreign firms.[65]

Yin's murderer (or murderers) has not been apprehended. But more than a dozen military officers have been arrested and a small number have been sentenced to life in prison. This scandal (and several others) has led some legislators—especially members of the DPP—to call for drastic changes in the current system for purchasing military equipment. They claim that the Yin murder is just "the tip of the iceberg, the procurement procedures are the same for the navy, army and air force."[66]

China's Threat to Taiwan

Although the PRC claims that it seeks the peaceful unification of China, it has not ruled out the use of force to take Taiwan. As described in Chapter 1, military officials in Taiwan have identified several situations they believe Beijing might employ as pretexts for an invasion of Taiwan. Authorities emphasize that, among the considerations that might lead the PRC to attack the island, "the most likely one under which the PRC would invade is if and when the ROC on Taiwan declares itself independent."[67]

Some Taiwanese—particularly members of the island's separatist movement—believe that the PRC threat is overstated. According to Shih Ming-teh, a leading DPP official and an independence activist, it is a "fantasy" to believe that China has the capability to invade Taiwan:

> I don't think mainland China has the capability to attack Taiwan. It is not that easy to launch an amphibious operation. China has never won an amphibious invasion in its history. China had conquered the Korean peninsula and Central Asia, but it had never conquered Japan or other islands. It is a mainland fantasy to think that it can take over Taiwan.[68]

Peng Ming-min, the 1996 DPP presidential candidate, has made similar arguments. Peng contends that "mainland China lacks sufficient military might to invade Taiwan" and claims "Taiwan has a combat force which could defend itself from any mainland attack."[69] Hsu Hsin-liang, Peng's rival for the 1996 DPP presidential nomination, also believes that "China will not and does not have the capability to use military force against Taiwan."[70] It is noteworthy that Hsu made this statement during the midst of Beijing's 1995 missile tests in the East China Sea. At roughly the same time, *Democracy and Progress,* the DPP's weekly newsletter, published an editorial claiming that "China does not have the required amphibious forces, equipment and training needed to succeed in an invasion of Taiwan."[71]

Some believe that the government uses the mainland threat to dampen support for Taiwanese independence. Others accuse the military of using "scare tactics" to ensure that Taiwan's legislature passes big defense budgets. Chu Feng-chi, a New Party lawmaker, claims that the military often exaggerates "the threat from Beijing to build support for the large defense budget."[72]

Government officials deny these allegations. They bristle at separatists' suggestions that "military confrontation is so remote to make the recent Chinese military actions laughable to the point of extreme merriment.... Taiwan is free to pursue its independence goals."[73] Military authorities argue that the PRC does have "enough military prowess to invade Taiwan" and that the probability of military confrontation across the Taiwan Strait is increasing.[74] They are especially irked by statements suggesting that mainland China would tolerate a declaration of Taiwanese independence. Sun Chen, Taiwan's former defense minister, says that such assertions prove only that the "people who deny that the Taiwan independence movement would lead the Chinese Communists to use force against Taiwan are basically very irresponsible and ignorant on the issue."[75]

Defense of Taiwan's Offshore Islands

In addition to the island of Taiwan, the ROC occupies the offshore islands of Penghu, Kinmen, and Matsu, and several islets scattered throughout the South China Sea. Penghu, Kinmen, and Matsu islands became the focus of heated debates and two international crises in 1954 and 1958. At the time, many believed that the islands—some of which are located within shouting distance of Fujian province—should be abandoned. But Generalissimo Chiang Kai-shek was determined to hold onto them. In his autobiography, President Dwight D. Eisenhower explained Chiang's reasoning:

> The most important [reason to retain possession of the islands] was Chiang's conviction that if he lost Quemoy [Kinmen] and Matsu, his main forces would lose their will to fight.... To Chiang and his people, Quemoy and Matsu would one day be stepping stones for the reinvasion of their

homeland. Meanwhile, the possession of these islands enabled Chiang to preserve for his forces a jumping-off place for guerrilla raids on the mainland.[76]

Chiang's forces did relinquish control of some islands. In 1955, the PRC conquered the ROC-held island of Ichiang, and ROC forces withdrew from the Tachen Islands. But for more than four decades, the ROC has continued to station thousands of troops on the remaining islands.[77] Few Taiwanese dared to question the wisdom of this deployment.

In October 1994, during the midst of a heated political contest, Taiwan's military occupation of the offshore islands emerged as a major campaign issue. On October 26, 1994, Shih Ming-teh, DPP chairman, told reporters that Taiwan should withdraw its forces from the islands of Kinmen and Matsu. Shih reasoned that, in an age of missiles and long-range attack fighters, the islands were no longer necessary for the ROC's security. He suggested that the government withdraw its troops "and not sacrifice their lives merely to gain early warning of any invasion."[78]

Shih's comments ignited a fierce public debate. President Lee Teng-hui declared that the territories "must be defended and developed."[79] Premier Lien Chan argued that the PRC would attack if Taiwan withdrew its forces from the islands:

> Although there are only some 80,000 residents, their safety and freedom are as important as that of other people in Taiwan and Penghu. Will the mainland not attack Taiwan because of the troop withdrawal from Kinmen and Matsu? Even Taiwan and Penghu will be at stake.[80]

Three of the ROC's leading business and industrial organizations—the National Federation of Industries, the General Chamber of Commerce, and the National Association of Industry and Business—threatened to pull their investments out of Taiwan if the two defense outposts were evacuated. The groups released a joint statement condemning the DPP proposal and saying that "evacuating troops and disarming the two defense outposts is like luring wolves to invade us and would put property and lives in Quemoy and Matsu at risk."[81]

Reacting to the public outcry, some DPP members attempted to back away from Shih's comments. It is noteworthy, however, that others support the party leader's controversial position. As Chiu Yi-jen, DPP deputy secretary general, explained, "these are long-term questions we will have to face at some stage."[82]

Recruitment and Retention of Military Personnel

Taiwan's military includes both volunteers and conscripts. According to Article 3 of the Military Service Law, "male persons shall be liable for military service on January 1 of the year immediately following the year during which they reach the age of 18, and shall no longer be drafted for service beginning on December 31 of the year during which they reach the age of 45."[83] In most cases, draftees complete two months of basic training before receiving a twenty-two-month assignment. Those whose education would be interrupted by military service, such as high school or university students, may defer their induction until after graduation.[84]

Defense officials contend that the Military Service Law needs to be amended. With most young people scrambling for high-paying careers, Taiwan's service academies are having trouble filling their entering classes. As one high-ranking naval officer complained, "there's no point in having new weapons if there's no one to use them."[85] Authorities also claim that "the required two-year military service for males is inadequate time to train personnel for the highly sophisticated equipment that Taiwan's defense forces are acquiring."[86]

Military officials are concerned about both the quantity and quality of conscripts. Loopholes in existing regulations allow draft-age males to evade military service. In fact, officials claim that "even if all those available for military service were drafted . . . conscript numbers would still be insufficient."[87] At the same time, the quality of draftees is declining—more than 15 percent of draftees fail to pass the physical examinations required to serve in the military.[88] Consequently, in March 1996, Taiwan's Ministry of National Defense and Ministry of the Interior jointly proposed new conscription regulations that would remove most of the exemptions traditionally granted to obese or underweight draftees. As one government official explained, "no matter what weight, every draftee has to go into the army as long as he can survive."[89]

Some disagree with the military's position. They point to studies suggesting that Taiwan's new military equipment requires fewer personnel to operate. For example, Taiwan's old World War II era destroyers "require a crew of at least 275, whereas the new Perry-class frigates need only 140."[90] They also oppose moves designed to close loopholes in the Military Service Law. Indeed, some DPP legislators have joined with the Association of Parents of Students Abroad to demand that the government lift all remaining restrictions on international travel by draft-age males.[91] Finally, the DPP opposes efforts to extend the compulsory two-year military service for males. Rather, the party advocates cutting the required military service to one year.[92]

Composition of Armed Services

Taiwan is reducing the size of its armed forces. Current plans call for downsizing the military into a defensive force of roughly 400,000 troops. Most Taiwanese—including members of the DPP—applaud this move. But some question the wisdom of continuing to place emphasis upon ground forces.

The ROC Army no longer trains to "retake the mainland." It continues, however, to make up over 50 percent of Taiwan's total armed services and enjoys a very large share of the island's defense budget (Table 2.4). Critics contend that Taiwan maintains "a military organization so vast it beats many of the world's militarist nations at their own game, and a massive standing army incompatible with its strategic objectives."[93]

Table 2.4 Comparison of ROC Ground, Naval, and Air Forces (force levels and share of defense budget)

	Troops	Budget (NT$ in millions)	Percentage of total budget
Ground forces	289,000	44,714.6	17.30
Naval forces	68,000	45,549.6	17.62
Air forces	68,000	32,109	12.42

Source: ROC Ministry of National Defense, *1993–1994 National Defense Report: Republic of China* (Taipei: Li Ming Cultural Enterprise Co., 1994), pp. 117–224. Translated from Chinese by Yang Lien-chung, Li Chang-hao, and Hsieh Yung-t'ien.

Some claim that the ROC government should bolster the combat capabilities of the navy and air force while slashing the army's share of the defense budget. They also question the army's need for new and expensive equipment—especially the 160 Korean War vintage M60-A3 tanks that it has agreed to purchase from the United States. Critics claim that these pricey behemoths will experience difficulties operating in Taiwan's hilly terrain and that they will be "sitting ducks" for the enemy's air force during an invasion.[94] These funds might better be used to strengthen the island's air and naval defenses.

The Defense Ministry disputes these charges. Officials point out that "upgrading naval and air forces will be given priority over the development of the Army."[95] ROC Army officers also resist calls for change. They claim that "if a war across the straits took place, the decisive battle would be on the land in Taiwan."[96] At that time, they argue, "there would be a strong need" for a large land army equipped with tanks.[97]

Further Concerns

The discussion above outlines only some of the major defense issues confronting Taiwan. A more complete analysis would include details of other concerns as well. These include demands that the government: (1) privatize the AIDC and other defense-related industries; (2) "depoliticize" the military; (3) review the armed forces' pension system and dissolve the Veteran Affairs Council; (4) increase the proportion of civilian positions in the armed forces; (5) reduce the number of high-ranking officers and adjust the ratio of officers to enlisted soldiers; (6) reduce the costs of foreign military equipment; and (7) eliminate the military's role on college campuses.

Summary

In recent years, Taiwan has undergone a metamorphosis. In fact, the island is well on the way to becoming one of Asia's few fully functioning democracies. Dramatic transformations in Taiwan's armed services have accompanied these changes.

Like the PRC, Taiwan is adopting a "crack troop" policy that stresses quality (in both weapons and training), rather than numbers of troops on the ground. The ROC also is placing greater emphasis on the modernization of its navy and air force while strengthening the research and development of defense technologies. Other recent changes include phasing out many noncombatant units (publishing, printing, entertainment), increasing the opportunities for young males to postpone (or evade) compulsory military service, and scaling back the compulsory service time for some draftees.

Unlike the PRC, defense issues in Taiwan are now subject to public scrutiny. After the lifting of martial law in 1987, questions began to be raised about Taiwan's security. Defense issues are now subject to widespread discussion and debate. The outcome of these quarrels—which range in scope from the nature of the PRC threat to veterans benefits—may well have real effects on the credibility of Taiwan's security policy.

It is possible, perhaps even inevitable, that Taiwan will make additional modifications in defense policy. Some changes could be significant, but this is to be expected. As one Taiwanese legislator observed, "Taiwan's changing society mandates new thought on national service and the role of the armed services."[98] The following chapter explores a major shift in Taiwanese military strategy—the move toward a policy of deterrence.

Notes

1. For more information, see Shu-Ming Chang, "ROC Defense Announces Merge Move," *China Post* (International Airmail Edition), November 5, 1993, p. 4.
2. ROC Ministry of National Defense, *1993–1994 National Defense Report: Republic of China* (Taipei: Li Ming Cultural Enterprise Co., 1994), p. 200. Translated from Chinese by Yang Lien-chung, Li Chang-hao, and Hsieh Yung-t'ien.
3. Ibid., p. 201.
4. See Tai Ming Cheung, "Still Gung-ho," *Far Eastern Economic Review*, May 18, 1989, p. 23.

5. See ROC Government Information Office, *The Republic of China Yearbook, 1995* (Taipei: Government Information Office, 1995), p. 160.

6. The subcommands include a Department of Political Warfare and offices of Personnel, Intelligence, Police Affairs, Logistics, Planning, Comptroller, Judge Advocates, and General Affairs. For more information, see ibid.

7. ROC Ministry of National Defense, *1992 National Defense Report, Republic of China* (Taipei: Li Ming Cultural Enterprise Co., 1992), p. 83. Translated from the Chinese by Major General Ma Kainan, ROC Army.

8. See James Kynge, "New Spending Plan Reveals a Nervous Taiwan," *China Post* (International Airmail Edition), November 11, 1994, p. 3.

9. Taiwan had planned originally to buy several hundred Stinger missiles (and launching and control systems) from the United States, but backed out of the deal after the United States declined to sell the shoulder-fired model. See Sofia Wu, "ROC Army to Buy 120 French Missiles," *China Post* (International Airmail Edition), March 18, 1995, p. 4.

10. See "Lee Inspects New Copters from U.S.," *China Post* (International Airmail Edition), November 16, 1993, p. 1. Following the 1996 Taiwan Strait crisis, however, the United States agreed to sell Stinger missiles to Taiwan.

11. See Dennis Van Vranken Hickey, *United States–Taiwan Security Ties: From Cold War to Beyond Containment* (Westport, Connecticut: Praeger, 1994), p. 55.

12. Ibid.

13. See "Ministry Admits to Developing Missiles," *China Post* (International Airmail Edition), November 11, 1994, p. 4.

14. See David Hughes, "Taiwan to Acquire Patriot Derivative," *Aviation Week & Space Technology,* March 1, 1993, p. 61.

15. For more information, see Vivien Pak-Kwan Chan, "Stingers to Deter Mainland Attack on Offshore Islands," *South China Morning Post,* May 25, 1996, p. 8.

16. For more information, see "Government Denies Missile Upgrade Plans," *China Post* (International Airmail Edition), December 28, 1995, p. 1; and "Taiwan Developing Medium-Range Missile?" *Asian Defense Journal,* February 1996, p. 120.

17. Quoted from Cheng-yi Lin, "ROC Defense Programs and Priorities: Current Assessment and Future Projections," paper presented at the International Conference on Taiwan in a Transformed Global Setting, Boston, Massachusetts, April 28–29, 1994.

18. Beginning in April 1994, the ROC Navy began to patrol the waters surrounding the Spratly and Pratas islands. For more information, see R. L. Chen, "ROC Steps Up Spratly Patrol," *China Post* (International Airmail Edition), March 29, 1995, p. 1; and Christopher Bodeen, "Patrol Boats Set Out for Spratlys," *China Post* (International Airmail Edition), March 31, 1995, p. 1.

19. ROC Ministry of National Defense, *1993–1994 National Defense Report,* p. 204.

20. Ibid.

21. Ibid., pp. 203–204.

22. Bear Lee, "Defense Minister Warns Against 'Provoking Beijing,'" Taipei, *CNA,* September 22, 1994, in *Foreign Broadcast Information Service, China* (hereafter *FBIS, China*), September 23, 1994, p. 92.

23. See "ROC Navy Studying Anti-Blockade Strategy," *CNA* (Taipei), January 25, 1992, in *Lexis/Nexis.*

24. Under the tactical concept of "controlling the sea from the land," Taiwan

reportedly is deploying land-based Hsiung-feng II missiles on the offshore island of Tungyin. Sources say that the missiles can hit targets in Fujian province and that all PRC ships operating in the Taiwan Strait are within range of the missiles. For more information, see Lu Chao-lung, "Missiles 'Secretly' Deployed on Offshore Islands," Taipei, *Chung-kuo Shih-Pao,* November 3, 1994, in *FBIS, China,* November 14, 1994, p. 93.

25. "Minesweepers Commissioned in Kaohsiung," *China Post* (International Airmail Edition), March 2, 1994, p. 1.

26. ROC Ministry of National Defense, *1993–1994 National Defense Report,* p. 209.

27. Ibid. For detailed information about Taiwan's air-defense tactics, see Arthur Cheng, "If Enemy Planes Should Strike: An Interview with Sherman Cheng," *Sinorama,* April 1991, p. 13.

28. For more information, see Andrew Yang, "Taiwan's Defense Build-up in the 1990s: Remodelling the Fortress," in Gary Klintworth (ed.), *Taiwan in the Asia-Pacific in the 1990s* (Canberra: Australian National University Printery, 1994), pp. 81–82.

29. Peter Kien-hong Yu, "Arms Balance Peace Insurance," *Free China Journal,* November 26, 1990, p. 5; see also ibid.

30. ROC Ministry of National Defense, *1993–1994 National Defense Report,* pp. 207–208.

31. See ROC Government Information Office, *The Republic of China Yearbook, 1995,* p. 161.

32. See Dennis Van Vranken Hickey and Christopher Craig Harmel, "U.S. Policy and China's Military Ties with the Russian Republics," *Asian Affairs* 20, No. 4, 1994.

33. See "Russia Sells PRC Fighter Plans," *China Post* (Domestic Edition), February 4, 1996, p. 1.

34. See "Defense Boss: Problems Dog Airspace Defense," *China Post* (International Airmail Edition), March 29, 1993, p. 4.

35. Hsieh Shu-fen, "Who Rules the Skies Over Taiwan?" *Sinorama,* April 1991, p. 13.

36. Ibid.

37. ROC Government Information Office, *The Republic of China Yearbook, 1995,* p. 159.

38. ROC officials have long acknowledged that the ROC defense forces may be inferior to those of the PRC. For more information, see R. L. Chen, "ROC Air Force Said Weaker Than Mainland, But Adequate," *China Post* (International Airmail Edition), October 29, 1992, p. 1.

39. Democratic Progressive Party, *Defense Policy Guidelines* (Taipei: Democratic Progressive Party, 1994), p. 1. This study was provided to the author by Geoffrey Fellows, foreign affairs adviser to the Democratic Progressive Party in Taipei, on May 16, 1994.

40. Ibid.

41. Jim Mann, "Targeting Taiwan for Arms Deals," *Los Angeles Times,* March 14, 1994, p. A1.

42. R. L. Chen, "ROC to Flex Military Muscle," *China Post* (International Airmail Edition), August 2, 1994, p. 1.

43. For more information, see Hickey, *United States–Taiwan Security Ties,* pp. 48–50.

44. See "Defense Ministry Gunning to Improve Public Image," *Free China Journal,* August 23, 1990, p. 2.

45. See Julian Baum, "Winged: Locally Made Jet Fighter Fails to Convince Critics," *Far Eastern Economic Review,* January 12, 1995, p. 21.

46. Ibid.

47. For example, in 1992, Taiwan's defense minister admitted during a meeting with legislators that the IDF program has suffered from "some problems." See Chen, "Air Force Said Weaker Than Mainland."

48. See "IDF Jet Fighter Crashed Off Taichung," *China Post* (International Airmail Edition), July 5, 1995, p. 1.

49. See "Jet Production to Be Suspended," *China Post* (International Airmail Edition), October 19, 1995, p. 1.

50. For more information, see "Defense Fighters to Be Examined," *China Post* (International Airmail Edition), July 5, 1994, p. 4; "Taiwan Battles Glitches, Expects IDF to Fly with Radar," *Defense News* 9, No. 28, July 18–24, 1994, p. 26; and "IDF Fighter Squadron Gets Commissioned," *China Post* (International Airmail Edition), December 29, 1994, p. 1.

51. See "Defense Fighters to Be Examined."

52. See Patricia Kuo, "ROC Jet Fighter Program Slammed," *China Post* (International Airmail Edition), October 15, 1992, p. 1.

53. Ibid.

54. See "Halt to Jet Development Is Proposed," *China Post* (International Airmail Edition), November 26, 1993, p. 4.

55. "IDF Fighter Squadron Gets Commissioned," p. 1.

56. "Halt to Jet Development Is Proposed," p. 4.

57. Officials remain divided over the IDF's export potential. See Alice Hung, "Taiwan-made Jets Not Good Enough for Export," *China Post* (International Airmail Edition), May 11, 1994, p. 4; and "Taiwan to Export Jet Fighter," *China Post* (International Airmail Edition), June 22, 1994, p. 1.

58. See Benjamin Yeh, "7 More Charged in Military Scandal," *CNA* (Taipei), April 22, 1994, in *Lexis/Nexis*.

59. Pat Cooper and Barbara Opall, "Taiwan, U.S. Disconnect on Provision of C3 Links," *Defense News* 9, No. 29, July 25–31, 1994, p. 28.

60. Ibid.

61. See "U.S. Sees No Need for Taiwan to Buy Mirage Fighters," *CNA,* November 18, 1992, in *Lexis/Nexis*.

62. Ibid.

63. "ROC Said Able to Develop Expertise to Link Various Weaponry," *CNA* (Taipei), July 27, 1994, in *Lexis/Nexis*.

64. Mann, "Targeting Taiwan for Arms Deals," p. A1.

65. According to some accounts, Yin's murder was connected to the French sale of LaFayette-class frigates to Taiwan. For more information, see "ROC Paid Double Price: Report," *China Post* (International Airmail Edition), March 1, 1994, p. 4.

66. Ibid.

67. ROC Ministry of National Defense, *1993–1994 National Defense Report,* p. 87.

68. Patricia Kuo, "Taipei to Find Common Interests with Washington," *China Post* (International Airmail Edition), February 10, 1993, p. 1.

69. "Chief Asks for Combat Readiness," *China Post* (International Airmail Edition), September 23, 1994, p. 4.

70. Yeh Ching, "Hopefuls Focus on Security," *China Post* (International Airmail Edition), August 7, 1995, p. 1.

71. "Knows the American Military Will Come to the Aid of Taiwan,"

Democracy & Progress: The Voice of the Taiwanese People 5, No. 28, September 1–8, 1995, p. 2.

72. "Military Using Scare Tactics to Get Big Budget," *China Post* (International Airmail Edition), March 17, 1994, p. 1.

73. The same report also argues that "China will not begin a war they are surely to lose." See "Knows the American Military Will Come to the Aid of Taiwan," p. 3.

74. See Dennis Van Vranken Hickey, "Special Report: Interview with Sun Chen, Taiwan's Defense Minister," *Asian Defense Journal,* February 1994, p. 35; and "Defense Boss: Problems Dog Airspace Defense," p. 4.

75. See Hickey, "Interview with Sun Chen," pp. 32–35.

76. Dwight D. Eisenhower, *Mandate for Change* (New York: Signet Books, 1963), pp. 552 and 561.

77. The exact number of ROC troops stationed on the offshore islands remains a secret.

78. Julian Baum, "Strategic Slip: Opposition Under Fire for Calls to Demilitarize Islands," *Far Eastern Economic Review,* November 17, 1994, p. 17.

79. "Lee Again Blasts Proposal for Isles," *China Post* (International Airmail Edition), November 12, 1994, p. 1.

80. "Legislative Brawl Over Islands," *China Post* (International Airmail Edition), October 29, 1994, p. 1.

81. "Taiwanese Outraged Over Call to Demilitarize Islands," *South China Morning Post* (Weekly Edition), November 5–6, 1994, p. 6.

82. Christopher Bodeen, "DPP Stands by Kinmen, Matsu Demilitarization," *China Post* (International Airmail Edition), October 29, 1994, p. 1.

83. ROC Government Information Office, *The Republic of China Yearbook, 1995,* p. 162.

84. Deferments also are granted to those in poor health, those who support elderly parents, and so on.

85. Hsieh Shu-fen, "Overcoming Adversity on the Seas—The Navy Plans for the Future," *Sinorama* 16, No. 9, September 1991, p. 91.

86. See Baum, "Winged"; and Shu-Ming Chang, "More Woes for the Navy," *China Post* (International Airmail Edition), November 3, 1993, p. 1.

87. See "Military Hit Hard by Draft-Dodging," *CNA* (Taipei), December 2, 1993, in *Lexis/Nexis.*

88. "Taiwanese Armed Forces Seen at Disadvantage," *China Post* (International Airmail Edition), November 12, 1993, p. 1.

89. "Draft: All Sizes Welcome," *China Post* (International Airmail Edition), March 4, 1996, p. 3.

90. See Shu-fen, "Overcoming Adversity on the Seas," p. 91.

91. Christopher Bodeen, "Group Wants Restrictions Lifted," *China Post* (International Airmail Edition), October 13, 1993, p. 1.

92. See "Vast Differences in KMT, DPP Proposals," *CNA,* October 29, 1992, in *Lexis/Nexis.*

93. Democratic Progressive Party, *Defense Policy Guidelines,* p. 5.

94. For more information on the controversial tank purchase, see "Decision to Purchase Used Tanks Splits Army," *China Post* (International Airmail Edition), January 3, 1994, p. 4; and "Korean War Vintage U.S. Tanks in Taiwan," *China Post* (International Airmail Edition), April 24, 1995, p. 1.

95. "Troop Cuts for 1994 Announced," *China Post* (International Airmail Edition), April 22, 1993, p. 1.

96. "Korean War Vintage U.S. Tanks," p. 1.
97. Ibid.
98. Bodeen, "Group Wants Restrictions Lifted," p. 1.

3

Taiwan's Security Strategy: Policies, Options, and Prospects

This chapter examines Taiwan's current defensive strategy and explores several options it might consider to augment its security. These include (1) the development of nuclear weapons, (2) joining a collective security organization, or (3) negotiating a nonaggression pact with the People's Republic of China. In conclusion, it suggests that, while recent transformations in the international system are generating challenges for Taiwan, it is unlikely that Taipei will adopt any of these alternatives. Rather, it is likely that Taiwan's security will continue to rest on two pillars—a formidable conventional military force and a close relationship with the United States.

Taiwan's Current Military Strategy

J. C. Wylie, author of the book, *Military Strategy: A General Theory of Power and Control,* once observed, "there are probably more kinds of strategy and more definitions of it, than there are varieties and definitions of economics and politics. It is a loose sort of word."[1] For the purposes of the present book, a broad definition of military strategy seems appropriate. Military strategy may be defined as "the employment of armed forces to achieve military and political objectives."[2]

At one time, the ultimate goal of the ROC military was to take back by force the mainland lost to the Chinese Communists in 1949 (*Fan-kung ta-lu*). Military planners concentrated on building an army capable of fielding forty or more divisions on the Chinese mainland.[3] But this policy has changed. At the present time, the chief objective of Taiwan's military is to *deter* a PRC attack by "keeping a mainland invasion [of the island] prohibitively costly in terms of casualties, materials and international image."[4] During an interview with the author, Stephen S. F. Chen, Taiwan's vice minister of foreign affairs, underscored his government's present position:

> These [weapons systems] are not for aggression. They are only for our defense. We are not going to use these systems to launch an attack on the mainland. . . . *We only want a credible defense so that the enemy will know*

that by launching an invasion, they would have to pay a price—a very high price [emphasis added].⁵

To accomplish this task, the island maintains a formidable military force and a close relationship with the United States.

A Formidable Military Force

In the early 1980s, the PRC launched a drive to modernize its military. Since that time, the program has accelerated. Taiwanese officials view this development with alarm. As Admiral Liu Ho-chien, ROC chief of staff, noted, "whatever their strategic goal in national development, their military buildup is a serious threat to us."⁶

Taiwan is aggressively upgrading its weapons systems to cope with the PRC buildup. Primary emphasis is being placed on building a more effective navy and air force. At the same time, the army is being downsized into a smaller defensive force.

Navy. Taiwan's navy is one of the ten largest navies in the world. But this statistic is misleading. Most ROC naval vessels are approaching obsolescence. In fact, Admiral Yeh Chang-tung, Taiwan's navy commander in chief, has acknowledged that "today they average over 45 years in service, and are almost at the stage where they are too old to use."⁷

In order to upgrade its naval power, Taiwan is manufacturing several varieties of missile-equipped fast-attack craft, refurbishing its World War II era destroyers, and developing plans to build a submarine. The navy also has launched an ambitious naval construction project aimed at the development of a second generation of warships (the Kuanghua I project), purchased over a dozen French LaFayette-class frigates, and leased several U.S. Knox-class frigates. All new ships will be equipped with state-of-the-art weapons and technology including Taiwan's locally developed antiship missiles (the Hsiung Feng I and Hsiung Feng II). To further beef up its antisubmarine warfare capabilities, the navy has purchased German minesweepers, U.S. antisubmarine helicopters and antisubmarine torpedoes, and formed an antisubmarine command "to study ways to counter possible moves by Communist Chinese subs to blockade the Taiwan Straits."⁸

Air Force. Taiwan is also putting more muscle into its air force. In January 1994, the armed forces began to take delivery of the domestically manufactured Indigenous Defense Fighter, a warplane designed originally to replace Taiwan's aging stock of eighty Lockheed F-104G and 300-plus Northrop F-5E/F aircraft. Current plans call for the acquisition of about 135 IDFs. The air force is waiting on the delivery of 150 U.S.-built F-16/AB fighters and sixty French-made Mirage 2000 warplanes. Finally, Taipei has signed a deal to lease T-38 jet trainers (enabling it to begin immediately to train pilots to fly F-16s) and drastically improved its surveillance capabilities with the purchase of several E-2T early-warning planes.

Army. Taiwan's army is being downsized into a smaller defensive force. Current plans call for the army to be reduced to 200,000 troops in ten years. At the same time, however, the Defense Ministry states that its goal is to develop the ground forces into "an armored, automated and 3-dimensional Army."[9] In order to achieve this objective, the army is being equipped with new tanks, combat helicopters, and other sophisticated military equipment.

Other developments. This discussion outlines only several major developments in Taiwan's armed forces. A more complete description would contain details about other enterprises as well. For example, the island has signed a deal to coproduce a derivative of the U.S.-built Patriot missile system (the Modified Air Defense System, or MADS), invested heavily in the military construction of air and naval bases (including underground shelters), and deployed an impressive array of domestically manufactured surface-to-air, air-to-air, and antiship missiles.

U.S. Support

With the abrogation of the U.S.-ROC Defense Treaty in 1979, the United States terminated its formal security commitment to Taiwan. However, the United States continues to play a critical role in Taiwan's defensive strategy. U.S. military equipment, technological assistance, and an informal or "tactic" alliance augment the island's defenses.[10] Furthermore, analysts also suspect that the United States cooperates militarily with Taiwan in other ways.

U.S. military equipment. According to the Taiwan Relations Act (TRA)—the legislation that guides official U.S. policy toward Taiwan—the United States will "make available to Taiwan such defense articles and defense services in such quantity as may be necessary to enable Taiwan to maintain a sufficient self-defense capability." Recent sales of U.S.-built military equipment have included missiles, advanced fighter aircraft, and sophisticated antisubmarine helicopters (Table 3.1). The United States also has transferred critical technologies to Taiwan. This technological assistance has enabled Taipei to domestically manufacture a wide range of military hardware, including advanced warplanes, missiles, warships, and tanks.[11]

U.S. security commitment. In terms of the U.S. security commitment to Taiwan, the TRA states that it is the policy of the United States "to consider any attempt to resolve the Taiwan issue by other than peaceful means, including boycotts or embargoes, a threat to the peace and security of the

Table 3.1 U.S. Foreign Military Sales Agreements with Taiwan and Commercial Arms Exports to Taiwan: Fiscal Years 1984–1993 (U.S.$ in thousands)

	FMS	Commercial	Total
1984	703.9	70.0	773.9
1985	697.6	54.5	772.1
1986	508.9	228.4	737.3
1987	507.1	210.0	717.1
1988	501.1	195.1	696.2
1989	524.7	84.8	609.5
1990	508.4	150.0	658.4
1991	475.7	160.0	635.7
1992	478.0	95.6	573.6
1993	6,275.0	346.0	6,621.0

Source: Defense Security Assistance Agency, *Foreign Military Sales, Foreign Military Construction Sales and Military Assistance Facts as of September 30, 1993* (Washington, D.C.: FMS Control and Reports Division, Comptroller, DSAA, 1993).

Western Pacific area and of grave concern to the United States." In the event that Taiwan is threatened, Section 3 of the TRA states:

> The President is directed to inform the Congress promptly of any threat to the security or the social or economic system of the people on Taiwan and any danger to the interests of the U.S. arising therefrom. The President and the Congress shall determine in accordance with constitutional processes, appropriate action by the U.S. in response to any such danger.

Some argue that the United States *must* come to the defense of Taiwan. These individuals are mistaken. The TRA provides the United States only with an *option* to defend Taiwan, it does not necessarily commit the United States to Taiwan's defense. The difference is important. The TRA is not a mutual defense treaty, and unlike the existing U.S. security relationships with the Republic of Korea or Japan, a U.S. response to hostilities directed against Taiwan is not guaranteed. Perhaps no one has underscored this fact more than Lee Teng-hui, Taiwan's president, who often warns the island-republic that it must maintain the capability and strength to handle an attack on its own.

Although the TRA is not a formal defense treaty, both sides of the Taiwan Strait agree that the prospect of U.S. military intervention has long played a key role in Taiwan's defense. For example, when cross-Strait tensions mounted in March 1996, the United States dispatched two naval battle groups to patrol international waters outside Taiwan and warned that any military attack on the island would lead to "grave consequences."[12] As Chang Shallyen, former ROC vice minister for foreign affairs, opined, the

U.S. "commitment to our security has never changed and this serves as a very effective deterrent."[13]

Other forms of military cooperation. Analysts have long suspected that the U.S. military support for Taiwan is not limited solely to arms sales and the TRA. For example, in 1995 reports surfaced that Washington was providing Taipei with critical intelligence information about the PRC's East China Sea missile tests. According to these reports, Taiwan depended "on American intelligence to say whether missiles have been fired and what type of weapons are involved."[14]

Analysis

Would a mainland invasion of Taiwan be prohibitively costly in terms of casualties, materials, and international image? Is Taiwan's defensive strategy working?

It is always difficult to determine whether a strategy of deterrence is working "since the absence of an attack could mean either that no attack was ever intended or that deterrence has succeeded."[15] But given Beijing's persistent refusal to rule out the use of force to take Taiwan, one may assume that the island is in danger. Indeed, a 1994 Gallup survey of Taiwanese residents found that roughly 75 percent of respondents believe that the PRC "is hostile to Taiwan."[16] Following China's 1995 missile tests in the East China Sea, that figure rose to 80 percent.[17] Moreover, a 1992 study commissioned by Taiwan's Government Information Office chronicled more than seventy-five instances between 1975 and 1991 in which high-ranking mainland authorities threatened to use force to resolve the Taiwan issue.[18]

It appears that Taipei's defensive strategy is succeeding: Taiwan's military buildup and its relationship with the United States deter PRC aggression.[19] At the same time, it should be stressed that Taiwan has taken concrete steps to defuse tensions across the Taiwan Strait.[20] Although a sudden resolution of the unification issue is unlikely, the explosion in economic, social, and cultural exchanges may ultimately draw the two Chinese governments toward a more stable and harmonious relationship.

Enhancing Taiwan's Security

Oskar Morgenstern once observed, "A strategy is a plan of action. It has to be continuously revised in the light of new information, new events in the world, and in view of possible changes in goals."[21] There is a range of options available to Taiwan should it desire to enhance, augment, or otherwise modify its current defensive strategy. These include (1) the development of nuclear weapons, (2) joining a collective security system, or (3) negotiating a nonaggression pact with the PRC. The discussion below examines each of these alternatives.

Nuclear Weapons

In July 1969, Taiwan established the National Chung Shan Institute of Science and Technology. The institute's missions include "the R & D [research and development] and design of defense science and technology, as well as the manufacture and production of research and development results."[22] The CSIST and its subsidiaries have played a critical role in the development of Taiwan's Indigenous Defense Fighter, the Ching Feng (Green Bee) surface-to-surface missile, the Tien Kung I and Tien Kung II (Sky Bow I and Sky Bow II) surface-to-air missiles, the Hsiung Feng I and Hsiung Feng II (Awe-Inspiring Air I and II) antiship missiles, and a host of other domestically manufactured weapons systems.[23] Since the creation of the CSIST, rumors also have circulated that the institute and a number of closely affiliated organizations—including the Atomic Energy Council's (AEC) Nuclear Energy Research Institute—are seeking to develop nuclear weapons.[24]

Nuclear weapons background. In 1988, Yen Chen-hsiung, then AEC director, acknowledged that when the Nuclear Energy Research Institute was first founded, "it was engaged in nuclear weapons research."[25] Yen stressed, however, that Taipei ceased all such activities after becoming a signatory to the Nuclear Non-Proliferation Treaty.[26] Despite such denials, Taiwan continued to engage in nuclear weapons research.

In 1976, reports surfaced that "Taiwan might be secretly reprocessing spent nuclear fuel—from its Canadian-supplied reactor or other sources—to produce weapons-grade plutonium for use in nuclear arms production."[27] Responding to the alleged activity, Washington sought and obtained a secret commitment from Taipei that it had "no intention whatsoever to develop nuclear weapons or a nuclear explosive device, or to engage in any activities related to reprocessing purposes."[28] In 1987, Wu Ta-you, then president of Academia Sinica (a prestigious Taiwanese think tank), confirmed that "the Taiwanese government had pledged to the U.S. in the 1970s that it would not make atomic weapons."[29] Indeed, the United States reportedly obtained assurances "that went well beyond those required by the international Nuclear Non-Proliferation Treaty."[30]

In 1988, following the mysterious disappearance of Colonel Chang Hsien-yi, one of four deputy directors of the Nuclear Energy Research Institute, reports again surfaced that Taiwan was attempting to develop a nuclear weapon. According to these, Colonel Chang—allegedly recruited by the Central Intelligence Agency (CIA) when he was a graduate student in the

Nuclear Engineering Department at the University of Tennessee—had informed U.S. officials of a secret CSIST nuclear research laboratory while visiting the United States in October 1987.[31] Shortly after his return to Taipei, representatives from the United States and the International Atomic Energy Agency "raided" the institute and asked to inspect the clandestine facility.[32] With CIA assistance, Colonel Chang fled shortly after the raid.[33]

Following Colonel Chang's much-publicized disappearance, U.S. officials refused to comment on whether Taiwan had been seeking to establish a plutonium-extraction installation, whether Taipei had violated understandings with Washington, or if Chang was a CIA agent.[34] But after one official suggested that "Taiwan is not engaged in activities which are inconsistent with its commitments," another explained that "this statement was correct at the moment it was spoken since Taiwan had stopped the nuclear activities that were being questioned."[35]

Taiwanese officials denied charges that CSIST had been building a facility to produce weapons-grade plutonium. Authorities argued that "according to both the international Non-Proliferation Treaty, to which the ROC is a signatory, and a trilateral agreement among the ROC, the U.S. and the IAEA, nuclear facilities and materials used by the ROC's nuclear plants are under the IAEA's strict supervision. . . . It would be impossible for the ROC to divert its nuclear wastes to the manufacture of atomic bombs."[36] Shaw Yu-ming, then director-general of Taiwan's Government Information Office, labeled as "absolutely groundless" stories that Taiwan was covertly developing nuclear bombs.[37] Finally, the government denied that Colonel Chang was a CIA agent and declared that "the so-called Chang Hsien-yi case was purely a personal affair."[38]

Following Colonel Chang's disappearance, Taiwan shut down its largest civilian nuclear research reactor—a unit that had been the focus of U.S. concern since it was delivered in 1969. When commenting on the closing, Taiwanese officials said only that it was being shut down for "economic reasons."[39]

Motivations for acquiring nuclear weapons. U.S. officials refuse to speculate on the possible motives that might have prompted Taipei to engage in nuclear weapons research. Others, however, have offered several explanations.

Although Beijing claims that it seeks the peaceful unification of China, it has not ruled out the use of force to take Taiwan. Some contend that Taipei might seek nuclear weapons in an effort to deter a PRC attack against the island. According to this view, a Taiwanese bomb "could probably deter any Communist invasion of the island. . . . [It] would be tactically useful against a Communist amphibious invasion, since amphibious forces classically have had to be concentrated to fight their way ashore."[40] In fact, in July 1995,

Taiwan's president hinted that the ROC might consider manufacturing nuclear weapons to confront Beijing's mounting threats.[41]

In February 1993, R. James Woolsey, CIA director, observed that collapse of the Soviet Union and the end of the Cold War have "jarred longstanding alliances and encouraged an increasing number of states to further bolster their own military capabilities, including developing weapons of mass destruction."[42] Officials in Taipei view the end of the era of superpower rivalry and the accompanying U.S. military drawdown in the Western Pacific with apprehension. In 1994, Sun Chen, then Taiwan's defense minister, cautioned that "taking advantage of the dissipation of Soviet power, the reduction in U.S. weapons and the U.S. plans to gradually reduce its military presence in this area, the Chinese communists are expanding their arsenal and strengthening their combat forces."[43] Analysts have long warned that "Taiwan might reconsider its nuclear choices if Peking significantly boosts its own defenses or comes to believe that the U.S. defense shield is unreliable."[44]

Taipei's stance toward nuclear arms also might be influenced by developments in North Korea. In fact, North Korea's nuclear aspirations have raised fears that other regional powers—including Japan, Taiwan, and South Korea—might opt to manufacture nuclear arms.[45]

Sentiment for Taiwan's de jure separation from mainland China has grown (Table 3.2). Following the 1994 Qiandao Lake tour boat murders, support for independence rose to an all-time high of 27 percent.[46] Given Beijing's persistent threat to use force if the island declares itself independent, some separatists see nuclear weapons as a means by which Taiwan can achieve independence.

Table 3.2 Support for Taiwanese Independence (percentage of respondents)

	Strongly support	Support	Oppose	Strongly oppose	No opinion	No answer
September 1989	5.4	10.4	28.9	28.4	25.2	1.7
December 1989	1.3	6.9	37.0	25.0	24.4	5.3
March 1990	4.5	11.3	33.4	28.9	13.7	8.1
June 1990	4.3	8.2	37.4	29.6	14.0	6.5
December 1990	3.8	8.2	30.6	31.1	21.7	4.3
June 1991	1.9	10.8	36.7	28.6	20.9	1.0
October 1992	4.7	10.4	33.8	29.5	16.0	5.5
May 1993	5.0	18.7	41.4	12.9	20.5	1.6
November 1993	3.8	16.2	39.8	14.9	24.1	1.2
April 1994	9.8	17.2	29.3	16.3	25.4	2.0

Source: Data provided to author courtesy of the Gallup Organization, Taipei, Taiwan, ROC.

Note: Polls from September 1989 to May 1993 were conducted by the Public Opinion Research Foundation. Polls from November 1993 and April 1994 were conducted by the Gallup Organization.

On April 12, 1994, Chou Po-lun, a Democratic Progressive Party legislator and an advocate of Taiwanese independence, called on the government to develop nuclear weapons as a hedge against the PRC threat. The lawmaker claimed that "peace in the region can be maintained only by the creation of mutual assurance of destruction over the skies of the Taiwan Strait" and that "developing nuclear weapons is necessary if Taiwan wants to be independent of mainland China."[47] In July 1995, another DPP legislator, Liu Hui-hsiung, also called on the Taiwanese government to develop nuclear weapons.[48]

Finally, one should note that only a handful of countries maintain formal diplomatic ties with the ROC. In fact, none of the world's important governments (with the possible exception of South Africa) recognize the Nationalist regime in Taipei. Some suggest that Taipei might attempt to acquire nuclear weapons to boost its prestige and "increase the international status of a government that is no longer formally recognized by many countries."[49] In short, a nuclear capability could bolster the regime's image both at home and abroad.

In sum, several considerations might lead Taipei to develop nuclear weapons. It remains unclear which, if any, of these factors led to Taipei's efforts to build nuclear arms in the 1970s and 1980s. But as one U.S. official observed, "they weren't doing it for the fun of it."[50]

Taiwan's current nuclear capabilities. At present, Taiwan possesses six nuclear power reactors housed in three nuclear power stations. Together, these units generate approximately 40 percent of the total electricity in the Taiwan area. Current plans call for the construction of a fourth power station. In addition to these peaceful applications of nuclear energy, however, reports that Taiwan is engaged in nuclear weapons research continue to surface. In fact, it is not uncommon for the popular press to suggest that Taiwan has successfully manufactured nuclear arms.

In 1986, a Hong Kong magazine claimed that Taiwan "has made several [nuclear] bombs."[51] According to another Hong Kong source, "Chinese Communist Party General Staff Headquarters' intelligence shows that Taiwan's Chung Shan Research Institute has successfully developed nuclear weapons in a mountain valley in Taiwan and that it also has the capability to manufacture such weapons."[52] The U.S. mass media also has speculated on Taiwan's nuclear capabilities and intentions. For example, in 1993, the U.S.-based National Broadcasting Corporation (NBC) reported that Taiwan and several other countries are "sparing no efforts to become members of the world's nuclear club."[53]

Taiwanese officials have long acknowledged that Taiwan "absolutely" has the capability to manufacture nuclear weapons.[54] But it is not clear whether this statement means that Taipei possesses the necessary "know-how" to manufacture nuclear arms, the required weapons-grade materials, or both.⁵⁵ Taiwanese officials do stress, however, that the island does not *possess* nuclear weapons. Current U.S. and Russian intelligence estimates support this assertion.

During U.S. congressional hearings in 1993, Senator John Glenn (Democrat–Ohio) asked Gordon Oehler, chief of the CIA's Non-Proliferation Center, about the status of Taiwan's nuclear weapons program. After observing that "Taiwan had a nuclear weapons program at one time" and that "they stood down with that program," the senator asked, "is that still in that same status, or have they started up again?"⁵⁶ Oehler replied that "they have stood down."⁵⁷ Russian intelligence reports also have confirmed that, while "having a developed industrial and scientific and technical potential, Taiwan is in a position, according to experts, to create weapons of mass destruction components and means of delivering them . . . *[but] Taiwan does not have nuclear weapons* [emphasis added]."⁵⁸

Collective Security

As Richard Betts has noted, "collective security is an old idea whose time keeps coming."⁵⁹ In fact, the concept has enjoyed widespread popularity during several periods in the twentieth century. A collective security arrangement "purports to provide security *for* all states, *by* the action of all states, *against* all states which might challenge the existing order by the arbitrary unleashing of their power."⁶⁰ Could such an organization enhance Taiwan's security?

Throughout the Cold War, the United States depended on a series of bilateral security relationships to provide a framework for peace and stability in the Western Pacific. For example, Washington negotiated bilateral defense treaties with Japan, South Korea, and Taiwan.⁶¹ It was widely believed that Asia's vast size and heterogeneity and the lack of a unified perception of a security threat would doom any drive to establish a multilateral security structure. Indeed, the Bush administration once rejected proposals for the establishment of a collective security forum or institution by suggesting that it would represent "a solution in search of problems."⁶²

With the end of the Cold War, new security concerns are emerging in Asia. There is a growing consensus among Asian governments that the U.S. network of bilateral alliances can no longer deal with the region's security problems. Even U.S. officials now acknowledge that multilateral solutions to security challenges are necessary to "manage or prevent emerging concerns such as arms races, the forging of competing alignments and efforts by one power or group of powers to dominate this strategic region."⁶³

In 1988, President Lee Teng-hui first raised the issue of Taiwan's participation in a collective security forum. Citing the U.S. drawdown in the Western Pacific, the rearmament of Japan, China's position toward the South China Sea, and the establishment of formal diplomatic relations between Seoul and Beijing as key factors, Lee told a U.S. delegation that Taiwan would be willing to contribute to a collective security system:

> A collective security system should be set up among Southeast Asian nations to ensure the region's stability. I think it's necessary to set up a collective security system and allow countries concerned to join. . . . Of course, the United States' economic power now is not enough to lead such a collective security organization, but we can set up a collective security protection fund and let the nations concerned contribute.[64]

Following Lee's initial call for Taiwan's participation in a multilateral security arrangement, other high-ranking Taiwanese officials took up the cause. Ma Ying-jeou, then vice chairman of Taiwan's Mainland Affairs Council, opined that "a collective security system could well be built along the lines of existing economic cooperation forums or organizations."[65] Fredrick Chien, Taiwan's foreign minister, observed that "this collective security system . . . would reduce the likelihood of conflicts flaring up and serve to eliminate mutual distrust."[66] Sun Chen, then Taiwan's defense minister, attempted to assuage fears that Taipei was calling for an anti-PRC alliance. Sun suggested that "we think the Asian-Pacific countries can consider establishing a collective security system without a mock enemy so that disputes can be resolved through dialogue."[67] As cross-Strait tensions escalated in 1995, however, it looked as if Taiwan was indeed pressing for an anti-PRC organization. When meeting with scholars at the 1995 Asia Open Forum in Kaohsiung, President Lee Teng-hui said that Asia Pacific countries should "study the feasibility of forming a joint security system" because "China has been building up its military power in recent years, posing threats to Taiwan and other Asia-Pacific countries and drawing international concern."[68]

A Nonaggression Pact

In 1991, the ROC government adopted the *Guidelines for National Unification,* Taiwan's blueprint for the peaceful unification of China. The *Guidelines* state that Chinese unification should be achieved over three stages: "a short-term phase of exchanges and reciprocity, a medium-term phase of mutual trust and cooperation, and a long-term phase of consultation and unification."[69] At the present moment, Taipei is attempting to persuade the PRC to respond positively to specific elements in the first phase.

Beijing rejects Taiwan's terms for unification. Scoffing at Taipei's call for treatment as an equal political entity, mainland authorities describe the island as a "renegade province" and argue that the ROC ceased to exist in 1949. But there is evidence that Beijing might change its position.

In 1993, the Hong Kong–based *Far Eastern Economic Review* reported that Beijing was pondering the feasibility of government-to-government negotiations. Perhaps more significant, one of the colony's leading newspapers, the *South China Morning Post,* has quoted Wang Daohan, head of the PRC's Association for Relations Across the Taiwan Straits (ARATS), as saying that relevant units in Beijing "are doing research on an adequate way, which is agreeable to both sides, to declare to the world that both sides have ceased their state of hostility."[70] Given the fact that the PRC represents the chief threat to Taiwan's security, some believe that the successful negotiation of a nonaggression pact could greatly augment the island's security.

Analysis

As described, each of the options above could enhance Taiwan's security. At the same time, however, each may be infeasible and/or undermine the island's security.

The Limited Utility of Nuclear Weapons

It is extremely difficult for a government to secretly launch a nuclear weapons program. Should Taipei adopt such a course of action, it is likely that Washington would learn of it. As in the past, the United States would attempt to force its "abandonment by at least implicit threats of suspension of military and economic aid and possibly other economic sanctions."[71]

If Taiwan did manage to develop nuclear weapons successfully, it is unlikely that the arms would enhance Taipei's international status. As President Lee observed, "everyone knows we once had this idea [to develop nuclear weapons], but it attracted international attention that might have had a grave effect on our national image."[72] Taiwan's hard-won international clout and prestige would plummet. Relations with the United States would suffer. In fact, in the eyes of much of the global community, Taiwan might join the ranks of Iran, Iraq, North Korea, and several other governments as an "international outlaw" or "rogue state."

It is difficult to gauge the PRC's response to a nuclear Taiwan. During the mid-1980s, Deng Xiaoping suggested that Beijing would use force against the island "if Taipei decided to build nuclear weapons."[73] Although PRC officials seem to have dropped this precondition for invasion, ROC military authorities still contend that the mainland will attack if the island develops nuclear weapons.[74]

Officials in Taipei also would have to consider the domestic political fallout that would accompany the development of nuclear weapons. Although some opposition lawmakers have called on the government to develop such arms, the DPP's platform states clearly that the party will "oppose production, procurement, storage and application of biochemical or nuclear weapons."[75] Indeed, opposition to nuclear power has soared in

Taiwan. Some of the most violent riots in Taiwan's history have been sparked by protests against the establishment of the island's fourth nuclear power plant.[76]

Finally, Taiwanese officials do not seem particularly concerned about nuclear weapons on the Korean peninsula. In fact, during interviews with the author, authorities expressed surprise at Western press reports that Taipei feels threatened by North Korea's nuclear ambitions. As one legislator noted, "Taiwan has no history of a problem with North Korea.... So far we think that only Red China is our enemy."[77] At the same time, however, it must be stressed that officials did express alarm at the prospect of Japan acquiring nuclear weapons.

Collective Security: Unlikely for Taiwan

Taiwan has expressed a strong desire to join any collective security system that might emerge in post–Cold War Asia. But no other states have extended an invitation for Taiwan to join such an organization. In fact, Taipei remains locked out of regional security discussions. As H. C. Wang, a member of the Legislative Yuan's Committee on National Defense, observed, it is unlikely that Taiwan will be able to gain membership in a collective security organization. The lawmaker explained that "I think that mainland China will force other Asian countries to not allow our country to participate."[78]

Governments are traditionally reluctant to enter into entangling alliances. This observation applies with special force to Taiwan—a state viewed by many as a breakaway province of China. If attacked, it is doubtful that any East Asian government would come to Taiwan's assistance—a fact appreciated by both Chinas. PRC authorities believe that "internationally, only the United States can react with hostility [to a PRC attack against Taiwan] but that it is unlikely to go to war with Communist China ... reactions from other countries are likely to fall under the following three categories: support, silence and verbal condemnation."[79] Taiwanese military authorities also have warned that the defense of Taiwan "is our problem ... [and] the ROC military must have the capability and strength to handle an attack on its own, without depending on outside help."[80] In sum, it must be emphasized that "no Asian state is likely to wish to be militarily involved in a major conflict between China and Taiwan."[81]

A Nonaggression Pact: Could It Be Trusted?

As described earlier, one of Taipei's preconditions for unification is that the PRC rule out the use of force to take Taiwan. According to some reports, Beijing is now studying Taipei's proposal. But would a nonaggression pact enhance the island's security?

Although Taiwan has called on Beijing to renounce the use of force to achieve unification, some insist that "it is too early to talk about signing a peace agreement between the two sides of the Taiwan Strait."[82] As John F. Copper, a noted authority on Taiwan's politics, has observed, Taipei realizes "that any promise of non-force is worth little or nothing (given the historical record of such promises) and may be a negative (in terms of lulling its own public into a sense of false security while encouraging the opposition to larger defense spending)."[83] Others believe simply that Beijing "has no intention of relinquishing the possibility of a military solution of the Taiwan issue."[84]

Despite such misgivings, ROC officials continue to express interest in a peace treaty with Beijing. During Taiwan's 1996 presidential election, Lee Teng-hui claimed that, if elected, signing a peace agreement with Beijing would be "the most important work" of his administration.[85] Immediately following his reelection, Lee indicated that he was willing to travel to Beijing to discuss peace with PRC leaders.[86] Other ROC officials also have begun to call vigorously for a cross-Strait treaty. Lien Chan, Taiwan's newly elected vice president, has said that "we are interested in seriously thinking about a peace treaty and a lot of preparations need to be done for that."[87] However, the vice president cautioned that "I think it takes time."[88] The president also has acknowledged that it "will be difficult" to negotiate with Beijing until after it has resolved the difficult succession issue.[89]

Conclusion: Taiwan's Security in the Post–Cold War Era

One of the most critical tasks facing a government today is the need to reassess its security now that the Cold War has come to an end. In the United States, government planners and bureaucrats speak happily of peace dividends and a new world order. But in Taiwan—a country that is fast emerging as one of Asia's few fully functioning democracies—the talk has turned to arms races, proliferation, and power vacuums.

As explained in following chapters, the end of the Cold War represents both opportunities and challenges for Taipei. But it is unlikely that Taiwan will significantly alter its current defensive strategy. Rather, Taiwan plans to strengthen military relations with the United States and upgrade its weapon systems to cope with the threats and uncertainties that are accompanying the end of the Cold War. The new arms—along with the U.S. security commitment and the growing linkages between Taipei and Beijing—will continue to be the foundation upon which Taiwan builds its strategy to deter PRC aggression and maintain peace and stability across the Taiwan Strait. As Lee Teng-hui has observed, "our primary task is establishment of a preventative, speedy response military capability, to let mainland China know of the terrible sacrifice that an invasion of Taiwan could entail, so that they might not likely take action."[90]

Notes

1. J. C. Wylie, *Military Strategy: A General Theory of Power and Control* (New Brunswick, New Jersey: Rutgers University Press, 1976), p. 13.
2. Samuel B. Gardiner, "Fundamental Strategic Concepts, Strategists and Their Ideas on War," in George Edward Thibault (ed.), *The Art and Practice of Military Strategy* (Washington, D.C.: National Defense University, 1984), p. 44.
3. See Shu-Ming Chang, "3 New Ships Feed Arms Buildup," *China Post* (International Airmail Edition), September 29, 1993, p. 1. Also see "ROC Defense Announces Merge Move," *China Post* (International Airmail Edition), November 5, 1993, p. 4.
4. Sun Chen, Taiwan's defense minister, has used these terms to describe Taiwan's current defense strategy. See "Defense Boss: Problems Dog Airspace Defense," *China Post* (International Airmail Edition), March 29, 1993, p. 4.
5. Author's interview with Stephen S. F. Chen, vice minister, Ministry of Foreign Affairs, Republic of China. Taipei, Taiwan, May 19, 1994.
6. "Mainland Strength Asked to Be Noted," *China Post* (International Airmail Edition), March 15, 1994, p. 4.
7. Hsieh Shu-fen, "Overcoming Adversity on the Seas—The Navy Plans for the Future," *Sinorama* 16, No. 9, September 1991, p. 85.
8. "ROC Navy Studying Anti-Blockade Strategy," *CNA,* January 25, 1992, in *Lexis/Nexis.*
9. ROC Ministry of National Defense, *1992 National Defense Report: Republic of China* (Taipei: Li Ming Cultural Enterprise Co., 1992), p. 83. Translated from the Chinese by Major General Ma Kainan, ROC Army.
10. Members of the U.S. legislative branch have argued that the Taiwan Relations Act is "tantamount to establishing an alliance with Taiwan against aggression." See statement of Representative Mark D. Siljander (Republican–Michigan), in U.S. Congress, House of Representatives, *Implementation of the Taiwan Relations Act,* Hearing and Markup before the Committee on Foreign Affairs and Its Subcommittees on Human Rights and International Organizations and on Asian and Pacific Affairs, May 7, June 25, and August 1, 1986 (Washington, D.C.: U.S. Government Printing Office, 1987), p. 42.
11. For a discussion of U.S. technology transfers to Taiwan, see Dennis Van Vranken Hickey, *United States–Taiwan Security Ties: From Cold War to Beyond Containment* (Westport, Connecticut: Praeger, 1994), pp. 41–75.
12. See Bill Wang, "Clinton's National Security Adviser Warns Beijing," *CNA* (Taipei), March 6, 1996.
13. Author's interview with Chang Shallyen, vice minister for foreign affairs, Republic of China. Taipei, Taiwan, January 8, 1992.
14. See Willy Wo-Lap Lam, "Beijing Reaps Rewards of War Games," *South China Morning Post,* July 24, 1995, p. 9. Also see "ROC Playing Intelligence Game with Beijing," *China Post* (International Airmail Edition), July 25, 1995, p. 4.
15. Alexander L. George and Richard Smoke, *Deterrence in American Foreign Policy* (New York: Columbia University, Press, 1974), p. 62.
16. Dennis Engbarth, "Lake Deaths Fuel Support for Taiwan Breakaway," *South China Morning Post* (International Weekly Edition), April 23–24, 1994, p. 6.
17. "Residents Say Beijing Is Acting Unfriendly," *China Post* (International Airmail Edition), July 24, 1995, p. 1.
18. See ROC Government Information Office, *A Study of a Possible Communist Attack on Taiwan* (Taipei: Government Information Office, 1992).
19. In fact, U.S. military officials have warned that "before Deng Xiaoping

decides to invade Taiwan, he should realize the invasion could fail—miserably. It's not a foregone conclusion China would win." See Tony Emerson, Jeff Hoffman, Kari Huus, and Marcus Mabry, "Would Beijing Dare Invade?" *Newsweek* (International Edition–Asia), December 23, 1991, p. 16.

20. Some analysts describe this as a critical element in Taiwan's defense strategy. For more information, see Cheng-yi Lin, "ROC Defense Programs and Priorities: Current Assessment and Future Projections," paper presented at the International Conference on Taiwan in a Transformed Global Setting, Institute for Foreign Policy Analysis and the Institute of International Relations, April 28–29, 1994, Boston, Massachusetts.

21. Oskar Morgenstern, "Military Alliances and Mutual Security," in David M. Abshire and Richard V. Allen (eds.), *National Security: Political, Military and Economic Strategies in the Decade Ahead* (New York: Praeger, 1963), p. 675.

22. See ROC Ministry of National Defense, *1992 National Defense Report,* p. 146.

23. For more information, see Hickey, *United States–Taiwan Security Ties,* pp. 41–76.

24. Although the Atomic Energy Council is an agency under the Executive Yuan, the CSIST is reportedly in charge of personnel at the AEC's nuclear energy research laboratories. For more information, see "Paper Claims U.S. Helps Nuclear Scientist Flee," *China Post* (Taipei), March 11, 1988, in *FBIS, China,* March 16, 1988, p. 53.

25. See "Taiwan Denies Plans to Build Nuclear Weapons," Hong Kong, Zhongguo Tongxue She, March 22, 1988, in *FBIS, China,* March 1988, p. 49.

26. The ROC signed the treaty on July 1, 1968. Although Taiwan's delegation to the International Atomic Energy Agency (IAEA) was ousted in 1971, Taipei has stated its intention to continue to cooperate with IAEA safeguards. In fact, Taiwan has signed three separate agreements pledging to use its nuclear facilities only for peaceful purposes. These include a bilateral agreement with Washington; a tripartite pact between the IAEA, the United States, and Taiwan; and another bilateral agreement with the IAEA. For more information, see Melinda Liu, "Taiwan's Power Game," *Far Eastern Economic Review,* December 17, 1976, p. 33. Also see "Executive Yuan Restates No Plan for Atomic Bombs," *CNA,* May 20, 1988, in *FBIS, China,* May 23, 1988, p. 65.

27. Taiwan officials publicly denied these charges. For more information, see Melinda Liu, "Accounting for the N-Factor," *Far Eastern Economic Review,* December 17, 1976, p. 32.

28. Quoted from Ralph Clough, *Island China* (Cambridge, Massachusetts: Harvard University Press, 1978), p. 119.

29. See Terry Cheng, "Taiwan Has 'No Need to Produce Atomic Bombs,'" *South China Morning Post,* January 7, 1987, p. 2.

30. See Stephen Engelberg, "Washington Talk: State Department; Making Policy and Such Public: The Whole Story," *New York Times,* April 22, 1988, p. A14.

31. See "Cabinet Denies Nuclear Official's Connections," *CNA* (Taipei), May 13, 1988, in *FBIS, China,* May 18, 1988, p. 69; and "Paper Speculates on CIA Role," *Agence France-Presse* (*AFP*) (Hong Kong), March 12, 1988 in *FBIS, China,* March 14, 1988, p. 57.

32. See "Paper Speculates on CIA Role."

33. According to Taiwanese press accounts, the CIA smuggled Chang off the island by way of a former U.S. military air base in central Taiwan. However, the American Institute in Taiwan (AIT), the "unofficial" U.S. embassy in Taipei, claimed that "nobody at the AIT knows anything" about Chang's disappearance. For more

information, see "Paper Claims U.S. Helps Nuclear Scientist Flee"; and "Defense Ministry Denies Producing Atomic Bombs," *China Post* (Taipei), March 9, 1988, in *FBIS, China,* March 16, 1988, p. 54.

34. See Stephen Engelberg and Michael R. Gordon, "Taipei Halts Work on Secret Plant to Make Nuclear Bomb Ingredients," *New York Times,* March 22, 1988, p. 1.

35. See Engelberg, "Washington Talk."

36. "Executive Yuan Restates No Plan for Atomic Bombs," p. 65.

37. "Nuclear Rumors Denied: Top Scientist Missing," *CNA* (Taipei), March 10, 1988, in *FBIS, China,* March 10, 1988, p. 54.

38. "Cabinet Denies Nuclear Official's Connections," p. 69.

39. See Engelberg and Gordon, "Taipei Halts Work on Secret Plant," p. 1.

40. See George H. Quester, "Taiwan and Nuclear Proliferation," *Orbis* 18, No. 1, Spring 1974, pp. 144–145.

41. See "No Nukes for Reunification: Lee," *China Post* (International Airmail Edition), August 21, 1995, p. 1.

42. See prepared statement of R. James Woolsey, director of central intelligence, in *Proliferation Threats of the 1990s,* U.S. Congress, Senate, Hearing Before the Committee on Governmental Affairs, 103rd Congress, 1st Session, February 24, 1993 (Washington, D.C.: U.S. Government Printing Office, 1993), p. 51.

43. Sun Chen has made this point on several occasions. For more information, see Dennis Van Vranken Hickey, "Interview with Sun Chen, Taiwan's Defense Minister," *Asian Defense Journal,* February 1994, pp. 30–35.

44. David K. Willis, "How South Africa and Israel Are Maneuvering for the Bomb," *Christian Science Monitor,* December 3, 1981, p. 14.

45. See Tai Ming Cheung, "Nuke Begets Nuke," *Far Eastern Economic Review,* June 4, 1992, pp. 22–23.

46. See Alice Hung, "27% Support Independence," *China Post* (International Airmail Edition), April 18, 1994, p. 1.

47. "No Nukes for Taiwan," *CNA,* April 12, 1994, in *Lexis/Nexis.*

48. See Christopher Bodeen, "Lee: Taiwan Not Ready to Go Alone," *China Post* (International Airmail Edition), July 29, 1995, p. 1.

49. See Joseph A. Yager, *Nuclear Nonproliferation Strategy in Asia* (McLean, Virginia: Center for National Security Negotiations, 1988), pp. 11–12.

50. Engelberg and Gordon, "Taipei Halts Work on Secret Plant," p. 1.

51. See "Defense Ministry Denies Development of Nuclear Weapons," *CNA,* March 15, 1986, in *Lexis/Nexis.*

52. "'Tangtai' CCP Conference on Taiwan Discusses Use of Force," *Tangtai* (Hong Kong), November 15, 1991, in British Broadcasting Corporation, *BBC Summary of World Broadcasts,* November 23, 1991, in *Lexis/Nexis.*

53. "ROC Denies Developing Nuke Device," *CNA,* December 27, 1993, in *Lexis/Nexis.*

54. One of the earliest references to Taiwan's ability to manufacture nuclear weapons was made in 1986 when General Chang Hui-yuan said that Taiwan "has the capability to manufacture nuclear arms." See "Ministry Denies Development of Nuclear Weapons," *CNA,* March 15, 1986, in *FBIS, China,* March 17, 1986, p. V1. Also see Hickey, *United States–Taiwan Security Ties.*

55. When asked directly what ROC officials meant by saying that Taiwan has a capability to develop nuclear weapons, Stephen S. F. Chen, ROC vice minister for foreign affairs, replied, "In a general sense. If we were determined to go that way we could. But we will not." From author's interview with Stephen S. F. Chen, Taipei, Taiwan, May 19, 1994.

56. See *Proliferation Threats of the 1990s,* p. 33.
57. Ibid.
58. See Foreign Broadcast Information Service, JPRS Report, March 5, 1993, "Proliferation Issues, Russian Federation: Foreign Intelligence Service Report, New Challenges After the Cold War: Proliferation of Weapons of Mass Destruction," in ibid., p. 103.
59. Richard Betts, "Collective Security and Arms Control in the New Europe," in Richard K. Betts (ed.), *Conflict After the Cold War: Arguments on Causes of War and Peace* (New York: Macmillan Publishing, 1994), p. 448.
60. See Innis L. Claude, Jr., *Power and International Relations* (New York: Random House, 1962), p. 110.
61. The U.S.-ROC Mutual Defense Treaty was terminated in 1979.
62. Susumu Awanohara, "Group Therapy," *Far Eastern Economic Review,* April 15, 1993, p. 11.
63. Winston Lord, assistant secretary of state for East Asian and Pacific affairs, made this point during his confirmation hearings. For more information, see ibid.
64. "Lee Urges Collective Security for Asia," *China Post* (International Airmail Edition), September 16, 1992, p. 1.
65. "Ma Calls for Collective Security System in Asia-Pacific," *CNA,* November 18, 1992, in *Lexis/Nexis.*
66. "The World Has Not Become Safer: ROC Foreign Minister," *CNA,* June 19, 1993, in *Lexis/Nexis.*
67. "Defense Minister Gives Interview to Jane's," *CNA,* July 9, 1993, in *Lexis/Nexis.*
68. Dennis Engbarth, "Lee's Poll Bid Brings Beijing War Threat," *South China Morning Post* (Weekly Edition), August 26, 1995, p. 1.
69. ROC Government Information Office, *The Republic of China Yearbook, 1993* (Taipei: Government Information Office, 1993), p. 149.
70. Willy Wo-Lap Lam, "Beijing Hints at End to Hostility," *South China Morning Post,* April 12, 1993, p. 6.
71. Yager, *Nuclear Nonproliferation Strategy in Asia,* p. 51.
72. Bodeen, "Lee: Taiwan Not Ready to Go Alone."
73. See Guo-cang Huan, "Taiwan: A View from Beijing," *Foreign Affairs* 65, No. 5, Summer 1985, p. 1068.
74. See Dennis Engbarth, "Taiwan Aims to Create More Flexible Military," *South China Morning Post,* March 24, 1994, p. 9. Also see ROC Ministry of National Defense, *1993–1994 National Defense Report, Republic of China* (Taipei: Li Ming Cultural Enterprise Co., 1994), p. 87. Translated from the Chinese by Yang Lien-chung, Li Chang-hao, and Hsieh Yung-t'ien.
75. Democratic Progressive Party, *Charter/Platform* (Taipei: DPP Headquarters, 1994), p. 27.
76. For more information, see "Violence Erupts in Talks on Funding Nuclear Plant," *China Post* (International Airmail Edition), June 22, 1993, p. 1; and "35 Hurt in Fierce Clash on Nukes," *China Post* (International Airmail Edition), June 26, 1993, p. 1.
77. From author's interview with H. C. Wang, legislator, Committee of National Defense, Legislative Yuan. Taipei, Taiwan, May 16, 1994.
78. Ibid.
79. "'Tangtai' CCP Conference on Taiwan Discusses Use of Force."
80. See "ROC Going to School on Gulf War Experiences, Defense Chief Says," *Free China Journal,* March 14, 1991, p. 2. More recently, the Taiwanese military stated that "should, one day, [the] PRC outrageously take rash action without think-

ing of any serious consequences, and rapidly settle the war situation, then it will probably be the case [that] these nations (the international community) would accept the fact of [the] PRC's occupying [the] ROC on Taiwan." See ROC Ministry of National Defense, *1993–1994 National Defense Report,* pp. 91–92.

81. Paul H. Kreisberg, "Asian Responses to Pressures on Taiwan," in Parris H. Chang and Martin L. Lasater (eds.), *If China Crosses the Taiwan Strait: The International Response* (Lanham, Maryland: University Press of America, Inc., 1993), p. 89.

82. See "'Too Early' for 'Peace Agreement' with PRC," *China Broadcasting* (Taipei), April 7, 1993, in *FBIS, China,* April 9, 1993, p. 19.

83. John F. Copper, "Taiwan and the New World Order," unpublished manuscript, 1994, p. 12.

84. Lin, "ROC Defense Programs and Priorities," p. 2.

85. See "We're Ready for Anything, Says Lee," *China Post* (International Airmail Edition), February 27, 1996, p. 1.

86. See R. L. Chen, "Lee Holds Out Olive Branch," *China Post* (International Airmail Edition), May 20, 1996, p. 1.

87. Apple Wan, "Vice President Holds Out Hope of Peace Treaty," *Hong Kong Standard,* March 28, 1996, on the World Wide Web at *http://www/hkstandard.com/.*

88. Ibid.

89. See Susan Yu, "Lee Links High-Level Talks to Mainland Tilt for Power," *Free China Journal,* May 17, 1996, p. 1.

90. Christopher Bodeen, "President Rebukes Mainland Threats," *China Post* (International Airmail Edition), July 28, 1995, p. 1.

Part 2

ENHANCEMENTS TO TAIWAN'S SECURITY

4

U.S.-PRC Relations

This chapter outlines the background and evolution of U.S.-PRC ties and shows how strategic considerations led the two governments to normalize relations in the 1970s. The chapter also suggests that, with the collapse of the Soviet Union, the raison d'être for U.S.-PRC rapprochement has vanished. Concerns Washington once overlooked for the sake of national security are emerging as major issues of contention. These strains—tensions elevated in part by the end of the Cold War and the accompanying demise of the so-called strategic triangle—are helping Taipei strengthen its ties with Washington.

Background and Evolution of U.S.-PRC Relations

Mao Zedong, chairman of the Chinese Communist Party (CCP), officially proclaimed the founding of the PRC on October 1, 1949. Since that time, U.S.-PRC relations have passed through several phases.

Phase One: Confrontation and Hostility

During the late 1940s, China was engulfed in a major civil war. Initially it appeared that the U.S.-equipped forces of the Kuomintang (KMT), which totaled roughly 3 million, were far superior to the 1 million Communist troops. Some even hoped for a quick victory. But the KMT regime had been predicting victory over the "Communist bandits" for many years. In 1934, the ROC government proclaimed confidently that it would be "foolish not to recognize the fact that the Chinese Government has dealt a smashing blow at the forces which for so long have been creating strife and fomenting discontent. . . . Communism in China is dying."[1]

By 1948, it was clear that the ROC government was losing both territory and popular support. In July 1948, John Leighton Stuart, the U.S. ambassador to China, summarized his views of the situation as follows:

> We can be sure that no amount of military advice or material from us will bring unity and peace to China unless indeed there are reforms sufficiently drastic to win back popular confidence and esteem. That these could even be attempted by those now in power or that the improvements could be rapid and radical enough to reverse the prevailing attitude is scarcely to be hoped for.[2]

As John King Fairbank observed, an "infinitude" of factors—including corruption, incompetence, factionalism, and economic collapse—contributed to the KMT's defeat.[3]

As the Chinese Civil War drew to a close, it appeared that the United States might be able to reach some sort of accommodation with the new Chinese government. Washington had reduced its aid to the Nationalist regime and was prepared to accept the PRC's conquest of Taiwan. But a number of factors hindered the development of cordial U.S.-PRC relations.

The continued support of the United States for Chiang, albeit reduced, aroused deep PRC suspicions. The Beijing leadership also was infuriated by Washington's reluctance to extend recognition to the new regime and its insistence that the Communists "have foresworn their Chinese heritage and have publicly announced their subservience to a foreign power, Russia."[4]

At the same time, Washington was outraged by PRC actions. On July 1, 1949, Mao denounced the "imperialism" of the United States and proclaimed that China would "lean to the side of the Soviet Union."[5] In November 1949, several U.S. diplomats were jailed for spying in China. In early 1950, the PRC seized U.S. property in Beijing and announced that it had successfully negotiated an alliance with the chief U.S. rival—the Soviet Union.

These developments contributed to strains in the U.S.-PRC relationship. But it was the outbreak of the Korean War that set the stage for roughly two decades of intense belligerence.

In June 1950, North Korean forces invaded South Korea. On June 27, 1950, U.S. president Harry S Truman ordered the Seventh Fleet to "neutralize" the Taiwan Strait.[6] As John Kuan observed, "The Korean War transformed American policy from abandonment of the Republic of China to the defense of Taiwan."[7] The United States had intervened in the Chinese Civil War.

Following Beijing's decision to enter the Korean conflict in November 1950, Washington sought to "contain" mainland China with a series of bilateral and multilateral alliances stretching from Japan and the Republic of Korea in the north to the South East Asian Treaty Organization (SEATO) and the treaty with Australia and New Zealand (ANZUS) in the south. Furthermore, the United States ruled out recognition of the Beijing regime and imposed a trade embargo on economic contacts with the PRC. Finally, for almost two decades, Washington sponsored a limited secret war against the PRC.[8] Throughout the 1950s and 1960s, U.S. intelligence agencies helped Taiwan stage raids on the Chinese mainland.

For its part, the PRC supported the Communist forces in North Korea and Vietnam. Beijing also proclaimed its intention to "liberate" Taiwan and attempted to seize ROC territory (the offshore islands) in 1954 and 1958. These crises almost led to a direct U.S.-PRC confrontation. However, a series of internal upheavals—including the disastrous Great Leap Forward in the late 1950s, the Tibetan uprising in 1959, and the Cultural Revolution (1966–1976)—gradually led the PRC to become more preoccupied with internal problems.

Phase Two: The Road to Reconciliation and Normalization

The Sino-Soviet alliance began to deteriorate in the late 1950s. By the late 1960s, it appeared that the two Communist giants might go to war. U.S. president Richard M. Nixon's startling announcement, during an August 14, 1969, National Security Council meeting, that the United States "could not allow China to be smashed" signaled a momentous transformation in U.S. policy.[9] Henry Kissinger explained: "It was a major event in American foreign policy when a President declared that we had a strategic interest in the survival of a major Communist country, long an enemy, and with which we had no contact."[10]

A wide range of considerations contributed to the president's decision. But global strategic concerns played a predominant role. The PRC had come to be viewed "as a desirable counterweight to the Soviet Union which was rapidly gaining strategic nuclear parity with the United States."[11]

For its part, Beijing had ample motivation to abandon its dual adversary strategy toward Washington and Moscow and pursue a policy of détente (or perhaps even a united front) with the United States. The 1960s had witnessed an escalation in Sino-Soviet tensions. Indeed, on more than one occasion, the Soviet Union had sought to enlist U.S. support for an attack on China:

> In 1970, the Soviet Union sought unsuccessfully to conclude an agreement with the United States directed against China . . . it was rejected, as had been earlier probes in 1969 of possible joint action to neutralize Chinese nuclear facilities.[12]

Moscow also attempted to line up Taipei's support for an invasion.[13] Threatened with the prospect of a preemptive Soviet nuclear strike, or worse, "rapprochement between Washington and Beijing was seen as a quick fix for the Communist Chinese as much as for the Americans."[14]

In order to improve relations, both parties proved willing to set aside temporarily their differences over certain volatile issues—matters that had previously rendered all prospects of a reconciliation hopeless. Perhaps most surprising was the delicate handling of the Taiwan question, an affair long considered an irredentist issue in U.S.-PRC relations. When addressing this problem, Mao said that "this issue is not an important one . . . the issue of the international situation is an important one."[15] After U.S. officials secretly promised that Washington would not support the Taiwanese independence movement, both parties easily and amiably reached an understanding whereby they would "agree to disagree" over Taiwan.[16]

Phase Three: Strategic Cooperation

On December 15, 1978, the United States announced the establishment of full diplomatic relations with the PRC, to become effective January 1, 1979. In order to achieve normalization, Washington acquiesced to Beijing's three long-standing demands: (1) termination of formal diplomatic relations with the ROC, (2) abrogation of the 1954 U.S.-ROC Mutual Defense Treaty, and (3) removal of all U.S. troops from Taiwan. At the same time, the United States acknowledged the PRC's position that it is the legitimate government of China.[17] As Zbigniew Brzezinski, then U.S. national security advisor, observed, the decision to formalize ties with Beijing was "definitely influenced by the Soviet dimension."[18]

During the 1980s, the United States sought to establish a tacit alliance with China. Secretary of State Alexander Haig and other White House officials convinced President Ronald Reagan that Beijing's continued strategic cooperation against Soviet expansionism outweighed any need to improve ties with Taipei.[19] The president even promised to reduce U.S. military support (in the form of arms sales) for Taiwan.[20] Reagan defended the change in policy by emphasizing Beijing's strategic importance:

> Building a strong and lasting relationship with China has been an important foreign policy goal of four consecutive American administrations. Such a relationship is vital to our long-term national security interests and contributes to stability in East Asia. It is in the national interests of the United States that this important strategic relationship be advanced.[21]

President Reagan also approved a change in policy permitting U.S. arms sales to the PRC. In June 1981, Haig announced that the United States would sell arms to Beijing on a case-by-case commercial basis.[22] In 1984, Reagan cleared the way for direct government-to-government transfers (foreign military sales) by declaring, as required by law, that such sales would "strengthen the security of the United States and promote world peace."[23] Table 4.1 outlines the growth in U.S. arms agreements and sales to the PRC from 1984 through 1989.

Table 4.1 U.S. Foreign Military Sales Agreements with the PRC and Deliveries to the PRC: Fiscal Years 1984–1989 (U.S.$ in thousands)

	Agreements	Deliveries
1984	629	6
1985	421	424
1986	36,045	547
1987	254,279	3,881
1988	12,913	39,122
1989	416	91,255

Source: Defense Security Assistance Agency, *Foreign Military Sales, Foreign Military Construction Sales and Military Assistance Facts as of September 30, 1991* (Washington, D.C: Data Management Division, Comptroller, DSAA, 1991).

Summary

A variety of economic, political, and strategic factors contributed to U.S.-PRC rapprochement. But strategic considerations were the driving force. In fact, the Central Intelligence Agency has revealed that the two governments "went to extraordinary lengths to cooperate with one another against Moscow . . . they regularly shared intelligence and teamed up devising anti-Soviet strategies."[24] Common opposition to Soviet expansionism brought the two governments together and for sixteen years the relationship was "sustained by this strategic assessment."[25]

U.S.-PRC Relations in the Post–Cold War Era

With the collapse of the Soviet Union, the raison d'être for U.S.-PRC rapprochement vanished. As Lloyd Bentsen, then a U.S. senator (Democrat–Texas), explained, "U.S. courtship of mainland China is no longer strategically imperative."[26] Tensions between Washington and Beijing have since escalated. Some analysts now suggest that "the U.S. considers mainland China to be its number one headache after the Cold War."[27] In fact, public opinion polls reveal that a majority of the U.S. public now thinks of China as either not friendly or as an enemy (Table 4.2).

Since 1949, the continued U.S. support for Taiwan has lingered as the most contentious issue in U.S.-PRC relations. From the PRC's viewpoint, it is the U.S. government, not the authorities on Taiwan, that stands in the way of a peaceful reunification of China. Officials in Beijing have long insisted that Washington's military support creates a climate encouraging Taipei's refusal to enter into reunification negotiations. But more than Taiwan separates the United States and the PRC. The following discussion explains how

Table 4.2 How the U.S. Public Views China

Close ally	Friendly	Not friendly	Enemy	Not sure
3%	25%	45%	24%	3%

Source: The Harris Poll 1995, No. 60, "Canada, Britain and Australia Top the List of Countries Which Americans Think of as Allies and Friends," October 2, 1995.

economic ties, human rights issues, and China's military policies—concerns Washington once overlooked for the sake of national security—have emerged as major issues of contention.

U.S.-PRC Economic Ties

U.S.-PRC trade has grown from a few million dollars in the early 1970s to more than $48 billion in 1994.[28] During the same period, U.S. investment in China soared. These economic ties have linked the two nations more closely, but they also have created frictions. China's trade surplus with the United States is approaching $30 billion per year, second only to that of Japan (Table 4.3).

Table 4.3 Top Ten U.S. Negative Trade Balances, 1994

U.S. deficit positions	Deficit amounts (U.S.$ billions)
1. Japan	65.7
2. People's Republic of China	29.5
3. Canada	14.5
4. Germany	12.5
5. Taiwan	9.6
6. Italy	7.5
7. Malaysia	7.0
8. Thailand	5.4
9. Venezuela	4.3
10. Nigeria	3.9

Source: Business America: The Magazine of International Trade, May 1995, p. 18.

Many believe that Beijing's burgeoning trade surplus is due to unfair trading practices. Ambassador Charlene Barshefsky, deputy U.S. trade representative, contends:

> China maintains one of the most protectionist trade regimes in the world. It has put in place multiple overlapping non-tariff barriers to imports and

maintains prohibitively high tariffs. While China's export regime has undergone a remarkable transformation over the past decade, turning China into one of the world's most formidable export engines, China's import regime remains in part the creature of central planners and state bureaucrats.[29]

In addition to maintaining import barriers on U.S. agricultural commodities, industrial goods, and many other products, U.S. officials claim that China's services markets are "largely closed" and "legitimate access for U.S. companies in most instances is not available."[30] Washington also has charged that "China has repeatedly engaged in violations of bilateral agreements controlling its exports of textiles and apparel to the U.S. market."[31] PRC transshipments, the practice of shipping textiles destined for the United States to a third country, where they are fraudulently labeled as having been manufactured in that country, are said to have assumed "massive proportions."[32]

One of the most contentious economic disputes—and an issue that brought the two governments to the brink of a trade war—involves the protection of intellectual property rights. U.S. authorities claim that businesses in the United States are losing more than U.S.$1 billion per year to Chinese pirates.[33] Bootlegged products range from jeans and sweatshirts to motion pictures and computer software. According to industry estimates, "copied software accounts for 94% of that used in China."[34]

U.S. and Chinese officials have hammered out several agreements to resolve troublesome trade issues. In 1994, negotiators reached an agreement whereby China promised to cooperate with the United States to prevent the transshipment and overshipment of textiles. Moreover, in 1995, Washington succeeded in forcing China to meet U.S. demands that it take steps to protect U.S. intellectual property rights.[35] But these negotiations have left sore feelings in both Beijing and Washington.

It is likely that economic issues will continue to plague U.S.-PRC relations. In China, officials resent what they perceive to be bullying tactics by the United States to achieve trade concessions. They also are deeply angered by what they see as a deliberate effort by the United States to block China's entry into the General Agreement on Tariffs and Trade/World Trade Organization (GATT/WTO). In the United States, officials and business leaders remain skeptical about China's pledges to reform its trading practices.[36] After all, China failed to abide by earlier accords, and it is an open question whether the central government has the ability to compel provincial and local authorities to comply with the new agreements. Finally, some U.S. officials question one of the basic premises for continued economic ties with China—namely, that bilateral trade creates jobs for U.S. workers. Representative Nancy Pelosi (Democrat–California) and other voices in Congress argue that the "reality" of the relationship is that "the U.S. is the job loser in the U.S.-China trade."[37]

Human Rights Issues

During the Cold War, the U.S. public felt uncomfortable with some aspects of realpolitik in foreign affairs. When making policy, it often seemed that strategic interests overrode moral considerations. Winston Lord, assistant secretary of state for East Asian and Pacific affairs, explained:

> We have always had multiple objectives, including during the Cold War—pursuing security, economics, human rights, other issues. But during the Cold War, we generally had a hierarchy; namely security came first. If we did not like a particular government, we sort of pulled our punches because we needed them as an ally against the Soviet Union. . . . Those days are over.[38]

Now that the Soviet Union has disintegrated, the United States is afforded an opportunity to attach a greater importance to human rights.

When the People's Liberation Army crushed China's 1989 pro-democracy movement, U.S. president George Bush responded by taking the following actions:

- Suspension of government-to-government arms sales
- Suspension of U.S.-PRC military exchanges
- Increased assistance to the Red Cross for work in China
- Sympathetic review of requests made by PRC students studying in the United States to extend their stay
- Review of other U.S.-China programs and activities

But these moves—measures that probably would not have been taken during the height of the Cold War—failed to satisfy many members of Congress and the media.[39]

The Tiananmen Square incident had a profound effect on U.S.-PRC relations. China is no longer viewed as a progressive country that practices "cuddly communism":

> In the 1980s China was seen as a possible model for reform in the socialist world. In the latter half of 1989, it was viewed by many in the same light as Vietnam, North Korea and Cuba.[40]

The bloody suppression of the democracy movement had shattered the domestic consensus on the U.S. China policy—a consensus that had endured for almost two decades.

Both President Bush and President Bill Clinton have attempted to stave off congressional initiatives to punish the PRC for its human rights abuses. Legislative attempts to impose stringent conditions on the renewal of China's most-favored-nation (MFN) status have failed.[41] But the annual tug-of-war over human rights and China's MFN status ultimately forced the Clinton administration to "delink" the two issues.

Many believe that China's human rights performance is not improving. Some even argue that "China has one of the worst human rights records in the world."[42] Numerous reports—including studies commissioned by the U.S. Department of State, Amnesty International, and Asia Watch—tend to support this view. Alleged violations include:

- Forced confessions and torture by police and prison authorities
- Arrest and imprisonment of political and religious activists—those who commit the "crime" of trying to practice universal basic freedoms
- Coercive birth control, including forced abortions and sterilizations
- The brutal occupation and colonization of Tibet
- Transplanting organs from executed criminals without their consent
- Restrictions on emigration and engaging in the practice of internal exile
- Jamming Voice of America broadcasts[43]

Other human rights abuses include

> denial of the right to strike (a concern of the labor movement in the West), denial of freedom of the press (raised by interest groups devoted to international press freedom), the kidnapping and abuse of women and girls, denial of the right to move one's legal residence, eugenics policies against the mentally defective, mistreatment of homosexuals, and interference with foreign journalists in China.[44]

These reports have inflamed passions in both Washington and Beijing.

It is unlikely that the human rights issue will go away—it most likely will linger as a contentious issue in U.S.-PRC relations. Voices in Congress and the media will continue to press for sanctions against China and will make it difficult for U.S. government leaders to get close to Beijing. As for the PRC, it views Washington's attempts to link trade with human rights as an infringement on China's sovereignty. In fact, China's State Council denies all reports of human rights abuses and claims that Washington "rigs up materials to attack China, in an attempt to mislead the world public and damage China's prestige."[45]

China's Military Policies

In addition to the two intertwined issues of trade and human rights, China's military policies are complicating the U.S.-PRC relationship. China's military buildup, arms sales, and territorial claims are fueling U.S. suspicions that the PRC is the post–Cold War "bogeyman."[46] As one congressional China expert observed, "there is a body of opinion in this country, I don't know how big, that thinks China is the enemy."[47]

Militarily, the PRC still lags far behind the United States. However, U.S. defense analysts are watching nervously as Beijing beefs up its military capabilities. According to a 1995 Rand Corporation study, "China's military budget stands at U.S.$140 billion—at least three times higher than the Pentagon's estimate of the People's Liberation Army spending."[48] The PRC is purchasing sophisticated Russian military equipment and technology—ranging from Kilo-class submarines to Su-27 warplanes—and upgrading its nuclear weapons arsenal. U.S. Defense Department officials caution that, although Washington should maintain a military dialogue with Beijing, it should not harbor "naive" illusions or engage in "wishful thinking" about the long-term prospects for U.S.-PRC military relations:

> They are building up their forces and brandishing their new-found political and military might. We ought to have a dialogue with them. But engaging in wishful thinking that the Chinese are our friends and that they have the same sort of world view as we do is a very naive approach to what the long-term security relationship in Asia is all about.[49]

The PRC is either a member or a participant in all leading nonproliferation agreements.[50] But it has supplied advanced weapons and technology to a number of governments—including Pakistan, Syria, Iraq, and Iran. Table 4.4 outlines the value of PRC arms agreements and deliveries during the years 1986–1993.

In August 1993, the Clinton administration imposed sanctions on roughly $1 billion in high-technology trade after intelligence indicated that Beijing had violated the Missile Technology Control Regime by shipping

Table 4.4 Chinese Arms Transfer Agreements and Deliveries to the World, 1986–1993 (constant 1993 U.S.$ in millions)

	Agreements	Deliveries
1986	2,268	1,649
1987	5,781	2,581
1988	2,990	3,557
1989	1,853	2,736
1990	2,558	1,660
1991	539	1,476
1992	306	827
1993	400	1,000

Source: Richard F. Grimmett, *CRS Report for Congress: Conventional Arms Transfers to the Third World, 1986–1993* (Washington, D.C.: Congressional Research Service, July 29, 1994), pp. 84–86.

M-11 missile components to Pakistan. But these sanctions, which were lifted only months after they were imposed, had little effect on Beijing. Personal appeals also failed. PRC officials were not impressed by U.S. energy secretary Hazel O'Leary's pleas for restraint:

> They basically told her to get lost—they'll stop [nuclear] testing by 1996, when they're good and ready. And meanwhile they'll sell whatever nuclear technology they please to whomever they please—Iran, Pakistan, what have you—under the heading of "atoms for peace."[51]

According to a congressional study, "China's willingness to abide by the guidelines on missile transfers set out in the MTCR is ambiguous at best" and Beijing "seems prepared to pursue arms sales opportunities it deems appropriate wherever they present themselves."[52]

The PRC's territorial claims are adding to the image of a Chinese government that is a threat to peace and stability in the Asia Pacific region. Beijing has long threatened to use force to take Taiwan or enforce its claims of sovereignty over the entire South China Sea. But current threats differ from those made in the past—they appear more credible. A 1995 simulation exercise conducted by the U.S. Department of Defense's Office of Net Assessment showed China taking over Taiwan.[53]

Finally, China's war games and "missile tests" off Taiwan's coastline put the United States and the PRC on a potential collision course during early 1996. Responding to China's "provocative" behavior, Washington dispatched two carrier battle groups to patrol the waters around Taiwan. For its part, Beijing threatened that if the armada entered the Taiwan Strait it might confront a "sea of fire."[54]

Conclusion: Implications for Taiwan

During the Cold War, Washington and Beijing successfully concluded what Zbigniew Brzezinski, former assistant to the president for national security affairs, described as "a de facto alliance or, if you will, an alliance by stealth . . . because of certain common and enduring geopolitical interests."[55] But the strategic rationale for this alignment crumbled along with the Berlin Wall. As described, the two governments now find themselves at odds over a wide variety of issues including trade, human rights, arms sales, and proliferation. Domestic political pressures and quarrels over Taiwan and Tibet are contributing to the tensions.

Charles W. "Chas" Freeman, a former high-ranking Defense Department official, has observed that "the current state of the [U.S.-PRC] relationship is the worst it has been since normalization of relations."[56] Despite presidential summits and other high-level meetings, most analysts see little chance for improvement during the foreseeable future. As one Western diplomat observed, "Sino-U.S. relations seem to have settled into an endless series of upsets that, taken one at a time, show a relationship that is neither steadily deteriorating nor rapidly improving."[57] Indeed, U.S. secretary of state Warren Christopher concedes that because of the leadership crisis in Beijing, there might be "some difficulties in some areas—especially trade, human rights and non-proliferation."[58]

PRC analyses share this pessimism. Chinese publications identify the United States as Beijing's "principal military adversary in the future" and suggest that "because of serious opposition and differences in ideology, social system and foreign policies between China and the United States during a fairly long period of time, it would be impossible to improve fundamentally Sino-U.S. relations."[59] Beijing's U.S. experts claim that "there is a union between [U.S.] liberals who oppose China on issues such as human rights and right-wing 'friends of Taiwan' who want to promote American hegemonism," and they predict that "anti-Chinese sentiments would remain equally strong if a Republican were to accede to the Presidency in 1996."[60]

Lawmakers in Washington are calling for significant changes in China policy. Representative Benjamin Gilman (Republican–California), chairman of the House Committee on International Relations, explains: "The bipartisan consensus is that our China policy needs to be overhauled. It has failed us on trade, human rights, proliferation and security matters."[61] A legislative "overhaul" of China policy does not bode well for the future of U.S.-PRC relations. After all, the new Congress is being described as the "most pro-democracy, pro-Taiwan, pro-Tibet, anti-Chinese Communist Party and anti-People's Liberation Army Congress in recent memory."[62] This sentiment escalated when China attempted to intimidate Taiwanese voters by conducting large-scale military maneuvers and missile tests off Taiwan's coast in March 1996. Responding to the crisis, both houses of Congress passed resolutions criticizing China's behavior and calling on the United States to assist in defending Taiwan if it came under attack.

From its perspective, the PRC now sees itself as "engaged in an international class warfare with the United States."[63] Hardliners in Beijing believe that the United States is "trying to divide China territorially, subvert it politically, contain it strategically and frustrate it economically."[64] Some Chinese officials believe that the time has arrived for Beijing to "stand up" to Washington. For example, in June 1993, 116 senior military officers in the People's Liberation Army reportedly petitioned Deng Xiaoping to "forcefully hit back at the rude acts of interference, subversion and extortion by the U.S. hegemonists."[65]

What do these persistent tensions in U.S.-PRC relations hold for Taiwan? In 1992, Chang Shallyen, then Taiwan's vice minister for foreign affairs, predicted that the end of the Cold War might lead Washington to strengthen its ties with Taipei:

The collapse of the Soviet Union has meant the disappearance of the so-called China card. The importance of mainland China in the eyes of the White House people definitely has decreased to a great extent because of the collapse of the Soviet Union—it is quite evident. In that regard, I think our ties with Washington, D.C. can be strengthened.[66]

Recent developments appear to support Chang's view.

On September 2, 1992, President Bush announced that he would approve the sale of up to 150 F-16 fighters to Taiwan—aircraft unavailable at any price during the Cold War. U.S. officials who might have opposed the sale during the 1970s or 1980s now supported the move. According to one account, "this time almost no one in the bureaucracy argued against antagonizing the Chinese by ending the United States' 10-year ban on weapons sales to Taipei."[67] The F-16 agreement is being followed by numerous other sales, including deals for Hawkeye E-2T early-warning aircraft, Mk-46 torpedoes, M60A3 tanks, Knox-class destroyers, Harpoon antiship missiles, Stinger missiles, and a derivative of the Patriot missile air defense system. These arms represent a significant boost to Taiwan's defensive capabilities.

In September 1994, the Clinton administration completed a comprehensive interagency review of U.S. policy toward Taiwan. After more than a year of study, the Department of State announced several adjustments in policy,[68] including the following:

- Senior U.S. economic and technical officials will be allowed to visit Taiwan
- Taiwan's leaders may make transit stopovers in the United States. However, senior Taiwanese officials—including Taiwan's president—will still be prohibited from visiting Washington or conducting official business in the United States.
- Taiwan will be permitted to change the name of its thirteen representative offices in the United States from the baffling "Coordination Council for North American Affairs" to the "Taipei Economic and Cultural Representative Office"
- The United States will support Taiwan's membership in international organizations where statehood is not an issue and will support opportunities for Taiwan's voice to be heard in organizations where it is denied membership[69]

It is noteworthy that the Clinton administration made these changes despite strong protests by Beijing.

In May 1995, the Clinton administration announced that Lee Teng-hui, Taiwan's president, would be permitted to pay a private visit to the United States to attend an alumni reunion at Cornell University. The announcement came only days after the State Department had explained that Lee would be denied a visa because "a visit by a person of President Lee's title, whether or not the visit were termed private, would unavoidably be seen by the PRC as removing an essential element of unofficiality in the U.S.-Taiwan relationship."[70] No president of the ROC had been allowed to visit the United States since 1979. Most officials shrugged off warnings that the visit would irritate Beijing. For example, when informed that the visit might jeopardize U.S.-PRC relations, some lawmakers replied, "So what?"[71]

It seems that Taiwan is gaining from changes in the nature of the U.S.-PRC dyad. Not only is Washington less receptive to PRC sensitivities about Taiwan, but an increasing number of voices in the Congress and the media advocate using the "Taiwan card" to strike back at China. For example, Representative Tom Lantos (Democrat–California) has declared that if improved U.S.-Taiwan relations and United Nations membership for Taiwan "make the Chinese uncomfortable, so much the better."[72] Others suggest that Washington should ignore Beijing's demands that Taiwan not follow it into the World Trade Organization, and they claim that U.S. support for Taipei's early admission would "send a message" to mainland China.[73]

So long as the strains in U.S.-PRC relations remain at a manageable level, Taiwan should benefit. However, Taiwanese authorities stress that they have no desire to be played as a "card." Furthermore, they caution that a precipitous deterioration in U.S.-PRC relations could actually threaten the island's security:

> From our point of view, we hope that the U.S. and the PRC relations will be stable. Stable, but not necessarily good. Good relations will hurt us too—we will be sacrificed again. But stable relations, within a range without big vibrations, would serve our interests.[74]

Authorities also stress that they have no desire to exacerbate strains in U.S.-PRC relations. As Su Chi, vice chairman of Taiwan's Mainland Affairs Council explained, "the PRC and the U.S. have enough problems and most of the problems have nothing to do with us."[75]

Notes

1. China Information Service, *Suppressing Communist-Banditry in China,* 2d ed. (Shanghai: China United Press, 1934), p. v.

2. *United States Relations with China* (Washington, D.C.: Department of State Publications, 1949), p. 277.

3. See John King Fairbank, *The United States and China,* 4th ed. (Cambridge, Massachusetts: Harvard University Press, 1980), pp. 344–349.

4. *United States Relations with China,* p. xvi.

5. "People's Democratic Dictatorship: Soviet Union Our Best Teacher," *Vital Speeches of the Day,* October 1, 1949, p. 749.

6. See "Statement by the President on the Situation in Korea," in *Public Papers of the President of the U.S.: Harry S. Truman* (Washington, D.C.: U.S. Government Printing Office, 1965), p. 492.

7. See John C. Kuan, *A Review of U.S.-ROC Relations, 1949–1978* (Taipei: Asia and World Institute, 1980), p. 10.

8. See Michael Schaller, *The United States and China in the Twentieth Century* (New York: Oxford University Press, 1979), p. 140.

9. Henry Kissinger, *The White House Years* (Boston: Little, Brown and Company, 1979), p. 183.

10. Ibid.

11. Steven L. Levine, "The Soviet Factor in Sino-American Relations," in Michel Oksenberg and Robert B. Oxnam (eds.), *Dragon and Eagle—United States–China Relations: Past and Future* (New York: Basic Books, Inc., 1978), p. 247.

12. Prepared statement of Hon. Raymond Garthoff, former U.S. ambassador to Bulgaria, in *The United States and the People's Republic of China: Issues for the 1980s*. U.S. Congress, House, Hearings Before the Subcommittee on Asian and Pacific Affairs of the Committee on Foreign Affairs, 96th Congress, 2nd Session, April 1, July 22, August 26, and September 23, 1980 (Washington, D.C.: U.S. Government Printing Office, 1980), p. 86.

13. See "ROC, Soviet Union Tried to Crush Mao," *China Post* (International Airmail Edition), May 22, 1995, p. 1.

14. A. James Gregor, *Arming the Dragon: U.S. Security Ties with the People's Republic of China* (Washington, D.C.: Ethics and Public Policy Center, 1988), p. 10.

15. Kissinger, *The White House Years*, p. 1062.

16. See Jim Mann, "U.S., China Coordinated Policy During Cold War," *Los Angeles Times,* June 13, 1994, p. A1.

17. The word "acknowledge" was deliberately chosen as it indicates cognizance of, but not necessarily agreement with, the Chinese position. For more information about the significance of this term, see Dennis Van Vranken Hickey, "United States Policy and the International Status of Taiwan," *Journal of East Asian Affairs* 7, No. 2, Summer/Fall 1993, p. 578.

18. Zbigniew Brzezinski, *Power and Principle* (New York: Farrar, Straus and Giroux, 1983), p. 197.

19. For more information, see Alexander M. Haig, Jr., *Caveat: Realism, Reagan and Foreign Policy* (New York: Macmillan, 1984), pp. 194–214.

20. For more information, see Dennis Van Vranken Hickey, "U.S. Arms Sales to Taiwan: Institutionalized Ambiguity," *Asian Survey* 28, No. 12, December 1986, pp. 1324–1336.

21. Quoted from Tan Qingshan, *The Making of U.S. China Policy from Normalization to the Post–Cold War Era* (Boulder, Colorado: Lynne Rienner Publishers, 1992), p. 101.

22. Commercial sales cover the delivery of arms purchased directly from U.S. manufacturers. In order to deliver, the manufacturers must be licensed and the sale approved by the U.S. Department of State's Office of Munitions Control and the U.S. Department of Defense. For more information, see Dennis Van Vranken Hickey, "America's Military Relations with the People's Republic of China: The Need for Reassessment," *Journal of Northeast Asian Studies* 7, No. 3, Fall 1988, pp. 29–41.

23. Ibid.

24. See Mann, "U.S., China Coordinated Policy During Cold War," p. A1.

25. See the Atlantic Council of the United States and the National Committee on United States–China Relations, *United States and China Relations at a Crossroads* (Washington, D.C.: Atlantic Council of the United States, February 1993), p. 1.

26. See "Senator Bentsen Urges Bush to Sell F-16s to ROC," *CNA* (Taipei), August 11, 1992, in *Lexis/Nexis*.

27. Professor Chen Wen-poh, a professor at the University of Wyoming, has made this point. For more information, see Shu-Ming Chang, "U.S. to Use ROC as Trump Card to Limit Mainland Military Buildup," *China Post* (International Airmail Edition), February 16, 1993, p. 1.

28. See "U.S. Trade Facts," *Business America: The Magazine of International Trade,* May 1995, p. 18.

29. See prepared statement of Ambassador Charlene Barshefsky, deputy U.S. trade representative on trade policy toward China, in *H.R. 4590, United States–China Act of 1994*. U.S. Congress, House, Hearing Before the Subcommittee on Trade of the Committee on Ways and Means, 103rd Congress, 2nd Session, July 28, 1994 (Washington, D.C.: U.S. Government Printing Office, 1994), pp. 105–107

30. Ibid.

31. See U.S. International Trade Commission, *The Year in Trade, 1993: Operation of the Trade Agreements Program, 45th Report* (Washington, D.C.: USITC Publications, June 1994), p. 102.

32. Overshipments, shipments that exceed China's quota limits, are another major concern. For more information, see ibid.

33. See Karl Huus, "Back to Normal: U.S.-China Trade War Looms Closer," *Far Eastern Economic Review,* January 19, 1995, p. 52.

34. Ibid.

35. For details of the agreement, see Dede Nickerson, "Relief After Mainland's Late Concessions Avert Trade War," *South China Morning Post* (Weekly Edition), March 4–5, 1995, p. 1.

36. See "Clinton Hails Agreement as a Victory for Aggressive Policy," *South China Morning Post* (Weekly Edition), March 4–5, 1995, p. 2 (Business).

37. Testimony of Representative Nancy Pelosi (Democrat–California), in *H.R. 4590, United States–China Act of 1994*. U.S. Congress, House, Hearing Before the Subcommittee on Trade of the Committee on Ways and Means, 103rd Congress, 2nd Session, July 28, 1994 (Washington, D.C.: U.S. Government Printing Office, 1994), p. 59.

38. See testimony of Winston Lord, assistant secretary of state for East Asian and Pacific affairs, in *U.S. Policy Toward China*. U.S. Congress, Senate, Hearing Before the Subcommittee on East Asian and Pacific Affairs of the Committee on Foreign Relations, 103rd Congress, 2nd Session, May 4, 1994 (Washington, D.C.: U.S. Government Printing Office, 1994), p. 25.

39. The president was severely criticized for coddling the "Butchers of Beijing" and for sending high-level officials on secret missions to Beijing in 1989.

40. The Atlantic Council of the United States and the National Committee on United States–China Relations, *United States and China Relations at a Crossroads,* p. 2.

41. During the Bush administration, these initiatives were thwarted only by presidential vetoes.

42. See opening statement of Representative Tom Lantos (Democrat–California), in *China: Human Rights and MFN*. U.S. Congress, House, Joint Hearing Before the Subcommittee on Economic Policy, Trade and Environment; International Security, International Organizations and Human Rights; and Asia and the Pacific of the Committee on Foreign Affairs, 103rd Congress, 2nd Session, March 24, 1994 (Washington, D.C.: U.S. Government Printing Office, 1994), p. 43.

43. Ibid., p. 41.

44. These abuses receive less attention in the West. See Andrew J. Nathan, "Influencing Human Rights in China," in James R. Lilley and Wendell L. Willkie II

(eds.), *Beyond MFN: Trade with China and American Interests* (Washington, D.C.: AEI Press, 1994), p. 79.

45. "Beijing Denies Report Claims," *South China Morning Post* (Weekly Edition), March 4–5, 1995, p. 1.

46. For more information, see Simon Beck, "Beijing Becomes the Bogeyman," *South China Morning Post* (Weekly Edition), October 2–3, 1993, p. 11.

47. Nayan Chanda, "Winds of Change," *Far Eastern Economic Review,* June 22, 1995, p. 16.

48. Simon Beck, "Beijing 'Spends U.S. $140b on Arms,'" *South China Morning Post* (Weekly Edition), June 10, 1995, p. 1.

49. Ibid.

50. In March 1992, China joined the Nuclear Non-Proliferation Treaty (NPT) and made a written commitment to abide by the guidelines and parameters of the Missile Technology Control Regime (MTCR). In January 1993, China became a member of the Chemical Weapons Convention (CWC).

51. Lincoln Kaye, "Trading Rights," *Far Eastern Economic Review,* March 9, 1995, p. 16.

52. Richard F. Grimmett, *CRS Report for Congress: Conventional Arms Transfers to the Third World, 1986–1993* (Washington, D.C.: Congressional Research Service, July 29, 1994), p. 8.

53. See Chanda, "Winds of Change," p. 16.

54. "Bush Says There Will Be No War," *Hong Kong Standard,* March 22, 1996, on the World Wide Web at *http://www.hkstandard.com/*.

55. Testimony of Zbigniew Brzezinski, in *United States–China Relations: Today's Realities and Prospects for the Future*. U.S. Congress, Senate, Hearing Before the Committee on Foreign Relations, 98th Congress, 2nd Session, May 17, 1984 (Washington, D.C.: U.S. Government Printing Office, 1984), p. 29.

56. Steven Mufson, "U.S.-Beijing Ties Said Worst Since Normalization," *China Post* (International Airmail Edition), June 23, 1995, p. 1.

57. Jane Macartney, "Mainland-U.S. Ties Seem to Be Languishing Despite Summits," *China Post* (International Airmail Edition), November 1, 1995, p. 2.

58. Willy Wo-lap Lam, "A Chill Wind Blows from Washington," *South China Morning Post* (Weekly Edition), February 11–12, 1995, p. 1.

59. See Patrick E. Tyler, "China's Military Regards U.S. as Main Enemy in the Future," *New York Times,* November 16, 1993, p. 8.

60. Lam, "A Chill Wind Blows from Washington," p. 1.

61. See Chanda, "Winds of Change," p. 15.

62. Nayan Chanda, "Storm Warning," *Far Eastern Economic Review,* December 1, 1994, p. 14.

63. See U.S. General Accounting Office, *National Security: Perspectives on Worldwide Threats and Implications for U.S. Forces,* Report to the Chairmen, Senate and House Committees on Armed Services (Washington, D.C.: U.S. Government Printing Office, 1992), p. 28.

64. For more information, see Seth Faison, "Beijing Sees U.S. Moves as Plot to Thwart China," *New York Times,* August 1, 1995, p. A2.

65. See "Generals 'Not Satisfied' with Policy on U.S." [Hong Kong, Cheng Ming, June 1, 1993], in *FBIS,* June 2, 1993, p. 33.

66. Author's interview with Chang Shallyen, vice minister of foreign affairs of the Republic of China, Taipei, Taiwan, January 8, 1992.

67. Thomas L. Friedman, "China Warns U.S. on Taiwan Jet Deal," *New York Times,* September 4, 1992, p. A3.

68. In order to underscore the continuing unofficial nature of U.S.-Taiwan relations, the Department of State refused to release a written account of the changes in U.S. policy.

69. For more information, see "Taiwan Policy Review," *Department of State Dispatch,* October 17, 1994, Vol. 5, No. 42, p. 11; and Jim Mann, "U.S. Slightly Elevates Ties with Taiwan," *Los Angeles Times,* September 8, 1994, p. 4.

70. Tony Walker and George Graham, "Reaction Was Predictable but Fallout Is Not: Washington's About-Face Sets Stage for the Taiwan Issue Overshadowing All Relations," *Financial Times,* May 24, 1995, p. 4.

71. Nigel Holloway, Julian Baum, and Lincoln Kaye, "Shanghaied by Taiwan," *Far Eastern Economic Review,* June 1, 1995, p. 15.

72. See prepared statement of Representative Tom Lantos in *China: Human Rights and MFN,* p. 44.

73. See Christopher Bodeen, "U.S., PRC Quarrel May Help ROC," *China Post* (International Airmail Edition), January 24, 1996, p. 4.

74. Author's interview with Su Chi, vice chairman of Mainland Affairs Council, Executive Yuan, Republic of China, Taipei, Taiwan, February 6, 1996.

75. Ibid.

5

Taiwan's Recent Arms Purchases

This chapter discusses Taiwan's foreign arms purchases during the post–Cold War era. It examines some of the advanced weaponry that Taipei is acquiring, analyzes a variety of considerations that have enhanced the island's ability to purchase arms overseas, and shows how these weapons augment Taiwan's security and help it to cope with new threats.

Taiwan's Recent Arms Purchases

Taiwan is one of the world's leading arms importers.[1] In fact, according to U.S. government estimates, "Taiwan ranked first among all Third World recipients in the value of arms transfer agreements in 1992, concluding $10 billion in such agreements."[2] The discussion below examines some of Taiwan's major arms acquisitions.

F-16 Warplanes

For more than a decade, Taiwan sought unsuccessfully to purchase jet fighters from the United States. As recently as June 1992, Washington had turned down Taipei's request for F-16s.[3] But on September 2, 1992, President George Bush announced that he would approve the sale of up to 150 F-16/A and F-16/B fighter jets to Taiwan.

First developed by General Dynamics (now Lockheed) in 1972, the F-16/A and F-16/B fighters are one-seater and two-seater aircraft, respectively. The jets have a thrust power of approximately 23,450 pounds and a radius of action of about 570 miles. Although a formidable dogfighter, many analysts consider the warplanes inferior to the later model F-16/C and F-16/D types that are equipped with improved fire radar controls and beyond-visual-range air-to-air missiles. Consequently, some ROC officials—including Lin Wen-li, commanding general of Taiwan's air force—complained that "we are not very satisfied with the A and B models."[4]

Sensitive to Taipei's complaints, but unwilling to provide it with the F-16/C or F-16/D, the United States agreed to sell updated versions of the

F-16/A and F-16/B. The warplanes will be equipped with the F-16 Mid-Life Upgrade (MLU)—an upgrade program developed originally for NATO forces in Europe. MLU modifications include "a cockpit similar to the F-16D Block 50s with wide angle head-up display, night vision goggle compatibility, modular mission computer, digital terrain navigation system, AN/APG 66 (V2A) radar upgrade, GPS navigation system, improved data modem and provisions for a microwave landing system."[5]

It is also noteworthy that the jets will be powered by an upgraded version of the original F-16 engine—a Pratt and Whitney F100-PW-220 afterburning turbofan unit. According to John Balaguer, president of Pratt and Whitney's Government and Space Propulsion Division, the 220 model "embodies state-of-the-art technology, derived from our newest generation of fighter power plants."[6] Although the engine is less powerful than the General Electric unit that powers the F-16/C and F-16/D, industry representatives claim that its lighter weight makes the plane more agile and provides it with an advantage in maneuverability, thus making it a better warplane for air-to-air missions.[7]

The proposed sale passed the required thirty-day congressional notification period without opposition. The deal was officially completed when formal letters of offer and acceptance for the planes, engines, and other equipment were signed by U.S. and Taiwanese representatives on November 12 and 13, 1992. In addition to the F-16s, the U.S.$6 billion contract includes forty spare engines, 900 Sidewinder missiles, 600 Sparrow missiles, 500,000 rounds of 20mm cannon shells, spare parts, technical documentation, and logistics service and personnel training.[8]

Since signing the F-16 agreement, both sides have agreed to several modifications to the original deal. For example, the F-16s will be equipped with Westinghouse Electric Corporation's latest model of the AN/APG-66 series of fire-control radars—the AN/APG-66(V)3.[9] Westinghouse representatives claim that the company is providing "its latest and best model to Taiwan."[10] Furthermore, Washington has agreed to sell eighty advanced electronic countermeasure pods to Taiwan. These technical devices, manufactured by the Electromagnetic Systems Division of Raytheon Corporation, enhance a warplane's electronic interference system and may be installed in both F-16s and the Taiwan-built IDFs.[11] The U.S.$150 million deal also includes "support equipment, spare and repair parts, technical publications and data, flight testing, U.S. government and contractor engineering and logistics personnel services, personnel training and training equipment, system software development and maintenance, and other related elements of logistics support."[12]

In addition to upgraded fire-control radars and countermeasure pods, Washington is helping Taipei train its pilots to fly the new jets. In September 1993, the United States agreed to lease forty T-38 trainer jets to Taiwan. Capable of reaching supersonic speeds, the T-38 is "an outstanding tool" for training new pilots, according to Taiwanese military officials.[13] The jets also will enable Taiwan's air force to transfer sorely needed fighters from training facilities to standard defense missions. Although the planes were leased free of charge, Taipei is paying Washington an estimated U.S.$49 million for delivery and maintenance.[14] In March 1995, the first twenty T-38s arrived in Taiwan.

In 1995, the United States agreed to sell four F-16 simulators to Taiwan for pilot training. The simulators have the same equipment and controls found on actual F-16 aircraft. ROC Air Force officers claim that "with simulators, pilots can practice dangerous operating skills that may be unfit for real aircraft."[15] The simulators, manufactured by ECC International Corporation, will cost about U.S.$9.3 million.[16]

Finally, U.S. and Taiwanese authorities have reached an agreement whereby Taiwanese firms will cooperate in building parts for the F-16s. In 1995, Lockheed announced that it had decided to purchase roughly U.S.$30.42 million worth of F-16 parts and components from Taiwanese manufacturers.[17] The components, which include air intakes, engine access doors, ventral fins, rocket launchers, and adapters, will be distributed to several countries that use the F-16. The deal is part of a U.S.$600 million offset agreement that was included in the original 1992 contract.[18]

Mirage 2000-5 Warplanes

The F-16 deal was not the only major warplane purchase that Taiwan negotiated successfully in 1992. Shortly after agreeing to buy the U.S. fighters, Taiwan agreed to purchase sixty Mirage 2000-5s from France. The U.S.$6 billion deal has been described by Serge Dassault, president of France's Dassault Aviation (the plane's manufacturer), as "a complete package."[19] It includes advanced Thompson-CSF RDY radar, electronic countermeasures, and 1,500 MICA missiles—air-to-air missiles that are comparable to U.S.-made AMRAAM missiles.

The Mirage 2000-5 has been described as a multirole fighter-bomber. It forms the backbone of the French Air Force's fighter squadrons.[20] The jet has a maximum speed of Mach 2.2, a service ceiling of 59,000 feet, and is capable of climbing 56,000 feet in one minute.[21] It also has a thrust power of approximately 21,385 pounds and a radius of action of more than 1,800 kilometers. Given the Mirage's formidable capabilities, U.S. officials argued that it is "an offensive weapon" and opposed the sale.[22] Taiwanese authorities, however, claim that the fighter-bomber is "purely for defensive purposes."[23]

The Mirage 2000-5s will be delivered between 1996 and 1999. Like the F-16 deal, Taiwan pushed hard for technology transfers and offset agreements. After prolonged negotiations, the French finally agreed to purchase an unspecified amount of parts from Taiwanese firms. Taiwanese officials "hope France will purchase at least U.S.$600 million worth of parts from Taiwan."[24]

Modified Air Defense System

In 1994, Taiwan agreed to buy an air defense system based on the U.S. Patriot missile.[25] Under the terms of the U.S.$1.3 billion deal, Raytheon will provide Taiwan with a Modified Air Defense System—a system intended to defend the island against both enemy aircraft and tactical ballistic missiles. The contract calls for Raytheon and Taiwanese firms to coproduce MADS:

> Raytheon will provide the missile forebody, ground support equipment, training, maintenance and technical support. Taiwan will produce the aft section of the missile, which will include the warhead assembly, propulsion and control sections, in accordance with a Raytheon technical data package.[26]

When deployed in the late 1990s, MADS will replace Taiwan's current air defense system, which is said to be incapable of defending the island against a possible PRC attack.[27] Chiang Chung-ling, Taiwan's defense minister, claims that "the existing air-defense system used by the ROC armed forces is not able to provide an early warning against the Chinese communist–developed M-series ballistic missiles, not to mention not having the capability to intercept them."[28] The M-series missiles, which have a range of 110–620 miles, have been deployed in China's coastal provinces.

U.S. industry sources concede that MADS is not perfect. But they claim that "MADS will in fact incorporate the latest available technology."[29] Since the Gulf War, Raytheon has spent more than U.S.$600 million to improve the missile's performance, and the company guarantees payment of *all* costs if MADS does not live up to its promised capability.[30]

Air-Warning Aircraft

In 1995, Taiwan began to take delivery of four E-2T "Hawkeye" air-warning aircraft (AWACS) that it had agreed to purchase from the U.S.-based Grumman Aircraft Company.[31] The planes are part of the military's "Strong Net" program to upgrade airborne detecting and combat capabilities. Taiwanese military sources claim that the turbo-prop planes will "help advance Taiwan's air-warning from the current five minutes to 25 minutes."[32] They add that "the new aircraft will also enable us to reconnoiter the flying activities of mainland Chinese military air bases west of its southeastern terrain."[33]

The E-2T is an updated version of the E-2C, an aircraft that has been in service with the U.S. Navy since the mid-1970s. Each plane is equipped with the same advanced APS-145 radar system found in the E-2C. This system is capable of reconnoitering a sea or land area of 238,000 square miles or an air space of 15 million cubic feet.[34] The E-2T's engine, however, is more powerful than that found in the E-2C.

Grumman has agreed to an offset agreement whereby Taiwanese companies will be provided with business opportunities worth roughly U.S.$161.43 million.[35] The U.S.$760 million deal should be completed by mid-1996.

Helicopters

In September 1992, Washington agreed to sell twelve SH-2F Light Airborne Multipurpose System helicopters and spare engines to Taipei for U.S.$161 million.[36] The helicopters will be stationed on Taiwan's newly acquired Knox-class destroyers and will greatly increase the ROC Navy's antisubmarine detecting and hunting capabilities. As one Western military analyst observed, these helicopters "could pose more of a threat to China's submarines than the handful of submarines the Taiwanese are now looking to acquire."[37]

Taiwan's army also is acquiring new helicopters. It is purchasing forty-two AH-1W Cobra attack helicopters and twenty-six OH-58D Kiowa warrior scout helicopters from the United States for U.S.$1.2 billion. The Cobras are armed with Hellfire antitank missiles and TOW air-to-ground missiles, Sidewinder air-to-air missiles, rockets, machine guns, and an M197 20mm cannon capable of firing 730 rounds per minute.[38] The Kiowas, which also are armed with Hellfire missiles and rockets, are capable of surveillance, intelligence gathering, support missions, and directing artillery fire. Each Kiowa is equipped with "a TV camera and image scanning system, which allows pilots on board to immediately locate targets within a range of eight kilometers."[39]

Taiwanese military authorities claim that the new choppers "expand the combat capability of the army's air force from the ground to the sky . . . and strengthens its reconnaissance capability."[40] The first Cobras and Kiowas were delivered to Taiwan in October 1993. Delivery should be completed in 1996.

LaFayette-Class Frigates

In 1991, France approved the sale of up to sixteen LaFayette-class frigates to Taiwan for U.S.$4.8 billion. Thus far, Taiwan has agreed to purchase six of the 3,500-ton warships for a reported U.S.$2.4 billion.

According to the terms of the original 1991 agreement, both France's state-run Thomson CSF and Taiwan's China Shipbuilding Corporation would build the frigates. France planned initially to build the hulks and ship them to Taiwan where China Shipbuilding would complete the assembly. In

1993, however, Paris backtracked and offered to equip all six ships with their standard weapons configurations.[41] The arms reportedly include U.S.$2.6 billion of sophisticated weaponry—including torpedoes, ship-to-ship Exocet missiles, 100mm rapid-fire cannon, and France's advanced Crotal naval ship-to-air missile system.[42] Taiwan accepted the offer, and delivery is scheduled to begin in 1996.

Knox-Class Frigates

As part of its effort to enhance its naval fleet, Taiwan also is leasing six Knox-class frigates from the United States. Although the frigates were first commissioned by the U.S. Navy in the early 1970s, the ships have been refurbished and updated to enhance their antisubmarine warfare capabilities. In addition to carrying a helicopter, each ship is equipped with three kinds of highly sophisticated sonar systems and armed with advanced weapons including Harpoon missiles and the Mk-15 Phalanx—a rapid-fire gun designed to protect the vessel from incoming missiles. In preparation for taking delivery of the warships, hundreds of ROC naval officers have received training in the United States.

The first three Knox-class frigates, renamed the Chiyang, Fengyang, and Fangyang, were formally commissioned into the ROC Navy in 1993. The total cost for the five-year lease was U.S.$236 million.[43] The second batch of warships, dubbed the Lanyang, Haiyang, and Huiyang, joined the ROC Navy in 1995.[44] These ships were leased for roughly U.S.$225 million. Taiwan hopes to purchase all six ships when the lease expires.

M60-A3 Tanks

In 1991, the ROC Army considered purchasing 110 Korean War vintage M60-A3 tanks from the United States for U.S.$199 million. However, the army decided against the deal. It opted instead to purchase the AH-1W Cobra attack helicopters and OH-58D Kiowa warrior scout helicopters described above. The army explained that the tanks "did not fulfill combat needs."[45]

In 1994, the ROC Army reversed its position. The Army General Headquarters announced that it planned to buy 200 M60-A3 tanks for U.S.$185 million.[46] The decision led to intense debate within both Taiwan's legislature and the military. Lawmakers claimed that the tanks were too old and too large to operate in Taiwan. Consequently, the army scaled back its original order to 160 M60-A3 tanks for U.S.$91 million.[47]

Taiwanese military authorities concede that the M60-A3s are old, but add that they will strengthen the army's combat capability. They claim that the tanks, which are equipped with thermal sights, grenade launchers, machine guns, and a 105mm main gun, will "serve as mobile land batteries against an invading force from mainland China."[48] By early 1996, Taiwan had taken delivery of thirty M60-A3s.[49]

Summary

Since the end of the Cold War, Taiwan has succeeded in purchasing an impressive array of sophisticated military hardware. U.S. sales include F-16 aircraft, AWACS planes, M60-A3 tanks, Knox-class destroyers, minesweepers, helicopters, Stinger missiles, and a derivative of the Patriot missile air-defense system. In addition to the U.S. sales, France has signed agreements to sell warships, Mirage 2000-5 fighters, and more than 1,000 short-range and medium-range air-to-air missiles to Taiwan. Paris also offered to sell its ship-to-ship Exocet missiles, Crotal and Mistral antiaircraft missiles, torpedoes, 100mm rapid-fire cannons, and electronic warfare systems to Taiwan.[50] Although France seemed to cave in to PRC demands that it limit future sales, it is now waffling on the issue.[51] In March 1995, Paris agreed to sell 120 Mistral shoulder-fired missiles to Taipei for U.S.$47.9 million.[52] Other governments—including Germany and the Netherlands—are reviewing their respective policies on arms sales to Taiwan. After all of the arms deliveries are completed, Taiwan's president boasts that the island "will be one of Asia's strongest nations militarily."[53]

Understanding Taiwan's Newfound Access to Arms

Why are numerous governments—including France, Germany, Russia, Belgium, and the United States—reviewing their respective policies on arms sales to Taiwan? Why are some now willing to provide Taiwan with advanced weapons—arms unavailable at any price during the Cold War? What do they hope to gain by such changes in policy? As with any other new initiative, many questions have been raised. The following discussion analyzes several considerations that may have influenced policy.

Collapse of the Strategic Triangle

During the 1950s and 1960s, the United States maintained a firm alliance with Taiwan, and massive amounts of economic aid and military equipment poured into the island. In the 1970s, however, Washington sought to enlist Beijing's strategic cooperation in a global drive to contain Soviet expansionism. In order to secure this support (and normalize relations with China), the United States severed diplomatic relations with Taiwan and agreed to reduce military support for the island.

In January 1982, Washington announced that it would not sell Taipei the FX fighter or any other advanced warplane because "no military need for such aircraft exists."[54] Shortly after this announcement, the United States promised to reduce its arms sales to Taiwan. In the August 17, 1982, U.S.-PRC joint communiqué, Washington said that "it does not seek to carry out a long term policy of arms sales to Taiwan" and pledged that it "intends to reduce gradually its sales of arms to Taiwan, leading over a period of time to a final resolution."[55] After that time, U.S. arms sales to Taiwan declined, as shown in Table 5.1.

Table 5.1   U.S. Foreign Military Sales Agreements with Taiwan and Commercial Arms Exports to Taiwan: Fiscal Years 1983–1989 (U.S.$ in millions)

	FMS	Commercial	Total
1983	689.0	85.0	774.0
1984	707.4	70.0	777.4
1985	700.2	54.5	754.7
1986	510.8	228.0	738.8
1987	509.0	210.0	719.0
1988	505.0	195.0	700.0
1989	526.3	84.7	611.0

Source: Defense Security Assistance Agency, *Foreign Military Sales, Foreign Military Construction Sales and Military Assistance Facts as of September 30, 1991* (Washington, D.C.: Data Management Division, Comptroller, DSAA, 1991).

The 1982 U.S.-PRC joint communiqué came as a devastating blow to Taipei. At the same time, European arms suppliers were reluctant to get close to Taipei. Despite its growing wealth, Taiwan found that it was unable to procure a new generation of fighter aircraft or other weapons deemed necessary for its defense. As Chen Li-an, then Taiwan's defense minister, explained, "we had the money, but nowhere to buy the aircraft."[56]

It is clear that strategic considerations led Washington to reduce military support for Taipei. But the collapse of the Soviet Union has led to the demise of the so-called China card and the strategic triangle, thereby diminishing China's importance to the United States and other Western nations. Governments are now more willing to risk Beijing's wrath and sell weapons to Taiwan.

Tiananmen Square

As described in Chapter 4, the Tiananmen Square incident shattered China's image as a progressive country that practices "cuddly communism." That event also had a profound effect on the PRC's relations with foreign governments, many of whom are no longer so anxious to get close to "the butchers of Beijing."

The bloody suppression of the student-led demonstrations in Beijing enabled the world to compare China's hardline response to popular demands for democratic reform with Taipei's commitment to democracy. Some argue that it no longer makes sense to ignore China's human rights violations or to cave in to its demands that the international community isolate Taiwan. David Laux, president of the U.S.-ROC Trade Council, explains: "Here's this one rich customer, Taiwan, and we can't sell them what we want because we have to please this pariah, the People's Republic of China. It just doesn't make sense."[57] As one Taiwanese observed, "Tiananmen gave Western countries the excuse to have a freer hand" in selling arms to Taiwan.[58]

Business Opportunities in Taiwan

Taiwan's economic stature is in sharp contrast to its second-class international status. The island boasts a per capita income of roughly U.S.$10,000, a gross national product of approximately U.S.$200 billion, and foreign exchange and gold reserves of almost U.S.$100 billion—among the highest in the world. Taiwan also has launched an ambitious Six-Year National Development Plan that calls for the expenditure of approximately U.S.$304 billion to upgrade the island's infrastructure. With about U.S.$100 billion of the work open to foreign bidding, U.S. officials have described the plan as "the best overseas market for major projects, bar none."[59]

As the world moves into an era of intense economic competition, many states are strengthening ties with Taipei. For example, all of the European Community (EC) nations have upgraded "unofficial" or "substantive" relations with Taiwan. Moreover, several Third World nations have been added to its diplomatic list, and a wide array of governments—both developed and underdeveloped—now support Taiwan in its bid to join (or rejoin) the world's major economic and financial organizations. Some governments also are more willing to risk Beijing's wrath by selling weapons to Taiwan. They believe that arms sales may provide them with an "inside track" in securing large commercial contracts in Taiwan.

When the United States sold 150 F-16 warplanes to Taiwan, the sale was not linked to any of the island's major commercial projects. However, U.S. officials and trade representatives did hope that the deal would help pave the way for U.S. firms to participate in Taiwan's Six-Year National Development Plan. As one business representative opined, "if we didn't get a nuclear contract [a contract to build one of Taiwan's nuclear power plants], it would be a bitter pill."[60]

The French decision to sell LaFayette frigates and Mirage 2000-5 warplanes to Taiwan also was influenced by the prospect of participation in the island's infrastructure improvement program. France had its eye on several major projects, including the construction of a high-speed railway, a subway, and a nuclear power plant. As one French official explained, "in Paris, they really hoped that the military sales would lead to big commercial contracts."[61]

Ironically, the prospect of losing lucrative commercial contracts to France may have played a role in the U.S. decision to sell F-16 warplanes to Taiwan. In August 1992, 100 members of the House of Representatives (fifty-three Democrats and forty-seven Republicans) signed a letter demanding that President Bush approve the F-16 sales and warning that "if we do not allow F-16 sales to Taiwan, they will buy French aircraft and will also make a commitment to purchase French nuclear power plants and railroad technology."[62]

Domestic Political Pressures

Domestic political pressures may also have led some governments to review their respective policies on arms sales to Taiwan. Western arms manufacturers, faced with bloated inventories, weak domestic economies, and reduced orders from abroad, are pressuring their governments to sell weapons to Taiwan. Ding Shou-chung, a Taiwanese lawmaker, explains:

> The Cold War system ended and the defense companies in the West faced shrinking defense budgets. Their markets at home were shrinking. Before, there were limits on selling weapons to Taiwan. But the companies pressure their governments to reduce the limits.[63]

In mid-1992, General Dynamics announced that, with the possible end of new F-16 orders, it would have to lay off 5,800 employees at its Fort Worth, Texas, plant by the mid-1990s. Scores of workers at F-16 suppliers scattered throughout forty-seven other states also would lose their jobs. As word of the F-16–related layoffs spread, U.S. lawmakers began to pressure the Bush administration to lift the ban on advanced fighter sales to Taiwan.

During congressional hearings, Senator Lloyd Bentsen (Democrat–Texas) described the F-16 deal as "a dream sale" and criticized the administration's refusal to approve it as "a senseless . . . dumb policy."[64] Governor Ann Richards (Democrat–Texas) accused the president of failing to deal in the global marketplace and said, "I don't know what deals have been made between George Bush and Communist China, but when it means the loss of 5,800 workers in Fort Worth, Texas, it's time to wake up and smell the coffee."[65] Dean Girardot, a spokesman for the International Association of Machinists, the labor union that represents about 10,000 General Dynamics employees, was even more direct. The labor leader bluntly called on the president to "get off his duff and let General Dynamics sell these F-16s to Taiwan."[66]

Domestic political considerations also helped convince French authorities to sell the Mirage 2000-5 to Taiwan. Indeed, the sale proved to be a "lifesaver" for Dassault:

For Dassault, the only remaining high-performance aircraft manufacturer in France to be privately owned, the Taiwan order was literally a lifesaver. The company had not made an export fighter sale in six years, had already laid off a number of employees, and was in danger of going out of business. French domestic pressure for the Mirage sale was almost entirely economic.[67]

Summary

In sum, the end of the Cold War and a conjunction of several other factors have led the United States, France, and other countries to revise their respective policies on arms sales to Taiwan. These developments also have enabled Taipei to increase its bargaining power vis-à-vis the arms-supplying nations. Taiwan has successfully pressured foreign governments to provide the island with offset agreements, technology transfers, and even lower prices.

Conclusion

Using both domestically manufactured and foreign-supplied arms, Taiwan has launched an impressive drive aimed at military modernization. With the end of the Cold War, however, Taiwan's leadership "hurriedly switched the focus of their own strategy—de-emphasizing the research and development of Taiwan's own weapons systems and stressing instead the procurement of advanced hardware from overseas."[68] Although the change in emphasis has contributed to some difficulties, Taiwanese officials believe that the benefits associated with foreign arms greatly outweigh the liabilities.[69]

Foreign arms augment Taiwan's security in several ways. First, the weapons boost the island's defensive capabilities, thereby deterring PRC aggression. Second, the drive by Taiwan to domestically produce the weapons necessary for its own defense was a cost-inefficient employment of resources. Foreign arms are generally of lower cost and higher quality than the island's domestically manufactured weapons. For example, foreign warplanes are both superior and cheaper than Taiwan's IDF fighter—the most expensive warplane in the world. Third, foreign arms help link the island to the international community. The weapons help Taipei construct "a web of relationships and situations . . . [that] constitute a political-economic 'situational deterrent,' which renders military attack by the PRC increasingly unlikely."[70] Finally, foreign arms help reassure Taiwan's business community. As Fredrick Chien, Taiwan's foreign minister, observed, the weapons "assure investors that Taiwan has the capacity to defend itself."[71]

Taiwan plans to purchase even more arms. Submarines are high on its list of priorities—Taipei has been attempting to buy them for more than a decade. Ku Chong-lien, Taiwan's naval commander in chief, has revealed that the ROC Navy hopes to purchase twenty-four submarines. He has warned that the navy "needs to buy ten submarines at least" to protect Taiwan's economic sea-lanes to other countries.[72] ROC officials acknowledge that the government is still experiencing difficulties in this area:

> Submarines are very sensitive. We have put in the request [with the United States] for such things, but so far that is not approved. Because the U.S. has a very strict interpretation of the word "defense" and submarines are not necessarily purely defensive.[73]

However, it is possible that China's provocative military maneuvers in March 1996 increased Taiwan's chances for acquiring U.S. submarines.[74]

In addition to submarines, Taiwanese authorities "hope to purchase from the United States warships, combat vehicles, missiles, electronic operations systems, and fighters that out-perform the Chinese communists' planes."[75] Deeply impressed with the remarkable display of Western weaponry during the Gulf War, defense officials are particularly interested in obtaining high-tech "smart weapons" and artillery-delivered high-precision munitions (ADHPMs). One military analyst explained, "we are in a new epoch where ADHPMs can have the impact of small nuclear warheads. If you have the battlefield all mapped out, ADHPMs can be highly deadly."[76] Reacting to Beijing's missile tests, Taipei also is showing interest in buying a theater-missile defense system and hopes to be included with other U.S. allies if Washington deploys the Star Wars–like system in Asia.

Notes

1. For more information, see U.S. Arms Control and Disarmament Agency, *World Military Expenditures and Arms Transfers, 1993–1994* (Washington, D.C.: U.S. Government Printing Office, 1995).

2. See U.S. Congress, Congressional Research Service, *Conventional Arms Transfers to the Third World, 1985–1992,* Richard F. Grimmett, (ed.), *CRS Report for Congress* (Washington, D.C.: U.S. Government Printing Office, July 19, 1993), p. 12.

3. See Barbara Starr and John Boatman, "U.S. Reconsiders F-16 Sale Ban," *Jane's Defence Weekly* 18, No. 16, August 8, 1992, p. 5.

4. P. T. Bangsberg, "Sale of F-16 Jets to Taiwan Strains U.S.-China Relations," *Journal of Commerce,* September 4, 1992, p. 3A.

5. Joris Janssen Lok, "U.S. Benefits from European MLU," *Jane's Defence Weekly* 18, No. 20, November 14, 1992, p. 8.

6. Tammy C. Peng, "F-16 Contract Finalized: Delivery to Begin in 1996," *Free China Journal,* November 17, 1992, p. 2.

7. Michael Towle, "Taiwan Hopes Election Pressure Will Aid F-16 Sale," *Fort Worth Star Telegram,* September 19, 1992, p. B1.

8. Ibid.

9. These devices provide pilots with heading and altitude information, enable them to spot enemy aircraft before they are in visual range, and guide air-to-air missiles to a target.

10. Bill Wang, "Advanced Radar for ROC Air Force," *China Post* (International Airmail Edition), December 7, 1994, p. 4.
11. See "Week in Review," *Free China Journal,* May 27, 1994, p. 1.
12. Bill Wang, "U.S. to Sell Taiwan Countermeasure Pods," *China Post* (International Airmail Edition), August 3, 1994, p. 4.
13. See "U.S. Trainer Jets to Arrive by December," *China Post* (International Airmail Edition), October 25, 1994, p. 1.
14. "On the Move," *Free China Journal,* March 31, 1995, p. 2. For information about objections to the terms of the agreement, see "Week in Review," *Free China Journal,* March 4, 1994, p. 1.
15. "U.S. Agrees to Sell Four F-16 Simulators to ROC," *China Post* (International Airmail Edition), March 24, 1995, p. 1.
16. Ibid.
17. See Sofia Wu, "F-16," *CNA,* February 25, 1995, in *Lexis/Nexis.*
18. See "Week in Review," *Free China Journal,* July 22, 1994, p. 2.
19. "French Deal with Taiwan Includes MICA Missile," *CNA,* December 13, 1993, in *Lexis/Nexis.*
20. France is upgrading its current fleet of Mirages to the same standard as the 2000-5 version. As Harlan W. Jencks noted, this is "a step it could not have afforded had not a substantial foreign sale brought down the unit price." For more information, see Harlan W. Jencks, "Taiwan in the International Arms Market," in Robert G. Sutter and William R. Johnson (eds.), *Taiwan in World Affairs* (Boulder, Colorado: Westview Press, 1994), p. 80.
21. See "Parameters for IDF and Other Jet Fighters," in *Free China Journal,* December 30, 1994, p. 1.
22. "U.S. Sees No Need for Taiwan to Buy Mirage Fighters," *CNA,* November 18, 1992, in *Lexis/Nexis.*
23. "Taipei Sees Mirage Fighters as Defensive Weapons," *CNA,* November 19, 1992, in *Lexis/Nexis.*
24. Sofia Wu, "France to Have Mirage Parts Made in ROC," *China Post* (International Airmail Edition), March 10, 1995, p. 3.
25. Negotiations began in September 1992.
26. David Hughes, "Taiwan to Acquire Patriot Derivative," *Aviation Week & Space Technology,* March 1, 1993, p. 61.
27. See "Week in Review," *Free China Journal,* March 12, 1993, p. 1.
28. "Military Chiefs Want Patriot to Counter Mainland's Missiles," *CNA,* February 25, 1995, in *BBC Summary of World Broadcasts* in *Lexis/Nexis.*
29. Barbara Opall, "Taiwan Balks at U.S. Deal for Patriot," *Defense News,* August 30–September 5, 1993, p. 28.
30. See ibid.; and Sofia Wu, "Patriot Missile Contract Signed," *CNA,* July 1, 1994, in *Lexis/Nexis.*
31. The deal with Grumman was concluded in 1989. The first E-2T was commissioned in May 1995.
32. "The Military: First AWAC Aircraft to Be Commissioned 'Later This Month,'" *CNA,* May 1, 1995, in *BBC Summary of World Broadcasts,* May 6, 1995, in *Lexis/Nexis.*
33. Ibid.
34. Ibid.
35. See Sofia Wu, "ROC Takes Delivery of Two 2-2T Aircraft," *China Post* (International Airmail Edition), September 4, 1995, p. 1.
36. See "Copters to Taipei Proposed," *Washington Times,* September 22, 1992, p. 3.

37. Julian Baum, "Prepare to Surface," *Far Eastern Economic Review*, February 4, 1993, p. 11.

38. For more information on the Cobra's formidable capabilities, see "Lee Inspects New Copters from U.S.," *China Post* (International Airmail Edition), November 16, 1993, p. 1; and Benjamin Yeh, "1st Combat Copter Squad in Service," *CNA*, March 2, 1994, in *Lexis/Nexis*.

39. Yeh, "1st Combat Copter Squad in Service."

40. "Lee Inspects New Copters from U.S.," p. 1.

41. See "France to Sell Missile System," *China Post* (International Airmail Edition), September 23, 1993, p. 4.

42. See ibid.; and Martin L. Lasater, *Changing of the Guard: President Clinton and the Security of Taiwan* (Boulder, Colorado: Westview Press, 1995), p. 191.

43. See "Frigates Formally Commissioned," *China Post* (International Airmail Edition), October 7, 1993, p. 1.

44. See Philip Liu and Sofia Wu, "Navy Gets 3 Knox-Class Frigates," *China Post* (International Airmail Edition), July 3, 1995, p. 1.

45. "Decision to Purchase Tanks Splits Army," *China Post* (International Airmail Edition), January 3, 1994, p. 4.

46. See "Week in Review," *Free China Journal*, January 7, 1994, p. 1.

47. See "Week in Review," *Free China Journal*, September 2, 1994, p. 1.

48. "Decision to Purchase Used Tanks Splits Army," p. 4.

49. See "Army Acquires Another 10 U.S.-made Tanks," *China Post* (International Airmail Edition), January 8, 1996, p. 1.

50. See "ROC Gets Big Offer of Arms," *China Post* (International Airmail Edition), October 22, 1993, p. 1.

51. In January 1994, Paris signed a communiqué promising to ban the sale of offensive weapons to Taipei. It appears, however, that France intends to continue sales of "nonoffensive" military equipment to Taiwan. For more information, see "ROC to Get Defensive Arms from Paris," *China Post* (International Airmail Edition), January 18, 1994, p. 4.

52. See Sofia Wu, "Mistral Missiles," *CNA*, March 18, 1995, in *Lexis/Nexis*.

53. See Bear Lee, "Lee Says Taiwan to Be One of Asia's Strongest Countries in 4 Years," *CNA* (Taipei), March 6, 1996.

54. "No Sale of Advanced Aircraft to Taiwan," *Department of State Bulletin*, No. 2059, February 1982, p. 191.

55. For a complete discussion of the document's meaning, see Dennis Van Vranken Hickey, *United States–Taiwan Security Ties: From Cold War to Beyond Containment* (Westport, Connecticut: Praeger, 1994).

56. "Peking Might Be Eyeing an Invasion of Taiwan, with World's Attention Focused on Middle East," *Free China Journal*, November 19, 1990, p. 2.

57. Jim Mann, "Targeting Taiwan for Arms Deals," *Los Angeles Times*, March 14, 1994, p. 1.

58. Ibid.

59. See testimony of Natale Bellocchi in *Departments of Commerce, Justice, and State, the Judiciary and Related Agencies Appropriations for 1993*. U.S. Congress, House, Hearings Before a Subcommittee of the Committee on Appropriations, 102nd Congress, 2nd Session, March 10, 1992 (Washington, D.C.: U.S. Government Printing Office, 1992), p. 1108.

60. Quoted from Jim Mann, "Targeting Taiwan for Arms Deals, Part 2," *Los Angeles Times*, March 15, 1994, p. A1.

61. Ibid.

62. Jackie Koszczuk, "Lawmakers Urging Bush to Approve Sale of F-16s to Taiwan," *Fort Worth Star-Telegram,* August 19, 1992, p. 10.

63. Mann, "Targeting Taiwan for Arms Deals," p. A1.

64. "Bush Warned Against Losing Multibillion Dlr Sale to France," *China Post* (International Airmail Edition), August 19, 1992, p. 1.

65. "Bush Would Reconsider Selling F-16s to Taiwan," *China Post* (International Airmail Edition), August 1, 1992, p. 1.

66. Ibid.

67. Jencks, "Taiwan in the International Arms Market," p. 81.

68. Mann, "Targeting Taiwan for Arms Deals," p. A1.

69. The acquisition of foreign weaponry has led Taiwan's military to scale back purchases of domestically manufactured arms, including the IDF fighter, the Tien Chien (Sky Arrow) missile, and the Tien Kung (Sky Bow) missile. For a discussion of other problems associated with foreign arms, see Chapter 2.

70. Jencks, "Taiwan in the International Arms Market," p. 99.

71. Mann, "Targeting Taiwan for Arms Deals," p. A1.

72. "Navy Chief on Long-Term Development Goals," *Tzu-Li Wan-Pao* (Taipei), October 23, 1995, in *FBIS, China,* October 31, 1995, p. 75.

73. Author's interview with Fredrick Chien, foreign minister of the Republic of China, February 7, 1996, Taipei, Taiwan.

74. In early March 1996, members of Congress called on the Clinton administration "to supply Taiwan with defensive weapons systems crucial to the security of Taiwan, including submarines and aircraft." See Han Nai-kuo, "House Resolution Calls for Defense of Taiwan," *CNA* (Taipei), March 5, 1996.

75. Dennis Van Vranken Hickey, "Special Report: Interview with Sun Chen, Taiwan's Defense Minister," *Asian Defense Journal,* February 1994, p. 35.

76. See David Silverberg, "Emerging Nations Hunger for Precision Weapons," *Defense News,* February 8–14, 1993, p. 9.

6
Taiwan's Democratization and Economic Clout

When measured on almost any scale of economic and political development, Taiwan is the most successful Chinese-run nation in more than 5,000 years of Chinese civilization. This chapter examines Taiwan's democratization and growing economic clout. It suggests that these considerations are contributing to the island's security in the post–Cold War era.

Taiwan's Democratization

Samuel Huntington contends that "a 20th century political system [is] democratic to the extent that its most powerful collective decisionmakers are selected through fair, honest, and periodic elections in which candidates freely compete for votes and in which virtually all the adult population is eligible to vote."[1] If we accept this definition, Taiwan may be considered as a model of democratization. Indeed, it has made remarkable strides toward political participation and freedom.

Prior to 1949, there had never been an island-wide election on Taiwan. In 1951, the first such election was held to elect a provincial assembly. In subsequent years, elections were held on both the provincial and national levels. But the island could hardly have been described as democratic.

During Chiang Kai-shek's rule, opposition parties were banned, dissidents were jailed, the press was muzzled, and parliamentary elections were restricted to a small proportion of the seats. Jaushieh Joseph Wu, an associate research fellow at National Chengchi University's prestigious Institute of International Relations, describes Taiwan's electoral contests during this period:

> Elections for the national legislature [Legislative Yuan], for example, could not alter the fact that the majority of legislators had been elected in mainland China in 1948. The Kuomintang was able to dominate the legislative chamber regardless of election results. Also, none of the key government offices, including the president, premier, cabinet ministers, and provincial governor, were open to public competition. The KMT's domination of these offices, through its guaranteed majority in the national

legislature, deprived Taiwan of democratic credentials in spite of the regularly held elections.[2]

As Alan Wachman observed, "the ROC was an authoritarian regime from the moment it retreated to Taiwan in 1949 until July 15, 1987."[3]

On July 15, 1987, President Chiang Ching-kuo lifted martial law. Democratization took another big step forward on July 20, 1989, when Taiwan's Legislative Yuan passed the Law on the Organization of Civic Groups. This law legalized the formation of opposition parties and paved the way for legitimate opposition parties to compete in elections.

On December 21, 1991, Taiwan held elections to elect a new National Assembly—the body that amends the constitution and selected the president until direct presidential elections were held in 1996.[4] Described as the island's "first major national election," it proved to be a victory for the KMT.[5] In December 1992, general elections were held to elect a new 161-seat Legislative Yuan—the first ever to be chosen in its entirety by the Taiwanese people. Although the ruling KMT retained control of Taiwan's legislature, the island's chief opposition party, the Democratic Progressive Party, made significant gains. The KMT won ninety-six seats, the DPP took fifty seats, the Chinese Social Democratic Party won one seat, and independent candidates won fourteen. In December 1994, the island held direct elections to select the provincial governor and the mayors of Taipei and Kaohsiung. The KMT managed to win both the gubernatorial election and the mayoral election in Kaohsiung, but the DPP candidate won the mayoral race in Taipei. Perhaps most significant, on March 23, 1996, Taiwan held its first-ever direct presidential election. In an electoral contest that included four major candidates, President Lee Teng-hui won roughly 54 percent of the vote (Table 6.1).

These and other moves—including the deregulation of the print media and the legalization of cable television—stand in stark contrast to the PRC's

Table 6.1 Results of Taiwan's 1996 Presidential Election

Candidate	Votes	Percentage
Lee Teng-hui (KMT)	5,813,699	54
Peng Ming-min (DPP)	2,274,586	21.13
Lin Yang-kang (independent)	1,603,790	14.9
Chen Li-an (independent)	1,074,044	9.98

Source: Information Division, Taipei Economic and Cultural Office in New York, March 25, 1996, on the World Wide Web at *http://www.Taipei.org/teco/cicc/news*.

hardline responses to popular demands for democratic reform. As one ROC official boasted, "we are not only a prosperous economy, but also a true democracy—a democracy in every sense of the word."[6]

Understanding Taiwan's Democratization

Taiwan's political development has caught much of the world by surprise. In fact, the island's democratization defies conventional wisdom at several levels:

> First, a former autocracy has evolved toward its opposite, a democracy. Second, such a development has avoided the trodden path of armed revolution. Third, this dramatic conversion of power distribution has been largely bloodless despite the recurrence of often galvanized pro-democracy urban protests. The process thus circumvented the all-too-familiar vicious circle of unrestrained civilian agitation and compelled government violence.[7]

Furthermore, scholars typically believe that "if there is not a commonly accepted view of the identity of the state in which a given population lives, it is not possible to transform that state into a democratic one."[8] But Taiwan's political development also challenges that assumption. Finally, some argue that democracy is incompatible with Chinese political culture. The centuries-old Confucian tradition that teaches that one should obey and respect the state, as the child obeys the father, means that a Chinese society cannot possibly break away from its authoritarian past.

How did Taiwan manage to overcome these obstacles and transform itself from an authoritarian state into a full-fledged democracy? What factors contributed to the island's remarkable political liberalization? Although it is beyond the scope of this study to fully explore and evaluate all competing theories of democratization, the following discussion examines several considerations that may have played a role in Taiwan's political transformation.

The Elites

Dankwart A. Rustow has observed that the ruling elite's determination to pursue democracy can be as important as the presence of certain socioeconomic conditions conducive to democracy.[9] Public opinion polls reveal that most Taiwanese credit the late president Chiang Ching-kuo as having made the greatest contributions to the island's democracy (Table 6.2). Chiang was responsible for lifting martial law, and he initiated steps toward many of the island's other political reforms. Indeed, it would be "hard to imagine that political liberalization could have proceeded far in Taiwan if Chiang

Table 6.2 Taiwanese Poll Ranking ROC Presidents by Contributions to Taiwan's Democracy

President	Percentage
Chiang Ching-kuo	38.7
Lee Teng-hui	19.2
Chiang Kai-shek	13.9
Yen Chia-kan (interim president)	0.3

Source: Poll commissioned by the Democratic Progressive Party in June 1995 as reported in Christopher Bodeen, "Lee's Popularity Soars After Visit to the U.S.," *China Post* (International Airmail Edition), June 19, 1995, p. 1.

Ching-kuo had actively opposed it—or that political reforms could have followed their recent trajectory if he had not paved the way for them."[10]

Chiang Ching-kuo's successor, President Lee Teng-hui, also has played a major role in Taiwan's political metamorphosis. The U.S.-educated Lee claims that his experience as a student in the United States taught him about democracy and inspired his political career.[11] As president, he has spearheaded numerous constitutional reforms.

Finally, the ruling party has contributed to the island's political transformation. During an interview with the author, retired general Chiang Wego suggested that the ROC's democratization might best be traced to Sun Yat-sen and KMT ideology:

> This was pre-planned and decided by Dr. Sun Yat-sen before the Republic was established. That means 85 years ago he already decided that our revolution would be completed in three phases. In the first phase, there was no government, so the military government made the final solution. The second period was the training period—to train the government and the people how to have a democratic government. And finally the third period will go into constitutional government.[12]

Although some Taiwanese might quarrel with Chiang's assertion, without the KMT's commitment to democratic reform it is unlikely that the democratization process would have been completed without bloodshed or turmoil. Surveys reveal that more than 50 percent of the Taiwanese population believes that the KMT contributed more than other political parties to the development of democracy on the island (see Table 6.3).

Economic Development

Some economists and political scientists have long suggested that democratization is related to economic development. In the late 1950s, Seymour

Table 6.3 Taiwanese Poll Ranking Political Parties by Contributions to the Development of Democracy in Taiwan

Party	Percentage
KMT	51.3
DPP	14.8
Other	2.9
Don't know	32.0

Source: Poll conducted by the 21st Century Foundation in November 1993 as reported in "KMT Contribution to Democratic Development Affirmed," *CNA,* November 10, 1993, in *Lexis/Nexis.*

Martin Lipset argued that the "more well-to-do a nation, the greater the chances that it will sustain democracy."[13] Barrington Moore suggested simply that "no bourgeois, no democracy."[14] Briefly stated, the theory is based upon the assumption that "a growing economic prosperity means a growing middle class, which in turn means a growing intolerance of political oppression and political impotence."[15]

Could Taiwan's democratization be related to its economic development? President Lee Teng-hui claims that "political and economic reforms are mutually indispensable; it is difficult to get anywhere by focusing on either one alone."[16] Hung-mao Tien, an authority on Taiwanese politics, also has suggested that "four decades of success in economic development have created social and economic preconditions favorable to a democratic surge in Taiwan's politics."[17]

Pressure by the United States

Since retreating to the island of Taiwan in 1949, the ROC's security has rested primarily upon two pillars: its own efforts with respect to military preparedness and its relations with the United States.[18] During this same period, the United States poured massive amounts of economic aid into the island and served as the chief destination for Taiwan's exports. Some believe that Washington used its leverage over Taipei to push the island toward democratic reform.

According to the terms of the Taiwan Relations Act, the law that guides U.S. policy toward Taiwan, "the preservation and enhancement of human rights of all people on Taiwan" are "objectives" of the United States. Following the passage of the law in 1979, the U.S. government (particularly the U.S. Congress) "increased its pressure on Taiwan to democratize in order to justify continued American economic and security guarantees and U.S. promises to prevent Taiwan from being absorbed against its will by the People's Republic of China."[19] Congress attempted to establish a linkage between U.S. military support and the island's democratic reform and threatened to curtail arms sales on several occasions.[20]

Did pressure by the United States play a role in Taiwan's democratization? John F. Copper, a noted authority on Taiwan's politics, contends that the United States played a "paramount" role in the island's political transformation: "The American Congress, the administration, the media and scholars have supported Taiwan's democratization. Sometimes they have used pressure and coercion. Clearly, the U.S. role has been a paramount one."[21] James R. Lilley, former U.S. ambassador to the PRC, concurs. He suggests that "the Republic of China on Taiwan is a clear example of how human rights and democratization have evolved from a long-term U.S. military and economic presence."[22]

Legitimation Crisis

At one time, many of the world's important governments recognized the Republic of China on Taiwan as the sole, legal government of China. This international support and the PRC's failure to gain recognition from most of the global community enabled the ROC government to occupy the Chinese seat in the United Nations (UN) and most other significant international organizations. As Cold War tensions eased in the early 1970s, however, Taiwan's position began to deteriorate.

By the 1980s, only a handful of foreign governments recognized the ROC, and it had lost its seat in the UN and most other important international forums. The ROC's position that it was the legitimate government of all China and that national elections must await the recovery of the mainland appeared increasingly ludicrous. Televised images of elderly and senile lawmakers—legislators who had not stood for election since 1948—being wheeled or carried into the Legislative Yuan (parliament) were deeply troubling to the Taiwanese population. In short, the regime confronted a legitimation crisis both at home and abroad.

Some suggest that Taiwan's political modernization may be traced to an effort by the ROC government to regain legitimation. According to this view, "the failure of Taipei's internationally based legitimation required it to replenish its supply of legitimacy by seeking deeper legitimation via democratization at home."[23]

Summary

The synergistic interplay of several factors—including an enlightened leadership, economic development, foreign pressure, and a legitimation crisis—contributed to Taiwan's rapid democratization. Other considerations, particularly the global communications revolution, may also have played a role.[24] As Lee Teng-hui observed, "there are many levels of reasons for this

[Taiwan's democratic] success, and . . . the factors at each level play a necessary role."[25]

Taiwan's Economic Power

When Chinese forces liberated Taiwan in 1945, the island's economy was in shambles. But the new government did little to improve matters. According to U.S. government accounts, corruption and mismanagement ultimately reached such proportions that they contributed to an aborted uprising on February 28, 1947:

> The economic deterioration of the island and the administration of the mainland officials became so bad that on February 28, 1947, popular resentment erupted into a major rebellion. In the ensuing days the Government put down the revolt in a series of military actions which cost thousands of lives.[26]

After the ROC national government retreated to Taiwan in 1949, conditions began to improve. By the early 1950s, the island's economy had recovered to prewar peaks.[27] At roughly the same time, Chiang Kai-shek came to the conclusion that his army would not be able to recover mainland China militarily. Consequently, the generalissimo agreed to transform Taiwan into a model province and thereby prove the superiority of the KMT's road to modernization. Chiang would employ political, rather than military, means to retake China.

By following what has sometimes been referred to as a "mixed" economic system—with heavy industries owned by the government, and virtually all light industries, services, and trading firms owned by private concerns—Taiwan's economy took off. As outlined in Table 6.4, between 1950 and 1994, the gross national product (GNP) increased more than 1,000 percent, the economic growth rate averaging 9.15 percent in the 1960s, 10.26 percent in the 1970s, and 8.25 percent in the 1980s. Between 1990 and 1994, Taiwan's economy grew at an average of 6.28 percent annually. Furthermore, the per capita national income (Table 6.5) has grown each year for the past twenty years. During this same period, the benefits of Taiwan's economic miracle were spread fairly evenly through society—in terms of the Gini income concentration ratio, the gap between the highest and lowest 20 percent of the wage earners is less than that which exists in the United States.[28]

The composition of Taiwan's labor force, a statistical characteristic that is often employed as a measure of national industrialization and modernization, reveals that the island's labor force began to experience a significant shift during the 1950s and 1960s. Whereas during the early 1950s

Table 6.4 Gross National Product of the ROC, 1952–1994 (constant 1991 NT$ in millions)

	Amount	Real growth rate (percentage)
1952	183,051	12.0
1955	237,027	8.1
1960	327,817	6.4
1965	515,097	11.0
1966	561,318	9.0
1967	620,856	10.6
1968	677,506	9.1
1969	738,820	9.1
1970	822,457	11.3
1971	929,450	13.0
1972	1,053,794	13.4
1973	1,188,513	12.8
1974	1,202,266	1.2
1975	1,255,539	4.4
1976	1,427,576	13.7
1977	1,573,984	10.3
1978	1,794,319	14.0
1979	1,946,103	8.5
1980	2,084,609	7.1
1981	2,204,510	5.8
1982	2,293,995	4.1
1983	2,492,409	8.7
1984	2,781,712	11.6
1985	2,936,389	5.6
1986	3,305,977	12.6
1987	3,711,281	12.3
1988	4,020,658	8.3
1989	4,341,409	8.0
1990	4,581,783	5.5
1991	4,927,801	7.6
1992	5,234,735	6.2
1993	5,549,861	6.0
1994	5,886,309	6.1

Source: Director-General of Budget, Accounting and Statistics, Republic of China, *Statistical Abstract of National Income, Taiwan Area, Republic of China, 1951–1995* (Taipei: Director-General of Budget, Accounting and Statistics, Republic of China, March 1995). Data supplied to author courtesy of the Chinese Information and Culture Center Library, New York City, New York.

approximately 52 percent of the labor force was engaged in agriculture and 20 percent in industry, by the early 1980s the percentage engaged in agriculture had dropped to 19 percent and the ranks of those employed in industry had swollen to 42 percent.[29] During the 1990s, the island is shifting from low-tech industry to high-tech industry and attempting to become a financial center of East Asia.

By the 1980s, Taiwan had evolved from a backward, agrarian society into an economic powerhouse. As one of the largest international traders, it

Table 6.5 Per Capita National Income in the ROC, 1955–1994 (constant 1991 NT$)

	Amount	Real growth rate (percentage)
1955	24,243	4.6
1960	27,994	2.1
1965	38,120	5.8
1966	40,500	6.2
1967	43,704	7.9
1968	46,602	6.6
1969	50,021	7.3
1970	54,324	8.6
1971	59,779	10.0
1972	66,233	10.8
1973	72,993	10.2
1974	71,307	–2.3
1975	72,797	2.1
1976	81,557	12.0
1977	87,559	7.4
1978	96,062	9.7
1979	102,338	6.5
1980	105,818	3.5
1981	108,237	2.3
1982	110,847	2.4
1983	118,384	6.8
1984	130,189	10.0
1985	135,331	4.0
1986	154,846	14.4
1987	173,038	11.8
1988	185,092	7.0
1989	198,468	6.2
1990	206,854	4.2
1991	219,637	6.2
1992	233,942	6.5
1993	244,692	4.6
1994	254,149	3.9

Source: Director-General of Budget, Accounting and Statistics, Republic of China, *Statistical Abstract of National Income, Taiwan Area, Republic of China, 1951–1995* (Taipei: Director-General of Budget, Accounting and Statistics, Republic of China, March 1995). Data supplied to author courtesy of the Chinese Information and Culture Center Library, New York City, New York.

commands the respect of the world's political and financial leaders (see Table 6.6).

Understanding Taiwan's Economic Miracle

Scholars have advanced numerous hypotheses in an effort to explain Taiwan's so-called economic miracle. During the 1970s, economists argued that Taipei's "adherence to the free market had allowed the nation to become

Table 6.6 Taiwan's Exports and Imports in World Merchandise Trade, 1994

Exporters	Importers
1. United States	1. United States
2. Germany	2. Germany
3. Japan	3. Japan
4. France	4. France
5. United Kingdom	5. United Kingdom
6. Italy	6. Italy
7. Canada	7. Hong Kong
8. Hong Kong	8. Canada
9. Netherlands	9. Netherlands
10. Belgium and Luxembourg	10. Belgium and Luxembourg
11. People's Republic of China	11. People's Republic of China
12. Singapore	12. South Korea
13. South Korea	13. Singapore
14. Taiwan	14. Spain
15. Spain	15. Taiwan

Source: World Trade Organization, "Press Release," April 4, 1995, p. 11. Information provided courtesy of Dan Gardner, International Trade Administration, U.S. Department of Commerce.

highly competitive in the global economy through 'getting the prices right.'"[30] In the 1980s, sociologists and political scientists suggested that the dynamics of rapid growth in Taiwan "represented a case of state-led development because of the considerable role that the government clearly played in the economy."[31] More recently, scholars interested in business administration have claimed that "the entrepreneurship of small businessmen stemming from 'Confucian capitalism' provides the best explanation for Taiwan's developmental history."[32]

Just as the interplay of several factors contributed to Taiwan's rapid democratization, it is likely that all of the interpretations above have some explanatory value. Sometimes overlooked, however, is the critical role that the United States played in the island's economic development. After all, it was the U.S. government that urged Chiang to undertake his highly successful land reform program. Furthermore, Washington poured massive amounts of economic aid into Taiwan (see Table 6.7).[33] In fact, U.S. aid accounted for roughly 40 percent of capital formation in Taiwan during the 1950s.[34] As Fredrick Chien, Taiwan's foreign minister, observed, the ROC "benefitted a lot from the generous economic aid from the U.S."[35] It is also noteworthy that the United States was willing to serve as the chief destination for Taiwan's exports. Without the U.S. market, it is unlikely that Taiwan's economy would have experienced such extraordinary growth.

Table 6.7 U.S. Economic Aid to Taiwan, 1951–1968 (U.S.$ in millions)

Fiscal year	Total arrival amount	Nonproject assistance	Project assistance
1951–1954	375.2	300.4	74.8
1955	132.0	96.4	35.6
1956	101.6	69.5	32.1
1957	108.1	66.2	42.9
1958	81.6	51.9	29.7
1959	128.9	73.7	55.2
1960	101.1	68.7	32.4
1961	94.2	70.4	23.8
1962	65.9	59.3	6.6
1963	115.3	113.5	1.8
1964	83.9	37.3	46.6
1965	56.5	56.1	0.4
1966	4.2	4.2	—
1967	4.4	4.4	—
1968	29.3	29.3	—
Total	1,482.2	1,100.3	381.9

Source: Council for Economic Planning and Development, Republic of China. Information provided courtesy of Moses Lu, Information Division, Taipei Economic and Cultural Representative Office, Chicago, Illinois.

Democracy, Economic Power, and Taiwan's National Security

In less than two decades, Taiwan has managed to transform itself from a backward, authoritarian state into a full-fledged democracy and an economic powerhouse. How have these developments contributed to Taiwan's security?

Enhanced International Legitimation and Support

Given Taiwan's political reforms, a new emphasis on human rights and democracy could yield big dividends for the island. U.S. lawmakers are calling on Washington to express support for Taiwan's democratization. Senator Paul Simon (Democrat–Illinois) has asserted, "Now, in light of the dramatically different ways in which the domestic situations of Taiwan and the mainland have evolved, I would argue that it is high time that we tilted the balance a bit toward a somewhat more official relationship with Taiwan."[36] Lloyd Bentsen has said that "the time has come to place our relations with the aging totalitarians in Beijing on a purely pragmatic basis, and to develop a new relationship with the new Taiwan."[37] After applauding Taiwan's "substantial strides in developing democratic representative institutions," Senator Joseph Lieberman (Democrat–Connecticut) has called on the United States to support Taiwan's bid to rejoin the United Nations.[38]

Other governments also are being pressured to recognize Taiwan's democratization. For example, Japanese officials are under mounting pressure to upgrade relations with Taipei. In 1993, Hisahiko Okazaki, former Japanese ambassador to Thailand, advised Tokyo to revise its policy toward the island because it is now "a completely free, democratic country."[39] In 1994, Akira Hatano, former Japanese justice minister, called on Tokyo to adopt a more "realistic Taiwan policy" because the island has developed into "a strong democracy and an economic powerhouse."[40] European lawmakers also are pressuring their governments to strengthen bilateral relations with Taiwan.[41]

In addition to Taiwan's political reform, the island's economic clout is contributing to its international stature. As the world moves into an era of intense economic competition, many states are strengthening ties with Taipei. Francis Mong, deputy director of Canada's Trade Office in Taipei, explained that his government upgraded relations with Taiwan because it had "to find a way to accommodate our trading partners . . . we cannot ignore an emerging economy like Taiwan."[42] Tarja Kuokkanen, Finland's representative in Taiwan, said that Helsinki established an office in Taipei because "we recognize the importance of developing a trading partnership . . . everything is happening here."[43] Officials in Washington also claim that economic considerations led to the Clinton administration's 1994 decision to upgrade relations with Taiwan. As one senior official explained, "the primary goal [of the recent changes in policy] is to make it easier to conduct business with Taiwan, which is now the United States' fifth largest trading partner and has more than U.S.$80 billion in foreign exchange reserves."[44] To underscore this position, the administration insisted that the new name of Taiwan's representative offices highlight the economic nature of U.S.-Taiwan relations. Taiwan's "unofficial embassy" is now called the Taipei Economic and Cultural Representative Office.[45]

In addition to the improvements in relations with the developed world, Taipei has managed to establish diplomatic relations or upgrade "unofficial" relations with many underdeveloped states. In fact, several Third World nations have been added to its diplomatic list, and it is primarily these states that now support Taiwan in its bid to join (or rejoin) the United Nations. The promise of bountiful aid packages, generous loans, or technical assistance may have been the decisive factor in enticing some developing nations to switch formal recognition to Taipei or to support its drive to return to the United Nations.[46]

As described in Chapter 7, these diplomatic triumphs contribute to several aspects of Taiwan's security. They bolster Taiwan's position that it is a political entity, undermine the PRC's claim of sovereignty over the island, and dampen sentiment for Taiwanese independence.

Increased Access to Foreign Arms

With roughly U.S.$100 billion in foreign exchange reserves, Taiwan is in a position to purchase arms overseas. Furthermore, Taipei is in a position to pressure foreign governments into providing the island with offset agreements, technology transfers, and even lower prices—concessions unthinkable during the Cold War.

In addition to Taiwan's economic clout, the island's democratic reforms may also have enhanced its ability to secure weapons. For example, Senator Claiborne Pell (Democrat–Rhode Island) has opined, "With Taiwan's continued political development . . . it will become increasingly difficult to deny it access to more modern military equipment."[47]

Domestic Support and Legitimation

Despite official statements to the contrary, Taiwan is not a perfect democracy. For example, both of the island's major political parties—the KMT and the DPP—have been accused of rampant vote-buying and corruption. But it is clear that Taiwan has taken major steps toward democratization.

The world has no perfect democracies. As Robert Dahl once observed, democracy is a condition that exists solely as an ideal.[48] It is never fully realized. As may be expected, some are unhappy with the island's political transformation. During an interview with the author, General (ret.) Chiang Wego, suggested that the democratization process has gone too far:

> A democratic country can have more than two political parties, but all the parties should be for the same country, the same constitution. If we allow some people who are not for China, and yet are working in our government, that is not natural. We are committing suicide. And what is the purpose of allowing such a party to exist?[49]

Others are shocked by the raucous behavior of Taiwan's legislators. Brawls in the National Assembly and Legislative Yuan have become so violent that the island's television stations are banned from broadcasting the proceedings. Still others are unnerved by the personal attacks and slanderous charges made by irresponsible politicians—offenses that were unthinkable only ten years ago.[50]

Taiwan is probably the noisiest democracy in Asia. It may even qualify as the most disorderly democracy in the world. But most Taiwanese support democratization nevertheless. This support, in turn, enhances the legitimacy of the government. Lung Ying-tai, a Taiwanese writer, explains: "Yes, the Taiwanese are breaking the heads of one another like clowns in parliament. But I would much rather see this sort of boisterous, tasteless farce than quiet and dignified ceremonies where oppositionists are locked up."[51] In short, few Taiwanese wish to return to the days when Generalissimo Chiang Kai-shek ruled the island with an iron fist.

Relations with China

During the mid-1980s, Taiwan's democratization and economic progress began to attract attention in the PRC. News of the "Taiwan miracle" was carried into China through a variety of channels, including the hundreds of thousands of "Taiwan compatriots" who journeyed to the mainland after 1987. As reported in the *New York Times* and other periodicals, the PRC was swept by "Taiwan fever" during the months that preceded the ill-fated 1989 democracy movement. The fever's symptoms included a fascination with the island's music, films, fashions, books, prosperity, and, ultimately, politics. Cheng Lin, one of the PRC's most famous pop stars, explained the attraction that Taiwan began to hold for young mainlanders: "Young Chinese envy Taiwan. We used to think Taiwan was a wretched place, but then we discovered it isn't like that. It's very rich and we envy it enormously. Life is so much better there."[52] A 1989 opinion poll of mainland Chinese students studying in both the United States and the PRC supported this view. When asked whether the PRC should learn from Taiwan's experience in economic development, 86 percent of the U.S. sample and 60 percent of the mainland sample said yes.[53] To the question, "Is Taiwan's economic development in the past 40 years successful?" 92 percent of the U.S. respondents and 76 percent of the mainland respondents replied in the affirmative.[54]

"Taiwan fever" spread rapidly from the PRC's younger generation into the population as a whole. During the brief "Beijing Spring" of 1989, when Chinese dared express their opinions openly, people from all walks of life began to praise the Taiwan experience. When discussing possible methods by which to democratize the mainland, a Beijing University professor said that the Chinese should "look at what Taiwan did, they first expanded freedom of the press—that's what we need to do, too."[55] Wu Jinglian, one of the PRC's leading economists, argued that Taiwan should be used as a model for economic development: "For the present period, our economy should be like Taiwan's. We have to build a system very close to Taiwan's or those of the other newly industrialized Asian countries."[56] Even members of the Chinese Communist Party dared to recognize the appeal that Taiwan was beginning to hold for the PRC population. Wu Jiaxiang, a leading CCP theorist, acknowledged that "across the nation, many people think that we should imitate Taiwan," but he cautioned that it is "a very complicated matter."[57]

Following the crackdown in Tiananmen Square, the view that Taiwan might serve as a model for Chinese political and economic development has continued to grow. Yan Jiaqi, an exiled democracy activist and former head of the Institute of Political Science at the Chinese Academy of Social Sciences, believes that "the people in Taiwan hold the democratic flag . . . this, I feel, is the fundamental basis for the reunification of Taiwan and China."[58] Liu Binyan, an exiled writer and journalist from the PRC, contends that "Taiwan is proof that the Chinese can attain democracy and prosper economically."⁵⁹ Su Shaozhi, another exiled activist, agrees. Su claims that the "course of democracy" in Taiwan is a "practical" one for the PRC in the future.⁶⁰ Acting on such beliefs, Taiwanese officials invited PRC reporters to cover the island's 1996 presidential elections.⁶¹

Individuals outside of China's pro-democracy movement also believe that Taiwan might serve as a model for political reform in the PRC. Christine Loh, a Hong Kong legislator, has cautioned that "Taiwan's attempts to turn itself into a more democratic country, with universal suffrage and a directly elected president, should neither be ignored nor belittled by other countries in the region."⁶² The lawmaker suggested that Taiwan is making a "special contribution to the development of a modern China, because it alone of Chinese societies is evolving into an authentic multiparty system."⁶³ Following a visit to the PRC, former British prime minister Margaret Thatcher also suggested that Beijing must "look to South Korea and Taiwan. . . . Taiwan got its prosperity and is going on to democracy."⁶⁴

Should China reform its political system, this development could enhance Taiwan's security. At a minimum, one might expect Beijing to adopt a more mature and (or) less rigid position toward the unification issue. On the other hand, the two Chinas might even negotiate a peace settlement. As Immanuel Kant observed, states are less likely to go to war when they've developed democratic political systems. In fact, as one political analyst noted, "democracies (almost) never fight each other."⁶⁵

Taiwan's economic clout, coupled with the magnitude of its investment in the PRC, might also reduce the threat from Beijing. According to PRC statistics, Taipei is now the chief investor in mainland China. Taiwan's investment is helping China modernize its economy, which, in turn, is creating new interest groups that will push China toward democratization. As Chang Shallyen, then Taiwan's vice minister for foreign affairs, observed, "They [the Chinese Communist Party] have missed one important point . . . political and economic reform must go side by side, like twins."⁶⁶

Finally, the scope of Taiwanese investment in mainland China could deter PRC aggression. As one Taiwanese businessman explained, "the communists can swear as much as they like, but they wouldn't dare raise a hand against us. We've got so many investors in mainland China they wouldn't want to lose them."⁶⁷

Summary

Taiwan's dramatic transformation from a backward, agrarian society into an economic giant has prompted many to rethink their views on economic modernization. Taipei's political reform also has caught much of the world by surprise. Irrespective of the causes of these dramatic changes, both developments augment the island's security.

Taiwan's economic power and political reform are helping the island to overcome obstacles erected by Beijing and to reintegrate into the global community. Many governments are now more willing to get close to Taipei. Fredrick Chien, Taiwan's foreign minister, explains:

> These two things combined to make a lot of countries in the world start to reassess their relationship with us. Because here is a case of a country—a very backward country with a rather authoritarian type of government—that in a period of 40 years progressed into one of the most open market societies and the most pluralistic societies and a very democratic government.[68]

Some nations are more willing to sell arms. Others are more willing to upgrade diplomatic linkages or criticize Beijing for bullying the island during its elections. At the same time, the ROC government enjoys increased legitimation both at home and abroad. Finally, Taiwan may serve as a catalyst for peaceful political and economic change in mainland China. Many scholars believe that a more democratic China would be a more peaceful China.

Notes

1. Samuel P. Huntington, *The Third Wave: Democratization in the Late 20th Century* (Norman: University of Oklahoma Press, 1991), pp. 6–7.
2. Jaushieh Joseph Wu, "The 1994 Elections in Taiwan: Continuity, Change, and the Prospect for Democracy," *Issues and Studies* 31, No. 3, March 1995, p. 93.
3. Alan Wachman, *Taiwan: National Identity and Democratization* (Armonk, New York: M. E. Sharpe, 1994), p. 30.
4. In June 1990, Taiwan's Council of Grand Justices had ruled that all mainland-elected deputies must retire by the end of 1991. Those elected in the 1986 supplementary elections, however, were not required to run for reelection. For more information, see June Teufel Dreyer, "Taiwan's December 1991 Election," *World Affairs* 155, No. 2, Fall 1992, pp. 67–70.
5. See Linda Chao and Ramon H. Myers, "The First Chinese Democracy," *Asian Survey* 34, No. 3, March 1994, p. 226.
6. Author's interview with Stephen S. F. Chen, vice minister, Ministry of Foreign Affairs, Republic of China. Taipei, Taiwan, May 19, 1994. The vice minister made this statement when asked to explain Taiwan's growing acceptance by the international community.
7. Chong-Ping Lin, "Introduction," *World Affairs* 155, No. 2, Fall 1992, p. 51.
8. Wachman, *Taiwan: National Identity and Democratization*, p. 32.
9. See Dankwart A. Rustow, "Transition to Democracy: Toward a Democratic Model," *Comparative Politics*, No. 2, April 1990, pp. 156–244.
10. Nicholas Eberstadt, "Taiwan and South Korea: The 'Democratization' of Outlier States," *World Affairs* 155, No. 2, Fall 1992, p. 88.
11. See Elizabeth Shogren, "Taiwan Leader Calls on U.S. to End Isolation," *Los Angeles Times,* June 10, 1995, p. A1.

12. Author's interview with General (ret.) Chiang Wego, Taipei, Taiwan, February 5, 1996.
13. Seymour Martin Lipset, "Some Social Requisites of Democracy: Economic Development and Political Legitimacy," *American Political Science Review* 53, 1959, p. 75.
14. Barrington Moore, Jr., *Social Origins of Dictatorship and Democracy* (Boston: Beacon Press, 1966), p. 418.
15. See Samuel S. Kim, "Taiwan in the International System: The Challenge of Legitimation," in Robert G. Sutter and William R. Johnson (eds.), *Taiwan in World Affairs* (Boulder, Colorado: Westview Press, 1994), p. 171.
16. "Li Addresses Democracy Conference," *CNA,* August 28, 1995, in *FBIS, China,* August 29, 1995, p. 80.
17. Hung-mao Tien, "Dynamics of Taiwan's Democratic Transition," in Steve Tsang (ed.), *In the Shadow of China: Political Development in Taiwan Since 1949* (Honolulu: University of Hawaii Press, 1993), pp. 103–104.
18. See Emerson Niou, "An Analysis of the Republic of China's Security Issues," *Issues and Studies* 28, No. 1, January 1992, p. 94.
19. John F. Copper, *China Diplomacy: The Washington-Taipei-Beijing Triangle* (Boulder, Colorado: Westview Press, 1992), p. 129.
20. Ibid.
21. Ibid.
22. James R. Lilley, "Trade and the Waking Giant—China, Asia and American Engagement," in James R. Lilley and Wendell L. Willkie II (eds.), *Beyond MFN: Trade with China and American Interests* (Washington, D.C.: AEI Press, 1994), p. 37.
23. See Kim, "Taiwan and the International System," p. 170.
24. Ibid., p. 171.
25. "Li Addresses Democracy Conference," p. 81.
26. U.S. Department of State, *United States Relations with China* (Washington, D.C.: Department of State, Division of Publications, Office of Public Affairs, August 1949), p. 308.
27. See Thomas B. Gold, "Taiwan: In Search of Identity," in Steven M. Goldstein (ed.), *Mini Dragons: Fragile Economic Miracles in the Pacific* (Boulder, Colorado: Westview, 1991), p. 28.
28. For more information, see Senator Paul Simon (Democrat–Illinois), "Proposals to Revitalize U.S. Policy in Asia," *Congressional Record,* Proceedings and Debates of the 102nd Congress, 1st Session, Vol. 137, No. 76, May 20, 1991, p. S6124.
29. See Chu-yuan Cheng, "Economic Development in Taiwan and Mainland China: A Comparison of Strategies and Performance," *Asian Affairs,* Spring 1983, pp. 69–70.
30. Cal Clark, "Dynamics of Development in Taiwan: Reconceptualizing State and Market in National Competitiveness," *American Journal of Chinese Studies* 2, No. 1, April 1994, p. 14.
31. Ibid.
32. Ibid.
33. U.S. aid was terminated in 1968.
34. Gold, "Taiwan: In Search of Identity," p. 28.
35. Author's interview with Fredrick Chien, foreign minister of the Republic of China, Taipei, Taiwan, July 14, 1992.
36. See prepared statement of Senator Paul Simon (Democrat–Illinois) in *Sino-American Relations: Current Policy Issues.* U.S. Congress, Senate, Hearings Before

the Subcommittee on East Asian and Pacific Affairs of the Committee on Foreign Relations, 102nd Congress, 1st Session, June 13, 25, and 27, 1991 (Washington, D.C.: U.S. Government Printing Office, 1991), p. 4.

37. "Senator Bentsen Urges Bush to Sell F-16s to ROC," *CNA* (Taipei), August 11, 1992, in *Lexis/Nexis.*

38. See *Congressional Record,* March 23, 1993, pp. S3531–S3532.

39. "Tokyo Leaders Urge Closer Official Ties with Taiwan," *South China Morning Post* (Weekly Edition), August 21–22, 1993, p. 7.

40. See "Japan Urged to Update China Policy," *CNA,* July 22, 1994, in *Lexis/Nexis.*

41. See "German Lawmakers Support Submarine Sales to Taiwan," *CNA* (Taipei), October 11, 1993, in *Lexis/Nexis.*

42. Julian Baum, "A Trend to Friends," *Far Eastern Economic Review,* November 29, 1990, p. 12.

43. Amy Lo, "Pragmatic Diplomacy, Creative Economics," *Free China Review* 41, No. 5, May 1991, p. 8.

44. Jim Mann, "Clinton to Ease Restrictions for Taiwan," *China Post* (International Airmail Edition), July 7, 1994, p. 1.

45. Taiwanese officials had hoped originally to change the name to Taipei Representative Office. For more information, see "Taipei Seeks Change of De Facto Embassy Title," *China Post* (International Airmail Edition), June 24, 1994, p. 1.

46. For more information, see Dennis Van Vranken Hickey, "U.S. Policy and Taiwan's Reintegration into the Global Community," *Journal of Northeast Asian Studies,* Spring 1992, pp. 26–28.

47. See U.S. Congress, Senate, *Trips to Taiwan, Hong Kong, Indonesia, and Papua New Guinea,* a Report to the Committee on Foreign Relations, April 1992 (Washington, D.C.: U.S. Government Printing Office, 1992), p. 6.

48. See Robert Dahl, *Polyarchy: Participation and Opposition* (New Haven, Connecticut: Yale University Press, 1971), pp. 1–5.

49. Author's interview with General (ret.) Chiang Wego, Taipei, Taiwan, May 17, 1994.

50. See James Kynge, "Despite Punch-ups, Taiwan's Democracy Marches On," in *Reuters World Service,* November 30, 1994, in *Lexis/Nexis.*

51. Philip Shenon, "Models for China: Either Filthy and Free or Clean and Mean," *New York Times,* February 5, 1995, Sec. 4, p. 1.

52. Nicholas D. Kristof, "In China, Disdain for Taiwan Turns to Envy," *New York Times,* May 4, 1989, p. A1.

53. See Li Shaomin, "A Chinese Student's Cultural Evolution," *Asian Wall Street Journal,* May 10, 1989, p. 10.

54. Ibid.

55. Kristof, "In China, Disdain for Taiwan Turns to Envy," p. A10.

56. Ibid.

57. Ibid.

58. "Wu'er Calls for All Chinese to Unite," *Free China Journal,* August 14, 1989.

59. "Exiled Chinese Dissidents in Taipei for Visit," *South China Morning Post,* December 12, 1989, p. 12.

60. "Mainland Fugitives Fly to Taiwan for Activities," *China Daily,* October 23, 1989, p. 1.

61. See "PRC Reporters May Cover Elections," *China Post* (International Airmail Edition), January 4, 1996, p. 1.

62. "ROC Called a Model for Asian Democracy," *CNA*, August 25, 1994, in *Lexis/Nexis*.

63. Ibid.

64. Jonathan Mirsky and Christopher Thomas, "Thatcher Endorses Deng's Road to Market Economy," *Times*, September 24, 1994, in *Lexis/Nexis*.

65. See Michael W. Doyle, "Kant, Liberal Legacies and Foreign Affairs," *Philosophy and Public Affairs* 12, No. 3, Summer 1983, pp. 205–235. For more information, also see Vincent Wei-cheng Wang, "Does Democratization Enhance or Reduce Taiwan's Security?" paper presented at the 1995 annual meeting of the American Political Science Association, Chicago, August 31–September 3, 1995.

66. Author's interview with Chang Shallyen, then director-general of Kuomintang Overseas Affairs Department and vice minister for foreign affairs, Republic of China, Taipei, Taiwan, February 15, 1990.

67. James Kynge, "ROC Hails President's U.S. Performance," *China Post* (International Airmail Edition), June 12, 1995, p. 1.

68. Author's interview with Fredrick Chien, foreign minister of the Republic of China, Taipei, Taiwan, February 7, 1996.

7

Pragmatic Diplomacy and Taiwan's National Security

As the Cold War came to a close in the late 1980s, Taiwan adopted a new approach to foreign policy—pragmatic diplomacy. The new approach to international relations is finding a receptive audience in the post–Cold War era. This chapter briefly outlines the background and evolution of Taiwan's diplomacy, discusses its new approach to foreign policy, and explains how pragmatic diplomacy contributes to the island's security.

Background and Evolution of Taiwan's Diplomacy

In 1949, Generalissimo Chiang Kai-shek and his Kuomintang government retreated to the island of Taiwan. Since that time, Taiwan's approach to international relations has gone through a complete cycle that started with active participation, moved to relative indifference and isolation, and finally returned to a passionate desire to participate. The following discussion examines each of these stages.

Phase One

During the first period—which extended from the early 1950s to the early 1970s—many important governments, including the United States and Japan, recognized the Republic of China on Taiwan as the sole, legitimate government of all China. Moreover, the KMT government continued to occupy the Chinese seat in the United Nations and most other significant international organizations. In fact, for roughly two decades, the United States and its allies successfully blocked Beijing's efforts to take Taipei's UN seat.

From 1951 to 1960, the ROC's friends and allies argued that the PRC did not meet the UN Charter's prerequisites that members must be "peace-loving states." In 1960, as support for Beijing's admission began to mount, the United States and other states switched tactics and barred the PRC's membership by claiming that the Chinese representation issue was an "important question" under Article 18 of the UN Charter and required a two-thirds majority vote of the General Assembly.[1] As Cold War tensions eased in the early 1970s, however, Taiwan's position began to deteriorate.

Phase Two

The second phase in Taiwan's diplomacy extended roughly from 1971—when Taiwan withdrew from the UN—until the late 1980s. During this stage, dozens of nations broke off diplomatic relations with Taiwan and recognized the PRC as the legitimate government of China. The most crushing blow came when the United States severed formal relations with Taipei in favor of Beijing.

In 1979, a grim-faced President Chiang Ching-kuo announced during a televised speech that Washington was switching diplomatic recognition to Beijing. In the aftermath of the announcement, security was tightened around the island and parliamentary elections were canceled. Nervous businessmen began to emigrate abroad. As Lee Cheng-chia, honorary chairman of Taiwan's Small and Medium Enterprise Association, recalled, "it was quite confusing at that time."[2]

It was also during this period that Taiwan withdrew from most international bodies. In an effort to patch up relations with Beijing, Washington reluctantly acquiesced to the position that the two-thirds rule was irrelevant to the Chinese representation issue. Rather than suffer the humiliation of expulsion, Chiang Kai-shek ordered his delegation to withdraw from the UN in 1971—a move some now contend was a diplomatic blunder.[3]

Following the ROC's withdrawal from the UN, Taipei lost representation in numerous other institutions. For example, in 1980 the ROC was forced to yield its World Bank and International Monetary Fund (IMF) seats to Beijing. By the mid-1980s, Taiwan had been expelled from most important international organizations.

During this time, Taiwan adopted a foreign policy posture that could perhaps best be described as "damage control"—it did not undertake bold initiatives in international relations.[4] Taiwan did, however, manage to establish "unofficial" or "substantive" relations with some foreign governments. In the case of the United States, political, economic, and cultural relations would be handled by the American Institute in Taiwan in Taipei and its counterpart, the Coordinating Council for North American Affairs (CCNAA) in Washington, D.C.[5] Despite similar arrangements with Japan and other states, Taiwan became increasingly identified as an "international orphan" or a "pariah state."

It is ironic that Taiwan's drift toward diplomatic isolation coincided with a period of rapid social and political change on the island and its emergence as a world-class economic power. As Professor Michael Y. M. Kau observed, "just as a large number of ROC citizens rushed abroad for business or pleasure, the country's international isolation worsened and the quality of its service in international interactions deteriorated."[6] In some instances, Taiwanese businessmen found themselves locked out of important international markets. Recalled one government official, "when the Europeans first cut relations—they cut them off—people couldn't even get a visa."[7]

Phase Three

The third phase of Taiwan's diplomacy extends from the late 1980s to the present. Reflecting President Lee's 1988 pledge that Taiwan must "strive with a greater determination, pragmatism, flexibility and vision in order to upgrade and break through a foreign policy based primarily on substantive relations," Taiwan has adopted a new diplomatic strategy described as "flexible" or "pragmatic" diplomacy.[8] By employing this approach, Taiwan hopes to recover its position in the international community.

Pragmatic Diplomacy

In recent years, Taiwan has undergone a metamorphosis. Changes in domestic policy include the lifting of martial law, the legalization of opposition political parties, and a revitalization of Taiwan's moribund legislative bodies. Dramatic transformations in the government's mainland policy—its relations with the PRC—have accompanied these changes. Bilateral trade has surged, Taiwanese investment in China has exploded, and Taipei now acknowledges the Chinese Communist Party's de facto rule over mainland China. Perhaps equally significant is Taiwan's new approach toward foreign policy—that of pragmatic diplomacy.

Shortly after Lee was sworn in as president of the Republic of China in January 1988, he began to promote a "pragmatic approach" to international relations. Pragmatic diplomacy calls for:

- The advancement and reinforcement of formal diplomatic ties
- The development of substantive relations with countries that do not maintain formal ties with Taiwan
- Admission or readmission to international organizations and activities vital to the country's national interest[9]

The following discussion explores Taiwan's progress in meeting these objectives.

Formal Diplomatic Relations

Taiwan is presently recognized by thirty states (see Table 7.1), most located in Central America and the Caribbean. Indeed, with the exception of Mexico, Taipei maintains formal diplomatic relations with all of the Central American nations.

Table 7.1 Nations Having Diplomatic Relations with Taiwan

The Bahamas	Malawi
Belize	Nauru
Burkina Faso	Nicaragua
Central African Republic	Panama
Costa Rica	Paraguay
Dominica	Saint Kitts and Nevis
Dominican Republic	Saint Lucia
El Salvador	Saint Vincent and the Grenadines
The Gambia	Senegal
Grenada	Solomon Islands
Guatemala	South Africa
Guinea-Bissau	Swaziland
Haiti	Tonga
Honduras	Tuvalu
Liberia	Vatican City

Source: Information provided courtesy of Moses Lu, Information Division, Taipei Economic and Cultural Representative Office, Chicago, Illinois.

Taiwan no longer considers its battle over diplomatic recognition with the PRC as a "zero-sum" game. The establishment of formal diplomatic relations with Grenada in 1988, a state that still maintained official ties with Beijing, signaled Taiwan's willingness to accept the principle of "dual recognition" (however, the PRC does not accept that principle). In 1995, Taiwan again indicated that it might be willing to accept dual recognition. When faced with the possibility that South Africa might switch recognition to the PRC, Du Ling, director of the ROC Foreign Ministry's African Affairs Department, explained that "what we value is the ROC's diplomatic relations with South Africa, [Pretoria's] relations with mainland China we do not question."[10]

These developments represent a dramatic turn in Taiwan's foreign policy. However, authorities stress that Taipei continues to adhere to the "one-China principle"—namely, that there is only one China and Taiwan is a part of China. During an interview with the author, Fredrick Chien, Taiwan's foreign minister, explained the government's position:

> We still adhere to the position of one China and that Taiwan is a part of China. But in China, there now exist two political entities—one mainland

China and one Republic of China on Taiwan. And that is really the theoretical basis of pragmatic diplomacy. Within the nation of China, there exists two political entities and each entity should have the capability of conducting its own diplomacy. They should, each one, have its own place in the world community.[11]

Officials also stress that, while the ROC government's established policy is to pursue a united China, "the 'one China' is not the People's Republic of China as claimed by Beijing . . . the united China that is envisioned by the ROC government is a country that features freedom, equality and the equitable distribution of wealth."[12]

Since adopting its new approach to foreign policy, Taipei has won a string of small victories in its struggle with Beijing over diplomatic recognition. Several countries, including Belize (1989), Grenada (1989), Guinea-Bissau (1990), Lesotho (1990), Liberia (1989), Nicaragua (1990), the Central Africa Republic (1991), The Gambia (1995), and Senegal (1996), have been added to its diplomatic list. Authorities are especially encouraged by the recent calls for Washington to "recognize Taiwan as a free country."[13] Even though Taiwanese officials concede that formal U.S. recognition appears unlikely, Chen Hsi-fan, Taiwan's vice minister of foreign affairs, has revealed that "re-establishing official relations with the U.S. has always been the top priority of the Foreign Affairs Ministry. . . . Our efforts toward this goal have not ceased for a single day."[14]

Although Taipei has won several important victories in its battle with Beijing over diplomatic relations, the island also has experienced two major defections—Saudi Arabia moved its embassy to Beijing in 1990 and South Korea switched recognition to the PRC in 1992.[15] As the date for the handover of Hong Kong to the PRC approaches, Taiwanese officials fear that Beijing will exert even more pressure on foreign governments to break relations with Taipei. The PRC has threatened to close the Hong Kong–based representative offices of several governments, including South Africa, Costa Rica, Panama, the Dominican Republic, and Guinea-Bissau, if they refuse to switch recognition to Beijing.[16]

Substantive Relations

Although Taiwan maintains formal diplomatic relations with only thirty nations, it maintains substantive trade, scientific and technological, and cultural relations with more than 120 countries and areas. Many now have representative offices in Taipei to carry out unofficial relations with Taiwan and provide services required by business travelers and tourists. When feasible, Taiwan will establish a counterpart organization in these countries. As outlined in Tables 7.2–7.5, Taiwan's informal diplomatic network spans the globe.

Table 7.2 Taiwan's Unofficial Representative Offices in North and South America

	Representative office title
Argentina	Commercial Office of Taiwan
Bolivia	Commercial Office–Consulate of the ROC
Brazil	Economic and Cultural Office of Taipei
Canada	Taipei Economic and Cultural Office
Chile	Economic and Cultural Office of Taipei
Colombia	Commercial Office of Taipei
Ecuador	Commercial Office of the ROC
Peru	Economic and Cultural Office of Taipei
Uruguay	Economic Office of Taipei
United States	Taipei Economic and Cultural Representative Office
Venezuela	Economic and Cultural Office of Taipei

Source: ROC Government Information Office, *The Republic of China Yearbook, 1995* (Taipei: Government Information Office, 1995), pp 789–791.

Table 7.3 Taiwan's Unofficial Representative Offices in the Asia Pacific Region

	Representative office title
Australia	Taipei Economic and Cultural Office
Brunei	Far East Trade and Cultural Center
Cambodia	Taipei Economic and Cultural Representative Office
Fiji	Trade Mission of the ROC
Hong Kong	Chung Hwa Travel Service
Indonesia	Taipei Economic and Trade Office
Japan	Taipei Economic and Cultural Representative Office
Macau	Taipei Trade and Tourism Office
Malaysia	Taipei Economic and Cultural Center
New Zealand	Taipei Economic and Cultural Office
Papua New Guinea	Trade Mission of the ROC on Taiwan
Philippines	Taipei Economic and Cultural Office
Singapore	Taipei Representative Office
South Korea	Taipei Mission in Korea
Thailand	Taipei Economic and Cultural Office
Vietnam	Taipei Economic and Cultural Office

Source: ROC Government Information Office, *The Republic of China Yearbook, 1995* (Taipei: Government Information Office, 1995), pp. 783–785.

Taipei is aggressively trying to cultivate or upgrade its substantive relations. In July 1992, Taiwan set up an economic cultural center in Portugal, making that country the last member of the European Community to approve a representative office for Taipei. In August 1995, Taiwan opened its first representative office in India—the Taipei Economic and Cultural Center.[17] Shortly afterward, Taiwan opened a representative office in Cambodia.[18] New trade offices also have been established in Australia,

Table 7.4 Taiwan's Unofficial Representative Offices in the Middle East and Africa

	Representative office title
Angola	Special Delegation of the ROC
Bahrain	Trade Mission of the ROC
Israel	Taipei Economic and Trade Office
Jordan	Commercial Office of the ROC
Kuwait	Commercial Office of the ROC
Libya	Commercial Office of the ROC
Mauritius	Trade Mission of the ROC
Madagascar	Special Delegation of the ROC
Nigeria	Trade Mission of the ROC (Taiwan)
Oman	Taipei Economic and Cultural Office
Saudi Arabia	Taipei Economic and Cultural Representative Office
Turkey	Taipei Economic and Cultural Office
United Arab Emirates	Commercial Office of the ROC
Zaire	Delegation of the ROC

Source: ROC Government Information Office, *The Republic of China Yearbook, 1995* (Taipei: Government Information Office, 1995), pp. 785–787.

Table 7.5 Taiwan's Unofficial Representative Offices in Europe (including Russia)

	Representative office title
Austria	Taipei Economic and Cultural Office
Belgium	Taipei Economic and Cultural Office
Czech Republic	Taipei Economic and Cultural Office
Denmark	Taipei Economic and Cultural Office
Finland	Taipei Economic and Cultural Office
France	Association for the Promotion of Commercial Exchanges and Tourism with Taiwan
Germany	Taipei Economic and Cultural Bureau
Greece	Taipei Economic and Cultural Office
Hungary	Taipei Trade Office
Ireland	Taipei Economic and Cultural Office
Italy	Cultural and Economic Institute of Taipei
Luxembourg	Taipei Economic and Cultural Office
The Netherlands	Taipei Economic and Cultural Office
Norway	Taipei Economic and Cultural Office
Poland	Taipei Economic and Cultural Office
Portugal	Taipei Economic and Cultural Center
Spain	Taipei Cultural and Economic Center
Sweden	Taipei Mission in Sweden
Switzerland	Cultural and Economic Delegation of Taipei
Russia	Representative Office in Moscow for the Taipei-Moscow Economic and Cultural Coordination Commission
United Kingdom	Taipei Representative Office

Source: ROC Government Information Office, *The Republic of China Yearbook, 1995* (Taipei: Government Information Office, 1995), pp. 786–789.

Canada, and Mexico. Although these gains are impressive, Taipei is finding some of its biggest diplomatic victories in its relations with the states emerging from the rubble of the former Soviet empire. Several have agreed to establish consular ties—a level of relations just below official recognition.[19] The Baltic states—Latvia, Estonia, and Lithuania—have all agreed to exchange legations with Taiwan. Taiwanese officials boast that these offices will enjoy "full diplomatic privileges."[20]

In addition to forging new bonds, Taiwan is upgrading existing ties. It has successfully renegotiated the titles and/or responsibilities of numerous foreign institutes and representative offices. In May 1992, the Japanese government allowed Taiwan to change the name of its organization in that country from the Association of East Asian Relations to the Economic and Cultural Representative Office of Taipei. In September 1994, Washington followed Tokyo's lead and allowed Taipei to change the name of its U.S. representative office from the cryptic Coordinating Council for North American Affairs—a name that gave no clue as to the identity of the country that it represented—to the Taipei Economic and Cultural Representative Office.

Taiwan is also managing to raise the acceptable level of government-to-government communication. In 1991, Roger Fauroux, French minister of industry, became the first European cabinet-level official to visit Taipei in more than two decades. This visit helped pave the way for calls by cabinet-level ministers from Italy, Ireland, Sweden, and Great Britain and probably contributed to the Bush administration's decision to send Carla Hills, then the U.S. trade representative, to Taipei. The Hills visit was fraught with symbolism as it represented the first time that a cabinet-level official had visited Taiwan since 1979. In 1994, the Clinton administration lifted the ban on high-level exchanges with Taiwan, and Federico Peña, U.S. transportation secretary, traveled to Taipei—a move heralded by Taiwan as "an important breakthrough" in U.S.-Taiwan relations.[21]

In addition to foreign dignitaries visiting Taiwan, high-ranking Taiwanese officials have traveled abroad to forge relations with other countries. Under the clever guise of "vacation" or "holiday" diplomacy, President Lee paid "unofficial" visits to the Philippines, Indonesia, and Thailand in 1994. In 1995, he visited the United Arab Emirates and Jordan and became the first ROC president ever to visit the United States. Shortly after Lee returned to Taiwan, ROC premier Lien Chan "sneaked" into Europe.[22] During his tour, Lien visited Austria, Hungary, and the Czech Republic, where he met with President Vaclav Havel. Lien is the highest-level ROC official to travel to Europe since 1949.

Finally, Taiwan is achieving significant breakthroughs in improving global transportation and communication linkages and otherwise strengthening cooperation with countries that no longer have diplomatic relations with Taipei. Taiwan recently established air links with Australia, Canada,

New Zealand, and Vietnam, and the island's state carrier, China Airlines, now serves several of the major cities of Europe (Paris, London, Frankfurt, and Amsterdam).

International Organizations

Taiwan participates in eleven governmental and 811 nongovernmental international organizations (see Table 7.6). It is excluded, however, from membership in most important international bodies including the UN, the IMF, the World Bank, and GATT. By employing pragmatic diplomacy, Taipei is making a strong bid to join (or rejoin) these institutions.

Table 7.6 Taiwan's Membership in International Nongovernmental Organizations

Nature of organization	Number of organizations
Science and technology	78
Medicine and hygiene	114
Agriculture, forestry, fishery, and animal husbandry	48
Religion	61
Charity and social welfare	12
Education	24
Journalism	17
Culture and arts	46
Politics and administration	33
Law and police administration	20
Labor	14
Women, family, and youth	13
Communications and travel	39
Recreation and refreshment	25
Trade, finance, and insurance	66
Mining	7
Engineering and telecommunications	43
Research and development management	49
Energy	10
Sports	92
Total	811

Source: ROC Government Information Office, *The Republic of China Yearbook, 1995* (Taipei: Government Information Office, 1995), p. 173.

Rather than be shut out of participation in international organizations by PRC protests, Taipei is now willing to bypass the sensitive China issue by using titles other than its official designation—the Republic of China. In 1988, Taiwan resumed participation in the Asian Development Bank (ADB) under the name "Taipei, China." In 1990, it formally applied for admission to GATT as the representative of "Customs Territory of Taiwan, Penghu,

Kinmen and Matsu." In 1991, it accepted membership in the Asia Pacific Economic Cooperation (APEC) forum under the title, "Chinese, Taipei." In 1992, Taiwan entered the South Pacific Forum using the name "Taiwan/Republic of China."

Although Taiwan is willing to employ creative means to achieve its diplomatic goals, authorities have no plans to change the name of the government and will adopt unofficial titles only under protest. Fredrick Chien explains the ROC position:

> We have joined non-governmental international organizations under different names. For example, in the Olympic Games we use "Taipei, China." But with regard to formal government organizations, we would still like to use the "ROC" as the name. This is the reason why, when the Asian Development Bank changed our name arbitrarily . . . we refused to attend for a number of years. Today, we will participate, but under pressure.[23]

As Koo Chen-fu, chairman of Taiwan's National Association of Industry and Commerce, observed, "we aren't happy with all the 'weird names' for us, but if we don't belong to international organizations, we don't have a forum to make our point. We can't seek to change things unless we're on the inside."[24] Once Taiwan is "on the inside," it attempts to upgrade the name under which it participates. For example, Taiwan has reportedly offered to give U.S.$1 million to the ADB if it removes the comma from "Taipei, China."[25] The ROC government reasons that the comma relegates it to the status of a "tributary part" of China.[26]

In addition to using a variety of names other than its official title, Taiwan no longer insists on the PRC's expulsion from an institution as a condition of membership. It also has agreed to participate in international meetings or activities conducted on the Chinese mainland. In April 1989, Shirley Kuo, then Taiwan's finance minister, led an official delegation to Beijing to attend the twenty-second annual ADB meeting. This trip marked the first time that an ROC official had set foot on mainland China since 1949.

Perhaps buoyed by these successes, Taiwan is now attempting to return to the United Nations. In 1993 and 1994, the permanent UN representatives of a group of Third World nations—some of whom have benefited from generous Taiwanese loans—asked UN Secretary-General Boutros Boutros-Ghali to place the issue of Taiwan's UN representation on the General Assembly's agenda for discussion.[27] In June 1995, Taiwan offered to provide U.S.$1 billion in assistance to developing nations if it was allowed to reenter the world body.[28] As President Lee Teng-hui explained, Taiwan's exclusion from the UN is an "aberrant situation . . . at variance with the principles and spirit of the UN Charter. It is high time for the UN to face this issue seriously and search for a solution."[29]

Pragmatic Diplomacy and Taiwan's National Security

Officials in Taipei suggest that there are several aspects of national security. As described in Chapter 1, according to Taiwan's *1992 National Defense Report,* "the main objective of national security is to protect the national interests from being violated and threatened."[30] Taiwan's national interests include the following:

- Under the stipulation of the ROC constitution, to safeguard all rights and interests to reach the goal of national unification
- To ensure territorial integrity and sovereignty
- To protect people's rights of security from invasion
- To maintain economic prosperity and social stability[31]

Does pragmatic diplomacy help Taiwan meet these objectives? Does it contribute to the island's security?

The Goal of National Unification

Both sides of the Taiwan Strait agree that there is only one China and that Taiwan is a part of China. They do not agree, however, on the terms for national unification. The PRC maintains that Taiwan is a "renegade province" and should return to China as a "special administrative region." The ROC, however, points out that "the ROC existed long before the PRC appeared and never in a day has Taiwan been ruled by the Chinese Communists."[32] ROC officials describe the PRC's position as "practically a joke."[33]

As a precondition for any unification discussions, Taipei insists that Beijing must treat it as an equal political entity. In this respect, there is an important relationship between pragmatic diplomacy and unification. After his 1995 visit to Europe, Premier Lien Chan outlined Taiwan's position: "We want mainland China to understand the goals of pragmatic diplomacy. We are working hard to reunite the country but this can only take place on an equal footing."[34]

Beijing rejects the ROC's terms for unification. Scoffing at Taipei's call for equal treatment, mainland authorities argue that the ROC ceased to exist in 1949. Consequently, the PRC refuses to negotiate on a government-to-government basis with the ROC (it calls for "party-to-party" talks or, more recently, "party-to parties" talks) and will not rule out the use of force to take Taiwan.

By contributing to Taiwan's diplomatic successes, pragmatic diplomacy bolsters the ROC's position that it is a political entity on an equal footing with the PRC. Taiwanese authorities point out that, in addition to having exercised effective control over Taiwan and several small islets for nearly fifty years, the ROC is recognized by thirty countries as the legitimate government of China. Taipei's other diplomatic linkages—particularly its successes in upgrading relations with Western countries and its growing acceptance by international organizations—also buttress this view.

Taiwanese officials hope that these gains may ultimately lead the PRC to adopt a more mature approach toward the unification issue. They also claim that international organizations may provide both Chinese governments with a forum in which they may discuss the thorny unification issue. In fact, Jason C. Hu, director-general of Taiwan's Government Information Office, claims that Taiwan's membership in the UN might accelerate the unification process:

> We are certain that, if the ROC were allowed an active presence in the United Nations, there would be many opportunities for the political entities on both sides of the Taiwan Straits to engage in constructive interaction and dialogue, to build mutual trust and to work toward the reunification of China.[35]

But Hu stresses that "for the sake of our own existence and development, and for the sake of our honor, dignity, rights and interests, we must establish a reasonable international presence *prior* to reunification [emphasis added]."[36]

Territorial Integrity and Sovereignty

Taiwan's pragmatic diplomacy is clearly beginning to yield some dividends. Since adopting the new approach to foreign policy, several countries have switched diplomatic recognition to the ROC, and dozens of others—including the United States, Japan, and most EC countries—have upgraded substantive ties with Taipei. Taiwan has also joined or rejoined several international bodies and applied for membership in GATT under the designation "Customs Territory of Taiwan, Penghu, Kinmen and Matsu." Finally, Taiwan is making a strong bid to return to the United Nations.

By helping to enhance Taiwan's international standing and prestige, pragmatic diplomacy weakens Beijing's claim of sovereignty over the island. On the other hand, the ROC's only alternative to the present policy— a continued drift into international oblivion—jeopardizes its security. As Chang Shallyen, deputy foreign minister of the ROC, observed, "if no countries recognize us, then we will be another Hong Kong."[37] In that case, foreign governments might confer on Beijing the right to pacify Taiwan by any means it thinks fit:

> If Taiwan is not able to establish its international identity, then it will, by default, be viewed as part of the PRC. This has important security impli-

cations, because the resolution of Taiwan's status would then be considered by most states to be an internal matter for Beijing to dictate.[38]

In other words, Taiwanese officials believe that "there is a need for the government to gain more international recognition in order to survive."[39]

Security from Invasion

Taiwan's military authorities believe that "the most serious threat to our national security at present is still the Chicom's [PRC's] use of force against Taiwan."[40] They believe that among those factors that might lead the PRC to attack, "the most likely one under which the Chicoms [PRC] would invade is if and when Taiwan declares itself independent."[41] In fact, PRC officials have implied that Beijing will use force against Taiwan *only* if the island declares itself independent.[42]

Taiwan's second-class international position helps fuel the movement for Taiwanese independence. Fredrick Chien explains:

> What has been pushing Taiwan independence is that mainland China is intentionally suffocating our existence in the international community. We want to be called the Republic of China because we never forgot that we are part of China. But Peking never allows the name anywhere but wants us to be called Taiwan. So they are the ones pushing independence.[43]

U.S. authorities concur with Chien's assessment. During congressional hearings, James Lilley, former ambassador to the PRC, testified that Beijing's "bullying of Taiwan in the international forum, humiliating Taiwan, only sparks Taiwan independence."[44]

Independence advocates emphasize that "it was the 'Republic of China' which was kicked out of the UN, and not Taiwan."[45] They reason that an independent "Republic of Taiwan" could more easily reestablish diplomatic linkages, gain admission into international organizations, and reintegrate into the global community. However, Taipei's successes in upgrading representative offices, President Lee's "vacation diplomacy," and the ROC's successful reentry to the ADB and other institutions undermines this argument and helps dampen the sentiment for de jure separation from the mainland.[46] In this critical respect, pragmatic diplomacy enhances the island's security.

Kau Ying-mao, executive director of Taiwan's 21st Century Foundation, has suggested that the ROC's new approach to foreign policy was adopted in part to "promote social and political stability in Taiwan and calm the movement for Taiwan's secession from mainland China.[47] U.S. analysts also have speculated that pragmatic diplomacy is intended partially to "preempt domestic advocacy of formal independence."[48] Following Lee Teng-hui's 1995 visit to Cornell University, Fang Chin-yen, ROC vice minister for foreign affairs, acknowledged that the government hoped that pragmatic diplomacy would "decrease the possibilities of our countrymen resorting to radical measures with a sense of frustration."[49]

Pragmatic diplomacy also may augment Taiwan's security environment in other ways. With the end of the Cold War and the accompanying drawdown of U.S. forces in the Asia Pacific region, many East Asian governments are calling for the construction of a multilateral security forum. Believing that such an organization could enhance its defense, Taiwan actively supports the proposal and hopes to join any regional security system that might emerge.[50]

Maintain Economic Prosperity and Social Stability

As an island nation that also happens to be one of the world's largest traders, the ROC is dependent on international commerce for its continued survival. Ironically, Taiwan's emergence as a world-class economic power coincided with its drift toward political nonexistence. In the absence of formal diplomatic ties, many Taiwanese firms found that what might otherwise have proved to be relatively simple chores—setting up telex services, shipping and insurance matters, and so forth—could become arduous tasks. For example, exclusion from the Universal Postal Union means that Taiwan has difficulties calculating international postal rates. As Fredrick Chien observed, "if figuring the cost of a stamp is such a headache, imagine the problems caused by not being a member of civil aviation and maritime organizations in charge of international shipping and transportation."[51]

Taiwanese officials also complain that they've played little or no role in the drafting of international agreements that could have an enormous impact on the island's economy. Su Chi, vice chairman of Taiwan's Mainland Affairs Council, explains:

> In 1995, an international fishing convention was passed. We had no say at all in that process. And we are the sixth largest fishing country in the world. In tuna fishing, we are the second largest; in squid we're number three and yet we had no say and no role at all in that convention. And that goes against our interests.[52]

Pragmatic diplomacy is enabling Taiwan to upgrade its relations with many of the world's most important trading nations and gain admittance to international organizations. These moves help Taiwanese businesses overcome the handicaps often associated with a lack of formal diplomatic ties. Officials believe that

> membership in world economic and trade organizations allows us to work through multilateral channels and international arbitration to gain reasonable treatment and ensure our economic interests, avoiding bilateral consultations, where we're often at a disadvantage because the other side is too strong.[53]

Moreover, pragmatic diplomacy is helping Taiwan establish the financial ties and economic linkages that ultimately pave the way for closer diplomatic relations. As David Liu, deputy director of market development at Taiwan's China External Trade Development Council, observed, "oftentimes these businessmen, who are also politically important, influence their government's decision on setting up representative offices here or upgrading the status of existing ones."[54]

Pragmatic diplomacy may promote Taiwan's economic interests in other ways as well. Membership in international organizations can help Taipei during the transition period away from an economy based on low-tech, labor-intensive exports (footwear, textiles, and so forth) and into a major financial and banking center of Asia. As one Taiwanese business leader observed, "joining financial organizations will help us to become an international financial center. . . . We should actively pursue entry to the IMF, which regulates the international financial system, and the World Bank, which aids developing countries."[55] Pragmatic diplomacy also helps Taiwanese businesses gain a foothold in the Third World—countries that may be employed eventually as "export platforms."[56]

Finally, Taiwanese authorities fear that the world is drifting into an era of protectionism and regional trading zones—a development that could threaten the island's economic security. In 1991, Vincent Siew, then Taiwan's economics minister, argued that "the global trend toward economic integration should be seen by Taiwan as pressure for strengthening its presence in Asian-Pacific trade organizations."[57] Officials also contend that GATT membership could offset some of the dangers associated with regional trading blocs by helping "ensure access to larger markets—more than 100 nations are members of GATT."[58]

In sum, pragmatic diplomacy plays an important role in helping the ROC government maintain economic prosperity in Taiwan. In fact, ROC officials believe that it plays a critical role:

> I ask you, if you have no foreign diplomacy, how can you have an economy? If you want to export or import, if you have no appropriate channels or appropriate relations with those countries, will they still buy and sell you things? Can you go to other countries to do business? No can do.[59]

Conclusion

As described in previous chapters, a conjunction of several factors is combining to strengthen Taiwan's position in the global community during the 1990s—pragmatic diplomacy is only one of these. The island's new approach to international relations is finding a receptive audience in the post–Cold War era. The new international environment and the new approach to international relations have enabled Taipei to win a string of small victories in its battle to reintegrate into the global community.

Some contend that pragmatic diplomacy does little to reduce the probability of a military confrontation across the Taiwan Strait.[60] Others even claim that some elements of pragmatic diplomacy—particularly Lee Teng-hui's vacation diplomacy and Taiwan's bid to rejoin the UN—serve only to antagonize Beijing. But ROC officials describe these critics as "spineless" and point out that Taiwan's security concerns are much broader than those relating to the immediate danger of an attack from the PRC.[61]

Pragmatic diplomacy contributes to several aspects of Taiwan's security. It bolsters the ROC's position that it is a political entity, undermines the PRC's claim of sovereignty over the island, dampens sentiment for Taiwanese independence, and promotes Taiwan's economic prosperity and social stability. As Tsai Cheng-wen, chair of the Department of Political Science at Taiwan's prestigious National Taiwan University, observed, "pragmatic diplomacy is a means of national survival."[62]

Notes

1. For more information, see Kuo-chang Wang, *United Nations Voting on Chinese Representation: An Analysis of General Assembly Roll-Calls, 1950–1971* (Taipei: Academia Sinica, 1984), pp. 11–27.

2. Quoted from R. L. Chen, "President Lee Heads for U.S.," *China Post* (International Airmail Edition), June 7, 1995, p. 1.

3. See Julian Baum, "In Search of Recognition," *Far Eastern Economic Review,* July 18, 1991, p. 26.

4. Szu-yin Ho uses this term to describe Taiwan's diplomacy in Szu-yin Ho, "Walking the Tightrope: The ROC's Democratization, Diplomacy, Mainland Policy," *Issues and Studies* 28, No. 3, March 1992, p. 10.

5. The U.S. Congress also passed the Taiwan Relations Act to rationalize and legitimize relations with Taiwan and to provide for its security.

6. See Michael Y. M. Kau, "The ROC's New Foreign Policy Strategy," in the Appendix of *Taiwan: The National Affairs Council and Implications for Democracy.* U.S. Congress, House. Hearings Before the Subcommittee on Asian and Pacific Affairs of the Committee on Foreign Affairs, 101st Congress, 2nd Session, October 11, 1990 (Washington, D.C.: U.S. Government Printing Office, 1991), p. 59.

7. Author's interview with Shuang Jeff Yao, counselor, Republic of China Government Information Office, and director, *Free China Journal,* Taipei, Taiwan, January 8, 1992.

8. Quoted from Kau, "The ROC's New Foreign Policy Strategy," p. 63.

9. For more information about the goals of pragmatic diplomacy, see "Fredrick Chien Speaks at Harvard: ROC Global Role Said 'Evolving,'" *Free China Journal,* November 26, 1991, p. 7; and ROC Government Information Office, *The Pragmatic Diplomacy of the Republic of China in Reference: ROC on Taiwan,* June 5, 1991.

10. Christopher Bodeen, "S. Africa May Recognize Both Governments: MOFA," *China Post* (International Airmail Edition), July 8, 1995, p. 1.

11. Author's interview with Dr. Fredrick Chien, foreign minister of the Republic of China, Taipei, Taiwan, July 14, 1992.

12. "Mounting Hostility Not to Affect UN Bid," *CNA* (Taipei), July 28, 1995, in *FBIS, China,* July 31, 1995, p. 94.

13. U.S. representative Newt Gingrich (Republican–Georgia) made these comments on the CBS news show, *Face the Nation.* For more information, see Christopher Bodeen, "ROC Welcomes Gingrich Call for Ties," *China Post* (International Airmail Edition), July 11, 1995, p. 1.

14. "Taiwan Reiterates 'One China' Policy at Meeting," *CNA* (Taipei), Central News Agency, July 19, 1995, in *FBIS, China,* July 19, 1995, p. 58.

15. Fredrick Chien described these defections as his greatest disappointments during his tenure as foreign minister of the ROC. During an interview with the author, he explained that "in both instances it was not the de-recognition that made us sad, it was the way it was conducted by those two governments. That is to say, they had told us that if anything should happen, they would come and discuss it with us." Author's interview with Fredrick Chien, Taipei, Taiwan, February 7, 1996.

16. See "Five Gov'ts Pressured via HK: PRC," *China Post* (International Airmail Edition), December 27, 1995, p. 1.

17. For more information, see Christopher Bodeen, "ROC-India Ties Strengthening," *China Post* (International Airmail Edition), July 1, 1995, p. 1.

18. See Debbie Kuo, "Cambodia Opens Taipei Office," *China Post* (International Airmail Edition), January 3, 1996, p. 1.

19. For example, Taiwan's trade office in the Ukraine will carry the name, Republic of China. See Jeremy Mark, "Taiwan Finds Diplomatic Gold Mine in Relations with New C.I.S. Nations," *Wall Street Journal,* February 7, 1992, p. A10.

20. See James L. Tyson, "Taiwan Besting China, Sets Up Ties to Baltics," *Christian Science Monitor,* December 27, 1991.

21. "U.S. Official Arriving on Monday," *China Post* (International Airmail Edition), December 1, 1994, p. 1.

22. When comparing Lee's "glorious trip" to the United States with Lien's visit to Europe, Lee Chin-yung, a DPP legislator, claimed that Lien "sneaked" into Europe. See "Premier Makes First Stop on Europe Trip," *China Post* (International Airmail Edition), June 17, 1995, p. 1.

23. Author's interview with Dr. Fredrick Chien, foreign minister of the Republic of China, Taipei, Taiwan, July 14, 1992.

24. Wei Hung-chin, "Opening Doors to International Organizations," *Sinorama* 17, No. 1, January 1992, p. 85.

25. See James Kynge, "Taiwan's Diplomacy, Is It Worth It?" *China Post* (International Airmail Edition), July 17, 1995, p. 2. Also see "Money Diplomacy Deplored," Central People's Radio, Beijing, July 21, 1995, in *FBIS, China,* July 24, 1995, p. 91.

26. Ibid.

27. For more information, see Susan Yu, "Seven Nations Ask UN to Consider ROC Role," *Free China Journal,* August 13, 1993, p. 1.

28. See Christopher Bodeen, "Lee Puts Forth Boldest ROC Pitch to UN So Far," *China Post* (International Airmail Edition), June 27, 1995, p. 1.

29. Ibid.

30. ROC Ministry of National Defense, *1992 National Defense Report: Republic of China* (Taipei: Li Ming Cultural Enterprise Co., 1992), p. 53. Translated from the Chinese by Ma Kainan.

31. Ibid., p. 52.

32. R. L. Chen, "Lee: Global Presence Is Key," *China Post* (International Airmail Edition), July 10, 1995, p. 1.
33. Ibid.
34. Christopher Bodeen, "Lien Back from Trip, Stresses Pragmatism," *China Post* (International Airmail Edition), June 23, 1995, p. 1.
35. Jason C. Hu, "How UN Seat Would Help Unify China," *Free China Journal*, September 22, 1995, p. 7.
36. Ibid.
37. Nicholas D. Kristof, "Taiwan Winning New Friends, Hopes for Another One in Clinton," *New York Times*, January 18, 1993, p. A12.
38. Martin L. Lasater, *U.S. Interests in the New Taiwan* (Boulder, Colorado: Westview Press, 1993), p. 101.
39. Jason Hu, director-general of Taiwan's Government Information Office, made this statement when explaining the goals of pragmatic diplomacy in 1995. For more information, see R. L. Chen, "Lee Defends Diplomatic Moves," *China Post* (International Airmail Edition), July 26, 1995, p. 1.
40. ROC Ministry of National Defense, *1992 National Defense Report, Republic of China*, p. 49.
41. Ibid., p. 55.
42. See Chen Guoqing, "'China Threat' Rings Hollow," *Defense News* 8, No. 19, May 17–23, 1993, p. 20.
43. Julian Baum, "Chinese Hurdle," *Far Eastern Economic Review*, November 14, 1991, p. 30.
44. "U.S. Congress Lauds ROC, Censures Mainland China," *Free China Journal*, May 25, 1993, p. 2.
45. Frank Hsieh, a Democratic Progressive Party lawmaker, has made this argument. For more information, see "Taiwan to Bid for UN Reentry," *China Post* (International Airmail Edition), September 14, 1991, p. 1.
46. Some PRC officials dispute this claim. For example, Qian Qichen, PRC vice premier, contends that "any move by Taipei to take part in UN activities would only fuel the pro-independence movement in Taiwan." For more information, see John Kohut and Chris Yeng, "Powers Warned Against Meddling," *South China Morning Post*, October 1, 1993, p. 7.
47. See Lin Ching-wen, "Equal Existence OK," *Free China Journal*, April 16, 1990, p. 5.
48. See Edwin A. Winckler, "Taiwan: Changing Dynamics," in William A. Joseph (ed.), *China Briefing, 1991* (Boulder, Colorado: Westview Press, 1992), p. 145.
49. "Vice Minister Emphasizes 'Pragmatic Diplomacy,'" Taipei, Chung-Yang Jih Pao, July 18, 1995, in *FBIS, China*, July 26, 1995, p. 63.
50. See "Lee Promotes 'Collective Security' in 'Prospects for Asia' Seminar," *China Post* (International Airmail Edition), November 13, 1992, p. 3.
51. Wei Hung-chin, "Opening Doors to International Organizations," pp. 84–85.
52. Author's interview with Su Chi, vice chairman, Mainland Affairs Council, Executive Yuan, Republic of China, Taipei, Taiwan, February 6, 1996.
53. Wei, "Opening Doors to International Organizations," p. 84.
54. See Amy Lo, "Pragmatic Diplomacy, Creative Economics," *Free China Review*, May 1991, p. 7.
55. Wei, "Economics Comes Before Politics: Koo on Joining International Bodies," *Sinorama* 17, No. 1, January 1992, p. 91.
56. Citing the North American Free Trade Agreement (NAFTA) as an example,

Taiwanese authorities believe that the world is moving toward regional economic blocs. By establishing a firm foothold in Latin America and other Third World countries, ROC officials reason that Taiwan can avoid being "locked out" of important foreign markets. For more information, see Lo, "Pragmatic Diplomacy, Creative Economics," pp. 4–9.

57. See "Siew Advocates Regional Footholds," *Free China Journal,* August 27, 1991, p. 3.

58. See Yvonne Yuan, "Pragmatic Diplomacy: Building Better Relations," *Free China Review* 43, No. 2, February 1993, p. 11.

59. Christopher Bodeen, "Opponents of Diplomacy Spineless: Chien," *China Post* (International Airmail Edition), September 5, 1995, p. 1.

60. Martin Lasater argues Taiwan's pragmatic diplomacy might increase the PRC's threat to Taiwan. According to Lasater, Taipei's recent diplomatic success "is at least a partial defeat of the PRC strategy to isolate Taiwan internationally. The failure of this strategy may lead to a re-examination of other options to see if they might be more effective in achieving reunification." For more information, see Martin L. Lasater, "Bill Clinton and the Security of the Republic of China," *Issues and Studies* 29, No. 1, January 1993, p. 54.

61. See Christopher Bodeen, "Opponents of Diplomacy Spineless: Chien," p. 1.

62. See Lin Ching-wen, "Equal Coexistence OK," *Free China Journal,* April 16, 1990.

Part 3

CHALLENGES TO TAIWAN'S SECURITY

8

The Taiwanese Independence Movement

Ever since large numbers of Chinese began to migrate to Taiwan, the question of sovereignty over the island has been haunting both sides of the Taiwan Strait. Is Taiwan a province of China, a state independent of China, or perhaps something else?

This chapter examines the international status of Taiwan—the so-called Taiwan question. It outlines the history of the island and shows how Beijing, Taipei, and Washington hold different views toward its sovereignty and future. The chapter also provides a brief overview of the Taiwanese independence movement and explains how the end of the Cold War is helping fuel the drive for de jure separation from mainland China. As Beijing threatens to use force to take Taiwan if it declares independence, this development undermines the island's security.

Historical Background

Little is known about Taiwan's early history. The island's first inhabitants—the aborigines who settled in Taiwan ten thousand years ago—did not keep written records. Furthermore, although some references to Taiwan may be found in ancient official documents of Chinese history, most of these are sketchy.[1] But it is known that imperial China sent an expeditionary force to Taiwan in A.D. 239 and that small numbers of Chinese began to emigrate to the island during the Tang dynasty (618–907).

The first permanent Chinese settlements in Taiwan were established in the sixteenth century, near the present site of Tainan. It was also during this period that Europeans began to explore the territory. The Portuguese, who named the island Ihla Formosa (island beautiful), were probably the earliest Western visitors. Spanish explorers also were attracted to the island. But it was the Dutch government that eventually gained control of Taiwan and ruled it for about forty years.

In 1644, the Ming dynasty collapsed. Shortly thereafter, forces loyal to the Ming retreated to Taiwan and expelled the Dutch colonialists. For several decades, an exiled army—aided by thousands of refugees from China's coastal provinces—held out against the alien Manchu (Ching) dynasty. At one point the loyal Ming troops—led by Cheng Ch'eng Kung (also known as Koxinga)—almost succeeded in recapturing Nanjing. In 1683, however, the island fell.

The Ching dynasty administered the island of Taiwan as a prefecture of the mainland China province of Fujian (Fukien) from 1683 until 1886, at which time Taiwan became a separate province of China. The two centuries of imperial Chinese rule facilitated migration to the island and the gradual spread of Chinese settlements. But Beijing's authority in Taiwan during this period could perhaps best be characterized as "careless and weak."[2]

In 1895, following China's defeat in the first Sino-Japanese War, Taiwan was formally ceded to the Empire of Japan by the Treaty of Shimonoseki. After several years, guerrilla forces—some of whom attempted to establish an independent Republic of Formosa—were finally subdued. For the next fifty years, Japan ruled Taiwan.

Japanese rule was often harsh and cruel. When confronted with resistance, soldiers destroyed entire villages.[3] But Japanese administration also had a positive side. Japan built the island's economic infrastructure—roads, harbors, and railroads—and greatly increased agricultural productivity. The imperial government also successfully launched an "island wide public health clean-up campaign" that greatly reduced mortality rates.[4] Finally, Tokyo strengthened Taiwan's educational system. With the establishment of modern universities and medical schools, "the island's literacy rate, technological skills, and knowledge of world affairs soon exceeded that of any part of China or, for that matter, any other area in Asia."[5]

By the beginning of World War II, many Taiwanese had become accustomed to Japanese rule. Thousands served in the Japanese military. But on December 1, 1943, the United States, the Republic of China, and the United Kingdom issued the Cairo Declaration, a document proclaiming the Allies' intention to return Taiwan to China. Specifically, the communiqué stated that:

> Japan shall be stripped of all the islands in the Pacific which she has seized or occupied since the beginning of the first World War in 1914, and that all territories Japan has stolen from the Chinese, such as Manchuria, Formosa and the Pescadores, shall be restored to the Republic of China.[6]

The Soviet Union approved the declaration four days later at the Teheran Conference. On July 26, 1945, the leaders of the United States, the Republic of China, and the United Kingdom declared in the Potsdam Proclamation that "the terms of the Cairo Declaration shall be carried out and Japanese sovereignty shall be limited to the islands of Honshu, Hokkaido, Kyushu, Shikoku and such minor islands as we determine."[7] Shortly afterward, the Soviet Union and France also indicated that they would adhere to the Potsdam Proclamation. When World War II ended, "the Supreme

Commander of the Allied Powers gave the Nationalist government of Chiang Kai-shek authority to accept the Japanese surrender and administer the island."[8]

The Taiwanese population was not consulted during the negotiations that led to the Cairo Declaration or other wartime agreements. Nevertheless, they initially welcomed the Chinese forces that oversaw the Japanese surrender on the island. As one Taiwanese observed, "if we had been given a vote in 1945, we probably would have approved Chinese rule."[9] This enthusiasm, however, proved to be short-lived:

> Within weeks we found that Governor Chen Yi and his commissioners were contemptuous of the Formosan people and were unbelievably corrupt and greedy. For eighteen months they looted our island. The newcomers had lived all their lives in the turmoil of civil war and of the Japanese invasion. They were carpetbaggers, occupying enemy territory, and we were being treated as a conquered people.[10]

In February 1947, resentment against corrupt mainland rule exploded into a near rebellion.

According to most accounts (including the official U.S. government report), the Chinese government overreacted to the crisis. After promising to meet popular demands for political and economic reform, Nanjing shipped 10,000 troops with heavy weapons to the island with orders to quell "the pro-Communist rebellion." During the weeks that followed, thousands of Taiwanese were killed, including most of the island's political elite. Although Chen Yi, the governor who ordered the massacre, was ultimately executed on Chiang Kai-shek's orders, the incident poisoned relations between mainlanders (those who arrived in Taiwan after 1945) and native Taiwanese (those who arrived in Taiwan before 1945) for decades to come.

In 1949, the remnants of the Kuomintang government retreated to Taiwan. Almost 2 million troops, bureaucrats, and refugees poured into the island to escape the Communist juggernaut. Most believed that the outpost would serve either as Chiang's last stand or as his base to recover mainland China. But the outbreak of the Korean War in 1950 changed that. Under President Harry Truman's orders, the U.S. Seventh Fleet "neutralized" the Taiwan Strait. Ever since that time, the ROC has thrived in Taiwan and a number of small islets—a constant reminder to Beijing of China's unfinished civil war.

The Taiwan Question

Is Taiwan a sovereign nation-state, a political entity, or a renegade province? Is it ruled by a government or a political clique? The following discussion explores how Beijing, Taipei, and Washington hold differing views toward these questions and shows how their positions have evolved over the past several decades.

The People's Republic of China

Prior to the establishment of the PRC in 1949, Chinese Communist Party leaders referred to Taiwan as being separate from China. Even Mao Tse-tung indicated that the territory did not belong to China.[11] He placed Taiwan "in the same category as Korea and other would-be 'friendly territories' on China's periphery . . . [and] apparently perceived that Taiwan was not part of China historically or legally."[12]

After gaining power, the CCP changed its position. Beijing now contends that "Taiwan has belonged to China since ancient times."[13] According to this interpretation, "Chinese governments of differing periods set up administrative bodies to exercise jurisdiction over Taiwan" and China always strived to "ward off foreign invaders" until the Ching government was "forced" to give Taiwan to Japan.[14] This act is described officially as a "wanton betrayal and humiliation [that] shocked the whole nation and touched off a storm of protests."[15]

When discussing the "origin of the Taiwan question," PRC authorities claim that, after the ROC government in Nanjing was "finally overthrown by the Chinese people" in 1949, the PRC became the sole, legal government of all China (including Taiwan). At that moment, however, "a group of military and political officials of the Kuomintang clique took refuge in Taiwan and, with the support of the then U.S. administration, created the division between the two sides of the Taiwan Straits."[16]

Beijing attempted initially to resolve the Taiwan question by force. In the late 1970s, however, it began to call for the "peaceful unification" of China under the banner of the so-called one country, two systems reunification formula. According to this arrangement, Taiwan would be allowed to "maintain a high degree of autonomy as a special administrative region."[17] It also would be permitted to maintain its present socioeconomic system and its own armed forces. Furthermore, both private property rights and foreign investment in Taiwan would be protected. Finally, Taiwanese authorities would be allowed to "take up posts of leadership in the PRC government."[18]

Since making the initial "one country, two systems" proposal, PRC officials have elaborated on some points. For example, Jiang Zemin, PRC president and head of the CCP, has promised that Beijing "would not send troops or administrative staff to be stationed in Taiwan."[19] Moreover, he claims that unification is "not a scenario whereby the mainland would swallow up Taiwan or Taiwan swallow the mainland."[20]

PRC authorities stress that many points in Beijing's unification proposal are negotiable. But some points are not. For example, Beijing insists that all unification negotiations must be held on a party-to-party basis or, more recently, a party-to-parties basis. The central government in Beijing refuses to negotiate with the central government in Taipei because it contends that the ROC ceased to exist in 1949. Furthermore, Beijing will not tolerate any unification formula that leads to the creation of "two Chinas" or "one China–one Taiwan." Finally, PRC authorities emphasize that Taiwan's democratization will have no effect on the island's status. In February 1996, Premier Li Peng declared that "whatever changes might occur in the way in which the leadership in Taiwan is chosen, they cannot change the fact that Taiwan is a part of China and its leaders only leaders of a region in China."[21]

In sum, Beijing argues that the PRC's sovereignty over Taiwan is "undebatable." Premier Li Peng explains:

> There is only one China in the world and the People's Republic of China is the sole government representing all China. Taiwan has been returned to the motherland for 50 years. Chinese people will never tolerate Taiwan's separating from the Chinese territory again.[22]

China is prepared to back up these claims with its military might. It argues that "any sovereign state is entitled to use any means it deems necessary, including military ones, to uphold its sovereignty and territorial integrity."[23] If Taiwan declares independence, the PRC has promised that the Chinese people "will certainly defend our country's territorial integrity with their blood and lives."[24] After the return of Hong Kong and Macau to China in 1997, Premier Li vows that "settling the Taiwan issue will be prominently put in front of all Chinese people."[25]

The Republic of China

The ROC has long maintained that there is only one China and that Taiwan is a part of China. Unlike the CCP, however, the KMT claimed that Taiwan was part of China prior to the 1940s. In fact, the wartime accords that "returned" the territory to the mainland may be traced, in part, to pressures exerted by Chiang Kai-shek and other KMT leaders. Like the PRC, however, the ROC's position toward this issue has evolved since the 1940s.

When the ROC government first retreated to Taiwan in 1949, the population was told that the island would serve as a staging area to retake mainland China. Although growing PRC power eventually led the generalissimo to conclude that the means of returning would have to be "70 percent political," he never abandoned his dream of "national recovery and national reconstruction."[26] Chiang's successor, Chiang Ching-kuo, also vowed that the "anti-Communist struggle will never cease until Communism is eliminated from Chinese territory and until the Chinese Communist regime has been destroyed."[27]

In addition to pledging to retake the mainland, the ROC did not tolerate calls for Taiwanese independence. For several decades, the government's position toward this issue was uncompromising—Taiwan was part of China and the ROC was the legitimate government of all China. Calls for independence were deemed seditious, and those who challenged this conviction were jailed, forced into exile, or otherwise silenced.

In the realm of international relations, the ROC viewed diplomatic ties as a "zero-sum" game. In keeping with the "one-China" policy, Taipei severed relations with foreign governments that recognized the Beijing regime. During an interview with the author, Fredrick Chien, Taiwan's foreign minister, described the ROC's position:

> We took the same position as mainland China. We both said that there was only one China. We both said Taiwan was part of China. And we said only the Republic of China was the legitimate government of China and they said only the People's Republic of China was the legitimate government of China. So, during this period we presented countries and international organizations of the world with a dilemma. They had to make a choice. They could not do it "both" or "and." They had to choose "either or."[28]

The ROC also refused to negotiate or otherwise establish meaningful linkages (such as travel, communications, or mail) with mainland China. Interestingly, however, retired general Chiang Wego, the generalissimo's last surviving son, has revealed that his father did maintain contact clandestinely with some leading PRC figures—including Lin Biao and Chou En-lai—during the 1950s.[29]

For more than three decades Taipei adhered to the rigid position outlined above. However, changes in the government's approach toward the Taiwan question accompanied the sweeping changes that occurred in Taiwan during the late 1980s. The ROC now acknowledges that the PRC exercises "de facto authority" over mainland China.[30] Again, Fredrick Chien outlines the ROC's position:

> We no longer consider the Communist Party in the mainland as a rebellious group. We consider them as a reality. They are, in fact, in control of the mainland. We, in contrast, can only exercise full and effective jurisdiction over Taiwan, Pescadores, Quemoy and Matsu. And this, as you can tell very easily, is the reality.[31]

Furthermore, Taipei has "formally and unilaterally renounced military force as a means of national unification" and will "no longer compete for the right to represent China in the international arena."[32] It also has signaled its willingness to accept the principle of "dual recognition" and to participate in international forums by using titles other than its official designation of the ROC.

Current ROC policy holds that both sides of the Taiwan Strait should be considered as "political entities" and that "while relations between the two sides of the Taiwan Strait are not those between two separate countries, neither are they purely domestic in nature."[33] Taipei disputes PRC claims that the ROC ceased to exist in 1949 and argues "that the ROC has been an independent sovereign state since its establishment in 1912 is an incontrovertible historical fact."[34] Authorities stress that "it's an unfortunate thing that China has been divided for the past forty-six years, but that is the reality."[35]

The ROC still adheres to the "one-China" principle. But it stresses that "one-China" does not mean the PRC, and officials disagree publicly over the precise meaning of the phrase. Some claim that the expression signifies the ROC whereas others suggest that it "refers to China in the historical, geographical, social and cultural sense."[36] Even Lee Teng-hui, Taiwan's president, concedes the meaning of "the word 'Zhongguo' [China] is confusing."[37]

Taiwan's own unification formula is embodied in the three-stage *Guidelines for National Unification* outlined in Chapter 1.[38] At the present time, ROC officials are attempting to persuade Beijing to treat the ROC as a political entity and to renounce the use of force, part of the first phase of the *Guidelines*. Taipei claims that, just as it has compromised in several key areas, Beijing should reciprocate. Vincent Siew, chairman of Taiwan's cabinet-level Mainland Affairs Council, outlines the ROC's position: "We have already given up the fight for orthodoxy, legitimacy and the rights to represent China. Until mainland China gives up its hostility towards Taiwan and its threats of force, we can't safely pursue unification."[39] In early 1996, ROC authorities hinted that they might be willing to sidestep the sensitive sovereignty question in order to hold discussions with Beijing. However, officials continued to stress that unification could occur only after economic and political liberalization takes root in mainland China.

The United States

Although the PRC and the ROC have long agreed that there is only one China and that Taiwan is a part of China, the U.S. position on this issue is unclear. It is not clear whether the United States considers Taiwan to be a part of China, a state independent of China, or perhaps something else. Furthermore, the United States does not take a position on the future of Taiwan other than to insist the resolution of the Taiwan issue is a matter for the Chinese themselves to decide and that it must be "peaceful."[40]

During the late 1940s, the U.S. position toward Taiwan's international status was clear—Taiwan was a province of China. For example, when asked during a 1949 news conference whether the U.S. policy of opposing aggression applied to Taiwan, President Truman responded, "I can't answer that question because that is not a free [independent] country . . . it is part of

Nationalist China."[41] During a news conference held on January 5, 1950, the president further stated:

> In keeping with these declarations [Cairo and Potsdam], Formosa was surrendered to Generalissimo Chiang Kai-shek, and for the past 4 years the United States and other Allied Powers have accepted the exercise of Chinese authority over the island.[42]

Secretary of State Dean Acheson defended administration policy by arguing that "when the United States takes a position it sticks to that position and does not change it by reason of transitory expediency or advantage on its part."[43] On this and other occasions Acheson would forcefully dismiss any suggestions that the status of Taiwan was uncertain or unsettled as "lawyers' doubts."[44] During private conversations with members of the U.S. Senate, the secretary reiterated this theme. Acheson argued that Taiwan was "essentially a Chinese territory" and that, in any event, like a number of other territories, its fate had been "morally sealed by some form of prior agreement."[45]

Calls for a change in U.S. policy toward Taiwan accelerated after the CCP won the Chinese Civil War. But it was only after the outbreak of the Korean conflict on June 25, 1950, that the Truman administration revised its policy. On June 27, Truman announced that he had ordered the Seventh Fleet to neutralize Taiwan and went on to add: "The determination of the future status of Formosa must await the restoration of security in the Pacific, a peace settlement with Japan, or consideration by the United Nations."[46]

Official U.S. policy still held out the promise that the question of Taiwan's international status would be resolved. A final settlement had been linked to several key events: (1) restoration of security in the Pacific, (2) a peace treaty with Japan, or (3) a settlement by the United Nations. Only during the interim period would the Taiwan issue remain unresolved. In time, however, the U.S. policy would be revised in such a way that a definitive policy on the Taiwan question would never materialize. The island's status was not determined by the UN, a peace treaty with Japan, or the restoration of security in the Pacific. Since that time, U.S. policy toward the Taiwan question has continued to be ambiguous and unclear.

Some individuals have argued that the United States has "unambiguously recognized the jurisdiction of the People's Republic over Taiwan."[47] But these people are mistaken. Other than an occasional statement to the effect that the status of Taiwan is undetermined or that the United States hopes that the Taiwan question will be settled peacefully, the United States has steadfastly refused to adopt a clear and readily identifiable position on the Taiwan question. U.S. officials have reiterated this position on numerous occasions.

The United States did not adopt a clear position on the Taiwan question when it concluded a mutual defense treaty with the ROC in 1954. When ratifying the treaty, the Senate noted that "nothing in the present treaty shall be construed as affecting or modifying the legal status or the sovereignty of Formosa or the Pescadores."[48] During hearings before the Senate Foreign Relations Committee at the time, Secretary of State John Foster Dulles testified that "in my opinion the status of the ROC in relation to Formosa is for all practical purposes unchanged and unaltered by this treaty."[49]

In the early 1970s, considerable speculation focused upon Taiwan's withdrawal from the UN and President Nixon's attempts to seek a rapprochement with the PRC. At that time, U.S. officials sought to dispel any rumors that Washington had revised its policy toward the Taiwan issue. Consequently, on April 28, 1971, the Department of State announced that "in our view sovereignty over Taiwan and the Pescadores is an unsettled question."[50]

Most often it is alleged that the United States declared that Taiwan is a part of China in the 1972 U.S.-PRC Shanghai communiqué, the 1978 U.S.-PRC normalization communiqué, or the 1982 U.S.-PRC communiqué. For example, some have argued that this "fundamental of American policy" was "enshrined" in the Shanghai communiqué.[51] A careful examination of each of these documents, however, reveals that the United States has consistently stated only that it *acknowledges* the Chinese position that there is but one China, and Taiwan is a part of China. This phrase was deliberately chosen as the key word—"acknowledge"—indicates only "cognizance of, but not necessarily agreement with, the Chinese position."[52] Interestingly, the PRC used the Chinese equivalent of acknowledge (*ren-shi*) in the 1972 Shanghai communiqué, but has used the Chinese equivalent of acceptance (*cheng-ren*) in all other communiqués.[53] In each of the U.S. communiqués, however, U.S. officials have consistently used the word "acknowledge" and "have stated that, in interpreting this phrase, the U.S. will adhere only to the English version."[54]

With the end of the Cold War, U.S. policy has not changed. In a 1990 study entitled, "A Strategic Framework for the Asian Pacific Rim: Looking Toward the 21st Century," the U.S. Department of Defense (DOD) referred to Taiwan, along with the Spratly and Paracel islands, as "unresolved territorial issues."[55] The description caused an uproar in Taipei and led Taiwan's Foreign Ministry to register a formal complaint against the report. The ministry complained that "we can neither understand nor accept any claim that Taiwan's status is uncertain."[56]

Responding to Taiwan's criticism, the DOD issued the following clarification:

> It was not our intention to indicate that Taiwan is an unresolved territorial issue. Our policy is unchanged. The United States *acknowledges* the

Chinese position that there is only one China and that Taiwan is a part of China. We believe that differences between the two sides should be resolved peacefully by Chinese on both sides of the Taiwan Straits [emphasis added].[57]

Taiwanese officials heralded this announcement as a major victory, even going so far as to declare that Washington had "reiterated the U.S. stand that America feels there is only one China and Taiwan is a part of China."[58] However, it is clear that U.S. policy did not change—U.S. officials had only reiterated their ambiguous position.

Another flap occurred in July 1995. At that time, Michael McCurry, White House spokesman, enraged independence activists when he said that "we [the United States] accept the view that Taiwan is a part of China."[59] However, the White House quickly clarified the statement and said that the United States "acknowledges" the Chinese position that Taiwan is a part of China.[60] Since that time, U.S. officials have stressed that Washington does not accept Beijing's claim that "Taiwan is part of the People's Republic of China."[61]

With regard to the future of Taiwan, Section 2(b) of the Taiwan Relations Act states that it is the policy of the United States "to make clear that the United States' decision to establish diplomatic relations with the People's Republic of China rests upon the expectation that the future of Taiwan will be determined by peaceful means." It is noteworthy also that in each of the U.S.-PRC communiqués, Washington has steadfastly expressed a desire that the resolution of Taiwan's future be peaceful. For example, in the 1972 Shanghai communiqué, the United States stated that it "reaffirms its interest in a peaceful settlement of the Taiwan question." In the 1979 U.S.-PRC normalization communiqué, the United States declared that it "continues to have an interest in the peaceful resolution of the Taiwan issue." Finally, in the U.S.-PRC joint communiqué of August 17, 1982, the United States stated that it "understands and appreciates the Chinese policy of striving for a peaceful resolution of the Taiwan question."

In addition to calling for a peaceful resolution of the Taiwan issue, U.S. policy stresses that the future of Taiwan is a matter that must be resolved by the Chinese themselves.[62] Washington has no intention of playing a mediator's role in negotiations between the two sides of the Taiwan Strait. Furthermore, U.S. policy does not address a host of other issues, including Taiwan's future international status, form of government, or economic system.[63] Indeed, the U.S. government "has not expressed any opinion on what form the ultimate resolution [of the Taiwan issue] might take nor on the procedures which the Chinese should follow to arrive at it."[64] As one U.S. official explained, U.S. policy toward the future of Taiwan is only that "one, the resolution of the Taiwan issue is a matter for the Chinese themselves to decide and, two, the United States has an interest in having that resolution be peaceful."[65]

Summary

Beijing, Taipei, and Washington hold different views toward the so-called Taiwan question. But these positions are not static. The policy of each government has shifted since the ROC gained control of the island in 1945.

The PRC, whose leaders once claimed that Taiwan was a foreign territory, now declares that it is an inalienable part of China. The United States, which once recognized Chinese claims of sovereignty over Taiwan, now refuses to take a clear and readily identifiable position on the issue. The ROC, which still pays lip service to the "one-China" principle, no longer competes with Beijing for the right to represent China and tolerates calls for de jure separation from China.

These policies hold important consequences for the future of Taiwan. Even the ambiguous U.S. position holds meaningful repercussions. Washington resists Beijing's calls that it "do something useful" to promote unification while simultaneously shielding the ROC with advanced arms and a de facto alliance. This has led the PRC to charge that the United States is "responsible for holding up the settlement of the Taiwan question."[66]

The Taiwanese Independence Movement and the End of the Cold War

Not all Taiwanese agree with the ROC's position toward the Taiwan question. Indeed, some don't agree with any of the positions outlined above and believe that Taiwan should declare its independence. The discussion below provides a brief overview of the Taiwanese independence movement and explains how the end of the Cold War is helping fuel the drive for de jure separation from mainland China.

Background

As described, the Ching dynasty ruled Taiwan for roughly two centuries. Throughout this period, corrupt and inefficient Chinese rule prompted constant uprisings and political instability. In fact, the population's reputation for insubordination and lawlessness led the island to become known as the "land of rebellion and unrest."[67] But most studies suggest that the origins of Taiwanese nationalism cannot be traced to these early peasant uprisings— insurrections that were endemic throughout imperial China.[68] It also is unlikely that the effort to establish a "Republic of Formosa," a move that was prompted by the Japanese occupation, reflected a sense of nationalism among the Taiwanese population. Rather, available evidence suggests that "the Chinese Governor in Taipei issued his 1895 declaration of independence only at the instigation of mainlander officials and without popular support inside Formosa."[69]

Many scholars trace the emergence of Taiwanese nationalism to the early years of Japanese rule. At that time, the Japanese government openly discriminated against the native population. After World War I, the Taiwanese began organizing to demand "home rule and an end to economic, social and political discrimination."[70] Although the imperial government grudgingly conceded to some demands, "discrimination continued in fact."[71]

The independence movement received another important boost shortly after the KMT took over administration of Taiwan in 1945. The ROC's mishandling of local affairs and its brutal suppression of the 1947 uprising "sowed the seeds of discord and hatred between the expatriate mainlanders and the indigenous Taiwanese and became the principal cause of the Taiwan Independence Movement."[72] Those activists who managed to escape the "white terror" of the 1940s and 1950s established resistance movements overseas. Some of these groups ultimately embraced a Marxist ideology whereas others resorted to terrorism.[73]

Throughout the 1960s and 1970s, Taiwan's separatist movement suffered from factionalism, intrigue, and impotence. Based largely in the United States and Japan, there was little the movement could do to influence the course of events in Taiwan. Within Taiwan, however, popular sentiment for an end to the mainlanders' continuous monopoly of political power grew. Authoritarian rule and increasing international isolation undermined the government's legitimacy. The arrest and persecution of dissidents also contributed to calls for greater Taiwanese participation in governmental decisionmaking. Finally, a 1979 riot in Kaohsiung helped persuade the ruling party to liberalize the political system and initiate a series of sweeping political reforms.

Taipei now tolerates calls for independence from China. In fact, the platform of the island's chief opposition party, the Democratic Progressive Party, endorses "the establishment of a sovereign and independent Republic of Taiwan."[74] Ironically, separatists who once served lengthy prison sentences for sedition now serve as lawmakers in the Legislative Yuan. Even some members of the KMT are calling for "abolishing the province and establishing the Taiwan country."[75]

End of the Cold War

In Taiwan, calls for independence from China are no longer deemed seditious. According to some surveys, support for de jure independence from China has grown to roughly 20 percent of the population. In fact, despite Beijing's bullying tactics, the DPP's candidate received 21 percent of the popular vote in the 1996 presidential election. In some respects, the new global environment is helping to fuel the movement.

The end of the Cold War encourages Taiwan's separatist movement in several ways. Citing the newly independent Baltic states and the disintegration of the Soviet Union and Yugoslavia as models, independence advocates see a global trend toward "self-determination" and "separatism." They argue that the time has arrived for the island to proclaim its de jure independence from China. According to the chairman of the Democratic Progressive Party, "People here on Taiwan want independence, just like the Baltic states. We don't want unification. . . . Our case is [like] the Baltic states' case. It's time we call the attention of the world to this."[76]

The recent acquisition of U.S. and French warplanes and other advanced arms—military equipment unavailable at any price during the Cold War—provides the independence movement with a newfound sense of security. Officials at the Formosan Association for Public Affairs, a Washington-based separatist organization, claim that "the [F-16] sale lessens the likelihood that China will respond with force once Taiwan declares itself independent, for the sale will come with an implicit guarantee of U.S. protection . . . [and] by selling to Taiwan as a country, the U.S. implicitly recognizes Taiwan's independent status."[77]

Finally, independence activists reason that, with the collapse of the Soviet Union, the United States is afforded a historic opportunity to abandon its outdated "one-China" policy. They argue that there is little that the PRC could do about a change in U.S. policy:

> In the past, the U.S. rationalized the alliance with China by saying that it was needed to counter the USSR. But the USSR is history. The U.S. no longer needs China. Indeed, it is quite the other way around. What can the PRC really do about arms sales to Taiwan or U.S. support for an independent Taiwan? Very little. . . . The fact is that China has virtually no cards to play in the Great Game. The Cold War is over.[78]

Conclusion

The end of the Cold War is not the only consideration that has led to an increase in support for Taiwanese independence. Numerous other factors—including the 1989 Tiananmen Square incident, the 1994 Qiandao Lake tour boat murders, and Beijing's unrelenting efforts to isolate Taipei internationally—also have played a role. But the ROC government acknowledges that the new international environment *is* helping "stimulate" the island's "separatist trend."[79]

The recent changes in the international system also have encouraged independence elements in other regions of China. For example, after the Muslim states in Soviet Central Asia won their independence in 1991, separatist sentiment intensified in neighboring Xinjiang. Beijing has transferred troops to the region and clashed with Uygurs attempting to break away from China and reestablish the Eastern Turkestan Republic.[80]

The separatist movement within China has grown and gained in popular support. But Beijing will not tolerate the establishment of an independent Republic of Taiwan, Tibet, or Xinjiang. In fact, Taiwanese independence is now identified as one of the four major threats confronting China.[81]

While sentiment for independence grows in Taiwan, China improves its capabilities to do something about it. Chapter 9 shows how the drive to modernize the People's Liberation Army—a program initiated during the early 1980s—has accelerated. Ironically, the collapse of the Soviet Union and the end of the Cold War have proven to be bonanzas for the PLA.

Notes

1. See John F. Copper, *Taiwan: Nation-State or Province* (Boulder, Colorado: Westview Press, 1990), pp. 18–19.
2. Douglas Mendel, *The Politics of Formosan Nationalism* (Berkeley: University of California Press, 1970), p. 13.
3. See Simon Long, *Taiwan: China's Last Frontier* (New York: St. Martin's Press), pp. 26–32.
4. See Peng Ming-min, *A Taste of Freedom: Memoirs of a Formosan Independence Leader* (New York: Holt, Rinehart and Winston, 1972), p. 8.
5. Copper, *Taiwan: Nation-State or Province*, pp. 23–24.
6. "Conference of President Roosevelt, Generalissimo Chiang Kai-shek and Prime Minister Churchill in North Africa," *Department of State Bulletin* 9, No. 232, December 4, 1943, p. 393.
7. "Proclamation Defining Terms for Japanese Surrender," *Department of State Bulletin* 13, No. 318, July 29, 1945, p. 137.
8. Chiao Chiao Hsieh, *Strategy for Survival* (London: Sherwood Press, 1985), p. 24.
9. Mendel, *The Politics of Formosan Nationalism*, p. 27.
10. Peng, *A Taste of Freedom*, p. 61.
11. See Edgar Snow, *Red Star over China* (New York: Random House, 1938), pp. 33–89.
12. Copper, *Taiwan: Nation-State or Province*, p. 28.
13. Taiwan Affairs Office, *The Taiwan Question and Reunification of China* (Beijing, China: Information Office State Council, August 1993), p. 1.
14. Ibid., p. 2.
15. Ibid., p. 4.
16. Ibid., p. 9.
17. Li Jiaquan, "Mainland and Taiwan: Formula for China's Reunification," *Beijing Review* 25, No. 5, February 3, 1986, p. 24.
18. Ibid.
19. Steven Mufson, "Beijing Assures Taiwan Will Not Be Swallowed," *China Post* (International Airmail Edition), October 16, 1995, p. 1.
20. Ibid.
21. Jasper Becker and Dennis Engbarth, "Taiwan Belongs to Us, Says Li Peng," *South China Morning Post* (Weekly Edition), February 3, 1996, p. 1.
22. "PRC Wants Progress Its Own Way," *China Post* (International Airmail Edition), October 25, 1995, p. 1.
23. See Taiwan Affairs Office, *The Taiwan Question and Reunification of China*, p. 19.

24. "Commentaries View Li, Taiwan Independence," Central People's Radio (Beijing), July 19, 1995, in *FBIS, China,* July 24, 1995, p. 90.
25. Becker and Engbarth, "Taiwan Belongs to Us, Says Li Peng."
26. See Copper, *Taiwan: Nation-State or Province,* p. 30.
27. The late president made this pledge during his 1979 New Year's message to the Chinese people. See *The Republic of China Is on the Move* (Taipei: Kwang Hwa Publishing Company, 1979), p. 8.
28. Author's interview with Fredrick Chien, foreign minister of the Republic of China, Taipei, Taiwan, February 7, 1996.
29. During a fascinating interview with the author, General Chiang was asked whether there was any truth to the rumor that his father, the generalissimo, had maintained contact with Lin Biao during the 1950s. The general replied, "Oh yes. Lin Biao and even Chou En-lai. Yes, but they were all killed—assassinated. Some people think Chou En-lai died in the hospital, but rumor comes out that he was poisoned. But very slowly—a slow process—and finally he died." Author's interview with General (ret.) Chiang Wego, Taipei, Taiwan, February 5, 1996.
30. See Mainland Affairs Council, *Relations Across the Taiwan Straits* (Taipei: Mainland Affairs Council, July 1994), p. 9.
31. Author's interview with Fredrick Chien, foreign minister of the Republic of China, Taipei, Taiwan, February 7, 1996.
32. Mainland Affairs Council, *Relations Across the Taiwan Straits,* p. 10.
33. Ibid., pp. 11–12.
34. Ibid., p. 12.
35. Author's interview with Fredrick Chien, foreign minister of the Republic of China, Taipei, Taiwan, February 7, 1996.
36. See David Wang and Lilian Wu, "Not Yet Time for Unification: Hu," *China Post* (International Airmail Edition), September 18, 1995, p. 1.
37. See "The Grief of Being Born a Taiwanese," a dialogue between President Lee Teng-hui and writer Ryotaro Shiba, reprinted from *Asahi Weekly,* May 6–13, 1994, in U.S. Congress, *Congressional Record,* Vol. 140, No. 96, 103rd Congress, 2nd Session, July 21, 1994, p. S9339.
38. ROC Government Information Office, *The Republic of China Yearbook, 1993* (Taipei: Government Information Office, 1993), p. 149.
39. Julian Baum, "Frankly Speaking," *Far Eastern Economic Review,* June 15, 1995, p. 24.
40. For more information, see Dennis Van Vranken Hickey, "America's Two-Point Policy and the Future of Taiwan," *Asian Survey* 28, No. 8, August 1988, pp. 881–896.
41. "President's News Conference of December 22, 1949," *Public Papers of the Presidents of the United States: Harry S. Truman, 1949* (Washington, D.C.: U.S. Government Printing Office, 1964), p. 586.
42. "President's News Conference of January 5, 1950," *Public Papers of the Presidents of the United States: Harry S. Truman, 1950* (Washington, D.C.: U.S. Government Printing Office, 1965), p. 11.
43. "United States Policy Toward Formosa," *Department of State Bulletin* 22, No. 550, January 16, 1950, p. 80.
44. See Ibid.
45. "Memorandum of Conversation, by the Secretary of State, January 5, 1950," in U.S. Department of State, *Foreign Relations of the United States: 1950,* Vol. 6 (Washington D.C.: U.S. Government Printing Office, 1976), p. 259.
46. "Statement by the President on the Situation in Korea," in *Public Papers of the Presidents of the United States: Harry S. Truman 1950,* p. 492.
47. Roy Medvedev, *China and the Superpowers* (New York: Basil Blackwell

Inc., 1986), p. 117; John Quansheng Zhao also argues that the United States recognizes Chinese sovereignty over Taiwan in "An Analysis of Unification: The PRC Perspective," *Asian Survey* 23, No. 10, October 1983, p. 1111.

48. Quoted from Lung-chu Chen and W. M. Reisman, "Who Owns Taiwan: A Search for International Title," *Yale Law Journal* 81, No. 4, March 1972, p. 616.

49. Hungdah Chiu, "The Question of Taiwan in Sino-American Relations," in Hungdah Chiu (ed.), *China and the Taiwan Issue* (New York: Praeger Publishers, 1979), p. 162.

50. Chalmers M. Roberts, "U.S. Suggests 2 Chinas Try Direct Discussions," *Washington Post,* April 29, 1971, p. A14.

51. See "Commentary Views Pentagon Report on Status," *CNA* (Taipei), in English, April 22, 1990, in *FBIS, China,* April 25, 1990, p. 75.

52. See statement of Fu-Chen Lo of the University of Pennsylvania in *The Future of Taiwan,* U.S. Congress, Senate, Hearing Before the Committee on Foreign Relations, 98th Congress, 1st Session on S. Res. 74, November 9, 1983 (Washington, D.C.: U.S. Government Printing Office, 1984), p. 12. Also see Victor Hao Li, "The Taiwan Question in U.S.-China Relations," in Hung-Mao Tien (ed.), *Mainland China, Taiwan and U.S. Policy.* (Cambridge, Massachusetts: Oelgeschlager, Gun and Hain Publishers, Inc., 1983), p. 199.

53. Li, "The Taiwan Question in U.S.-China Relations," p. 199.

54. Ibid.

55. See "A Strategic Framework for the Asian Pacific Rim: Looking Toward the 21st Century," in *The President's Report on the U.S. Military Presence in East Asia,* U.S. Congress, Senate, Hearings Before the Committee on Armed Services, 101st Congress, 2nd Session, April 19, 1990, p. 37.

56. "U.S. Report Criticized," *Hong Kong Standard* (Hong Kong), April 21, 1990, p. 6.

57. "EPF 507: Defense Department Report, Friday, April 20 (Wolfowitz Testimony)," *East Asia/Pacific Wireless File,* April 20, 1990, Press and Cultural Section, Consulate General of the United States of America, Shanghai, People's Republic of China.

58. "U.S. Issues Report on Taiwan Territorial Disputes," Taipei, International Service in English, April 22, 1990, in *FBIS, China,* April 26, 1990, p. 65.

59. See Paul F. Horvitz, "U.S. Restates 'One-China' Policy to Placate Beijing," *International Herald Tribune,* July 14, 1995, in *Lexis/Nexis.*

60. For more information, see "What Is a 'One China' Policy?" *Taiwan Communiqué* (International Edition), No. 67, August 1995, p. 13.

61. See "U.S. Won't Accept Claim That Taiwan Part of PRC," *China Post* (International Airmail Edition), November 9, 1995, p. 1.

62. Each of the U.S.-PRC communiqués has emphasized that the issue of Taiwan's future is a matter for the Chinese themselves to decide. The TRA, however, does not address the issue. For more information, see Dennis Van Vranken Hickey, "America's Two Point Policy and the Future of Taiwan," *Asian Survey* 28, No. 8, August 1988, pp. 881–896.

63. Contrary to popular misconception, the United States does not recognize Chinese sovereignty over Taiwan. In each of the U.S.-PRC communiqués, the United States states only that it *acknowledges* the Chinese position that there is one China and Taiwan is part of China. The term "acknowledge" was deliberately chosen as it indicated cognizance of, but not necessarily agreement with, the Chinese position. For more information see ibid., p. 883, and Dennis Van Vranken Hickey, "U.S. Policy and the International Status of Taiwan," *Journal of East Asian Affairs* 7, No. 2, Summer/Fall 1993.

64. See prepared statement of William A. Brown, deputy assistant secretary of state for East Asian and Pacific affairs, in *The Future of Taiwan,* U.S. Congress, Senate, Hearing Before the Committee on Foreign Relations, 98th Congress, 1st Session on S. Res. 74 Expressing the Sense of the Senate Concerning the Future of the People on Taiwan, November 9, 1983 (Washington, D.C.: U.S. Government Printing Office, 1984), p. 8.

65. Ibid.

66. See Taiwan Affairs Office, *The Taiwan Question and Reunification of China,* p. 12.

67. Copper, *Taiwan: Nation-State or Province,* p. 21.

68. See Mendel, *The Politics of Formosan Nationalism,* pp. 14–15.

69. Ibid., p. 16.

70. See Peng, *A Taste of Freedom,* p. 13.

71. Ibid., p. 14.

72. Hsin-hsing Wu, *Bridging the Strait: Taiwan, China, and the Prospects for Reunification* (New York: Oxford University Press, 1994), p. 227.

73. For more information, see Simon Long, *Taiwan: China's Last Frontier* (New York: St. Martin's Press, 1991), p. 66.

74. *Democratic Progressive Party Charter and Platform* (Taipei: DPP Headquarters, 1993), p. 17.

75. See "KMT Politician Advocates De Jure Independence," *Taiwan Weekly,* April 8, 1995, in *FBIS, China,* July 25, 1995, pp. 44–45.

76. Hsu Hsin-liang, then chairman of Taiwan's Democratic Progressive Party, made this statement in 1991. See David Holley, "Changes in Europe and Taiwan Linked," *Los Angeles Times,* December 23, 1991, p. A16.

77. "F-16s and Independence," *Washington Post,* September 17, 1992, p. 20.

78. See statement of David W. Tsai in *Congressional Record,* October 9, 1992, E 3110–E 3112.

79. See Mainland Affairs Council, *Relations Across the Taiwan Strait,* p. 21.

80. See Charlene L. Fu, "Racial Tensions Remain in Far Western Mainland," *China Post* (International Airmail Edition), January 16, 1996, p. 2.

81. See "Beijing 'War Plan' in Bid to Isolate Taiwan," *South China Morning Post* (Weekly Edition), September 10–11, 1994, p. 1. The three other "major threats" to China are (1) U.S. and Western attempts to contain China, (2) the challenge posed by the rapid economic growth of other Asia Pacific nations, and (3) instability in countries and areas of critical importance to China such as North Korea.

9

The PRC Military Buildup and the East Asian Arms Race

In the early 1980s, the PRC launched a drive to modernize its military. With the end of the Cold War, the program has accelerated. This chapter discusses China's military budget, examines its defensive capabilities, and analyzes its intentions. It also examines the accompanying East Asian arms race and its likely consequences. In conclusion, the author suggests that these developments represent real challenges for Taipei.

China's Military Budget

All defense budgets contain hidden costs. But most analysts agree that China's official defense budget—which stands at roughly U.S.$7 billion—is "ridiculously low."[1] It includes primarily "salaries and personnel expenses and some operating and maintenance expenses, such as fuel for training."[2] The official budget does not include the cost of major weapons acquisitions (which are funded from other budget accounts), most military research and development costs, or revenues generated from the People's Liberation Army's sprawling business empire.

Given China's lack of transparency, it should come as little surprise that estimates of its actual military budget vary significantly. In fact, the U.S. Congress General Accounting Office claims that "it is impossible to determine [China's] total defense spending."[3] Western analysts also concede that "we've no idea where the money is coming from. Maybe other budget headings, but we don't know which."[4]

Taiwanese military authorities contend that "mainland China's inflation rate has been overstated to justify its military buildup . . . its actual military expenditures will be *at least four times as large as the official figure* [emphasis added]."[5] As outlined in Table 9.1, U.S. estimates range from the Central Intelligence Agency's figure of approximately U.S.$20 billion to around U.S.$140 billion by the RAND corporation. Some private estimates suggest that China is spending roughly U.S.$90 billion.[6]

Although estimates of China's defense budget may vary, even Chinese analysts concede that Beijing's military expenditures are rising. Indeed, the official budget has been increasing since the late 1980s:

Table 9.1 U.S. Estimates of China's 1995 Defense Budget (U.S.$ in billions)

Source	Estimate
Central Intelligence Agency	20
Pentagon	40
Arms Control and Disarmament Agency	50
RAND Corporation	140

Source: Simon Beck, "Beijing Spends U.S.$140 Billion on Arms," *South China Morning Post* (Weekly Edition), June 10, 1995, p. 1.

> After a decade of declining defense budgets, official Chinese military budgets started to grow in 1988, and the increase in 1993 was the fourth consecutive rise. Since 1988 Chinese budgets have nearly doubled in current prices, from 21.5 billion yuan to 42.5 billion yuan.[7]

But Chinese military officials claim that, when adjusted for inflation, there has been very little growth in China's actual defense spending.[8]

Why has the PRC's defense budget increased? Why does it continue to grow? The following discussion examines several possible reasons.

Tiananmen Square Incident

In the mid-1970s, China adopted the so-called Four Modernizations. This program called for the modernization of agriculture, industry, science and technology, and defense. But defense received the lowest priority. Throughout the 1980s, the PLA's appropriations fell.

Following the PLA's suppression of the 1989 Democracy Movement—a campaign that represented the greatest challenge to the Chinese Communist Party's monopolization of political power since 1949—defense budget outlays began to rise. Some believe that "Beijing's leaders reversed earlier defense budget reductions apparently as a reward for the PLA's contribution to restoring order in Tiananmen Square."[9] According to this view, increased expenditures "are one way in which the PLA exacts its price for supporting and sustaining the Communist Party in power."[10]

Bargain Prices

During the early 1980s, economic conditions in the Soviet Union began to deteriorate. With the disintegration of the Communist regime, the slide toward financial collapse accelerated. In December 1991, Robert Gates, then CIA director, warned:

> The former Soviet defense industries, enterprises involved in special weapons and missile programs that face cuts in military funding, may well try to stay in business by selling equipment, materials and services in the international market place. The hunger for hard currency could take precedence over proliferation concerns, particularly among Republic and local governments with high concentrations of defense industry and little else that is marketable.[11]

In October 1993, the CIA reported that "Russia has been actively promoting military sales to China this year to secure needed hard currency and to help defense industries cope with declines in domestic procurement."[12]

The cash-starved republics that are emerging from the rubble of the former Soviet Union are scrambling to sell a wide range of arms and technology to the PRC. According to U.S. sources, PRC officials "are going into the former Soviet Union and picking the shelves clean at fire-sale prices—they are buying not only weapons, but advanced technologies so that they can upgrade their own weapons."[13] Major Russian sales reported since 1990 include:

- Mi17 helicopters
- Su-27 Soviet fighters (and production rights to produce the warplane)
- Il heavy transport planes
- T-72 tanks
- In-flight refueling technology
- S-300 surface-to-air missiles (similar to the U.S. Patriot), with mobile launchers
- Rocket engines and missile guidance technology
- Kilmov/Sarkisov RD33 jet engines
- Kilo-class submarines[14]

As Andrew Yang, a military analyst at Taiwan's prestigious Sun Yat-sen Center for Policy Studies, observed, "this is a great moment for China to acquire modern weapons and technology at a cheap price."[15]

The Gulf War

With almost 3 million active military personnel, the PLA is the largest military establishment in the world. But this statistic is misleading. Much of China's military equipment is antiquated and obsolete.

The Allied victory in the 1991 Gulf War had a profound impact on China's military leaders. It convinced them that the PLA required modernization. Ronald Montaperto, a senior fellow at the National Defense University's Institute for National Strategic Studies, explains:

> More than any other event, the rapid successful conclusion of that conflict settled lingering questions about the proper direction for developing China's future military capabilities. The PLA is totally committed to building the mix of capabilities that will guarantee the successful prosecution of so-called Local Wars of Limited Duration.[16]

Following the war, Jiang Zemin, now PRC president, commented on the "lessons" of the conflict:

> The realities of regional war—especially the recent one—tell us that modern warfare is high-tech warfare. . . . It is warfare involving land, sea and air forces. It is electronic war, guided missile war. To fall behind means to get thrashed.[17]

Fluid Security Environment

PRC officials believe that the Russian military threat has diminished with time. China's security specialists no longer plan for a general war in which the entire country must mobilize in order to preserve its territorial integrity against a full-scale invasion. However, the post–Cold War international environment appears highly fluid and potentially threatening to Chinese leaders.

PRC defense planners hope to be prepared for a wide range of contingencies. These include renewed border conflicts with Vietnam or India, separatist movements within China, a possible war over the Spratly Islands, and military threats from some of its neighbors—particularly Japan. In order to meet these potential challenges, Beijing may have "adopted the philosophy that the best defense in uncertain times is a strong offense."[18]

Dominant Regional Power

With the end of the Cold War, the strategic balance in East Asia is shifting. Some believe that the PRC is increasing its defense budget in an effort to acquire the power required to fill the military-political vacuum left in the wake of the U.S. and Russian regional drawdowns. For example, one senior Pentagon analyst claims that "China is attempting to change the balance of power in the region."[19] Ross Munro, coordinator of the Asia Program at the Foreign Policy Research Institute, warns that "much of the increase [in military spending and acquisitions] is committed to a military buildup aimed at giving China its first capability to project naval and air power well beyond its shores."[20] In 1993, Sun Chen, then Taiwan's defense minister, charged that "the Chinese Communists are continuing to import high-performance, high-tech equipment. It is expected that by the year 2000, they will become a new hegemony in Asia."[21]

China's behavior during Taiwan's 1996 presidential elections supports the view that Beijing is seeking to use its military power to influence events and engineer outcomes in the Western Pacific region. Many analysts believe that the war games and missile tests—actions described as routine by the PRC—were designed to intimidate Taiwanese voters.

Summary

Several considerations appear to be driving China's increase in defense expenditures. These include (1) rewarding the PLA for its loyalty and support, (2) lessons learned from the brilliant Allied victory in the 1991 Gulf War, (3) the availability of state-of-the-art weapons and sophisticated military technology at affordable prices, (4) the unpredictable post–Cold War international environment, and (5) a long-term desire to become a dominant regional power.

China's Military Capabilities

Operationalizing the concept of military power is a difficult task. After all, a nation's power is dependent upon numerous variables. Some of these, including weapons, territory, population, natural resources, and level of economic development, may be subject to quantification. But other critical factors, including a state's political system, leadership, cohesiveness, popular will, and morale, do not lend themselves easily to measurement.[22] Further complicating matters is the fact that all power is relative. As Kenneth Waltz observed, "an agent is powerful to the extent that he affects others more than they affect him."[23]

The following discussion is not intended to provide readers with a comprehensive assessment of China's military power. Rather, it shows how Beijing is channeling some of its growing defense budget into the PLA. It examines recent changes in the PLA Navy, Air Force, and ground forces and analyzes Beijing's attempts to modernize its nuclear arsenal.

PLA Navy

In the mid-1980s, PRC military officials revealed that China's naval strategy had shifted from a "coastal" defense to a "near-sea" defense.[24] Since that time, the PLA Navy (PLAN) has been developing, constructing, or purchasing new classes of surface combatants (Luhu-class destroyers and Jiangwei-class frigates), supply ships (Dayun-class resupply ships), missile boats (Houjian and Houxin-class missile patrol craft), and nuclear and conventional submarines (Ming-class submarines and Russian Kilo-class submarines). These new warships, "with their marked improvements in weapons and electronic systems, represent an enormous advance in capability."[25] The PLAN also has improved its amphibious and airborne capabilities with the establishment of the PLA Marine Corps and the modernization of naval bombers that can be equipped with antiship missiles and torpedoes.

Looking to the future, the PLAN hopes to enhance its antisubmarine warfare capabilities and strengthen shipborne air defense capabilities. It also hopes to develop the capability to conduct sustained operations and develop an amphibious warfare capability. Finally, while plans to purchase the Varyag, an incomplete Russian aircraft carrier, have been scuttled, the PLAN continues to show interest in acquiring a carrier.

PLA Air Force

Most of the PLA Air Force's (PLAAF) inventory of roughly 5,900 warplanes is comprised of obsolete variants of Soviet-designed aircraft. With the help of foreign technology and hardware, however, the PLAAF hopes to catch up with Western combat aircraft.

In 1992, the PRC purchased a squadron of advanced Russian Su-27 "Flanker" jet fighters.[26] Reports indicate that Beijing has negotiated a follow-on purchase of twenty-two additional aircraft, bringing the total close to fifty.[27] Perhaps more significant, in late 1995 the PRC successfully negotiated a U.S.$2 billion deal to manufacture the warplane.[28] According to the terms of the agreement, Moscow will supply Beijing with plans and train PRC personnel.

Although the number of imported Su-27s is small, the new warplanes provide the PLAAF with an instantaneous qualitative boost. The combat jet is an air superiority fighter designed for air-to-air combat and is equipped with Russia's most advanced avionics.[29] It has a range of 2,500 miles on internal fuel tanks and a combat radius of approximately 1,000 miles.[30] According to reports, "the Su-27 could in some flight envelopes exceed the performance of the U.S. F-16 and F-18, and is a rough match for the F-15—the top U.S. air superiority fighter."[31] If based in southern China, the PLAAF could gain the capability to control the skies over the South China Sea.[32]

In addition to the Su-27s, the PRC has purchased up to twenty Russian Il-76 military transport planes (aircraft that could serve as air-refueling or AWACS platforms) and one hundred Russian Kilmov/Sarkisov RD-33 jet engines, which will be used to upgrade the PLAAF's domestically produced F-7 fighter.[33] Beijing also has bought several batteries of the Russian SA-10 surface-to-air missile defense system—a system comparable to the U.S.-built Patriot system—and has reportedly acquired in-flight refueling technology from Israel, Russia, or Iran.[34] Future acquisitions may include Russian MiG-31 fighters (and production technology), Russian Tu-22M bombers, and Russian AN-124 transport planes—an aircraft larger than the U.S.-built C-5.35

PLA Ground Forces

Beijing has put a priority on upgrading the major weapons systems in the PLAN and PLAAF. But it also is attempting to modernize the PLA's ground forces. In addition to reducing its size to roughly 2.3 million troops and creating a number of highly mobile elite or "fist" units, "the main feature of the ground force's modernization has been the streamlined organization, a relatively improved command and control system, and better training for soldiers."36

As the PLA's ground forces have received the lowest priority in the PRC's drive to modernize its military, purchases of sophisticated foreign equipment and technology have been quite limited. Nevertheless, some hardware and technology is being acquired. The PRC has reportedly purchased fifty T-72 tanks from Russia and "is negotiating with Russia to obtain other advanced technologies and coproduction rights for advanced munitions and weapons."37 High on the PLA ground forces' list of priorities are "attack helicopters, ground-based radars, electronic equipment, night vision devices, laser range finders, and advanced munitions."38

PLA Nuclear Forces

The PRC is a nuclear power with air, land, and sea-based warheads. The air-based leg of Beijing's nuclear triad consists of long-range, medium-range, and short-range bombers. Although nuclear capable, most of these aircraft "are based on 1950s and 1960s technology and would have limited operational capability against modern air defense systems."39 The land-based leg of the PRC's nuclear triad includes several varieties of intermediate and long-range ballistic missiles. A handful of these could strike the continental United States. The sea-based leg of its triad consists of one Xia-class submarine that can carry up to twelve ballistic missiles.

Although the PRC's nuclear weapons program is no match for the United States or the former Soviet Union, analysts agree that it contains "pockets of excellence."40 Furthermore, Beijing appears determined to enhance its nuclear war-fighting capabilities. According to reports, it is developing solid-fuel missiles and attempting to MIRV its missiles. In fact, Robert Karinol, Asia Pacific editor of *Jane's Defence Weekly,* contends that the aim of China's recent nuclear tests is "to develop a better offensive capability, not a defensive one. . . . They [the PRC] are looking for improved range and guidance for their missiles [and] trying to increase the number of devices [they] could place aboard a Multiple Re-entry Vehicle to make each missile substantially more effective."41

Summary

Like arch-rival Taipei, Beijing is attempting to build a "leaner and meaner" military establishment. It has reduced its force structure and put a priority on upgrading the major weapons systems in the PLAN and PLAAF. The PRC is also modernizing its strategic nuclear triad, and U.S. officials suspect that it is stockpiling offensive chemical and biological weapons.[42]

The drive to enhance the PLA's strategic and conventional military capabilities is beginning to show results. As William J. Perry, U.S. defense secretary, observed during his 1994 visit to China, the PLA's "capabilities in all areas, including the military areas, are growing by the day."[43]

China's Intentions

A state's military capability does not, in itself, constitute a threat to other states. Mexico and Canada do not feel threatened by the military strength of the United States. But Israel is vitally concerned with the military posture of Iran and Iraq. In other words, a state's intentions are as important as its capabilities. The problem, of course, lies in deducing the nature of another state's intentions.

A nation's strategic intentions can be evaluated in two ways. First, one may examine a government's military doctrine, where military doctrine is defined as "a set of approved, shared ideas about the conduct of warfare that guides the preparation of armed forces for future wars."[44] It may provide an analyst with a basic understanding of how a state plans to deploy military forces in the future. Second, one may examine a state's actions. Do a state's actions indicate that it is content with the international status quo? Does it have a history of using force to resolve disputes? How often and under what circumstances does it threaten to use military coercion? Answering these questions may help one ascertain the degree to which a government is willing to upset the international equilibrium.

PRC Military Doctrine

The PRC's strategic doctrine has gone through three distinct phases. During the first period—which extended from the 1930s until the mid-1970s—the PLA followed a military doctrine described as "People's War." Developed by Mao Zedong (who borrowed heavily from Sun Tzu, the classical Chinese strategist), People's War was a strategy by which small numbers of guerrillas could defeat an objectively stronger enemy. Enemy forces would be lured deep into China and then surrounded, attacked, and ultimately defeated:

> People's War doctrine envisioned swift and mobile guerrilla harassment of an aggressor's over-extended supply line. . . . This active and total defense strategy is based on the PRC's strengths of geography, manpower, organization, and size. It is a total war concept in which the entire population plays a role.[45]

The doctrine is said to have contributed to CCP victories during World War II and the Chinese Civil War.

In the late-1970s, People's War was replaced by the doctrine of "People's War Under Modern Conditions." PRC defense specialists concluded that People's War was ill-equipped to deal with the changing nature of modern warfare, which includes nuclear weapons, advanced conventional arms, new technologies, and new strategies and tactics. Military strategists also feared that "by the time an enemy had been lured deeply enough into the People's Republic for this [People's War] to work, the enemy would have destroyed much of the country's vital industries and transportation nodes."[46]

People's War Under Modern Conditions called for major revisions in PLA tactics, organization, and operations. June Teufel Dreyer, an authority on China's military, explains:

> The doctrine is characterized by greater attention to positional warfare, modern weaponry, and combined arms. The concept of luring an enemy deeply into China and then surrounding and attacking him was amended to include the possibility of forward defense.[47]

In keeping with the new doctrine, the PRC began to move first-line military units closer to the tense Sino-Soviet border.[48] It also launched an ill-fated "defensive counterattack" against Vietnam in early 1979. Although the new doctrine continued to pay lip service to Mao's contributions to military strategy, most security analysts agree that the new doctrine represented a sharp break with the past.

In the mid-1980s, PRC leaders concluded that the possibility of a major confrontation with the Soviet Union (or the United States) was remote. Deemed more likely was the possibility of small or local wars erupting somewhere along China's vast borders. These conflicts would require a distinctly different strategy than the principles of protraction and attrition that guided People's War or even People's War Under Modern Conditions. Consequently, the PLA is now oriented toward a new doctrine—the doctrine of "Limited and Local Wars."

Defense analysts argue that the new doctrine, with its emphasis on quick decisive results and high technology, represents a "complete break" with the past.[49] Limited War doctrine "emphasizes rapid reaction, limited conflict, flexible response, preemptive action, and limited power projection to China's 'strategic boundaries.'"[50] As the new approach indicates that the PLA wishes to operate beyond China's geographic borders, power projection now represents a critical element in the PLA's military doctrine.

PRC Actions

Since 1949, Beijing has elected to employ force to resolve a number of disagreements. These include:

- Occupation of Tibet (1950–1951)
- Korean War (1950–1953)
- Offshore islands crises (1954 and 1958)
- Sino-Indian border war (1962)
- Sino-Soviet border clash (1969)
- Occupation of some of the Paracel Islands (1974)
- Sino-Vietnam border war (1979)
- Occupation of some of the Spratly Islands (1988)

More worrisome for the future, the PRC will not rule out the use of force to settle other territorial disputes, particularly its claims to Taiwan and the entire South China Sea.

Threats to use force to take Taiwan have escalated as the island has attempted to raise its international profile. Provocative actions have accompanied these threats. In February 1995, Taiwanese authorities revealed that the PRC had redeployed elements of an artillery division that includes M-9 and M-11 missiles to Fujian province—the coastal province opposite Taiwan.[51] With ranges of 600 kilometers and 290 kilometers, respectively, these missiles are within striking distance of the island. Even more alarming, Beijing conducted a series of threatening military exercises and "missile tests" in the East China Sea and the Taiwan Strait during 1995 and 1996. The Hong Kong press described the tests as "the moral equivalent of an invasion."[52]

Beijing also appears determined to back up its claims to the entire South China Sea. In addition to conducting regular military maneuvers in the region, the PRC has constructed military installations on some of the disputed islands located on Mischief Reef.[53] Described by U.S. defense specialists as "a wake-up call," the bases are located seventy miles within the Philippines' 200-mile economic exclusion zone.[54] The Mischief Reef affair represents Beijing's "first direct challenge to the Philippines' claims in the South China Sea, prompting fear and outrage in Southeast Asia."[55]

Summary

As described, a state's military capabilities do not necessarily constitute a threat to other states. It is both power *and* intentions that matter. Although intentions always are difficult to ascertain and subject to rapid change, an analysis of a state's military doctrine and its willingness to use force may provide some indication of a state's ambitions. In the PRC's case, such an examination is not reassuring.

The recent shifts in strategic doctrine indicate that Beijing is preparing to project its power beyond the nation's geographic borders. Furthermore, the PRC has a history of using coercion to settle disputes and appears prepared to take up arms to enforce its territorial claims over Taiwan and the South China Sea. When viewed together, these developments seem to present a picture of a Chinese government that is seeking to project its power in order to threaten, intimidate, or even subjugate its neighbors.

Asian Arms Race

With the collapse of the Soviet Union and the end of the Cold War, many Western governments have scaled back military expenditures. In the Asia Pacific region, however, defense spending is on the rise. Instead of a peace dividend, the end of the Cold War seems to be fueling a costly arms race in the region.[56]

There are many explanations for the escalation in defense spending. Some nations cannot resist the bargain prices being offered by the former Soviet Union. As Andrew Mack, head of Australian National University's International Relations Department, observed, "you can just about cut any deal with the Russians these days . . . they'll sell anything to anyone if they can."[57] Others are simply awash in cash and anxious to replace obsolete Vietnam-era arsenals with state-of-the-art equipment. Finally, some fear that, with the collapse of the Soviet Union and the withdrawal of the United States from the Philippines, a power vacuum is emerging in the region. These governments are uneasy about the PRC's increasing military capabilities and its strategic intentions.

A 1995 U.S. Department of Defense study, *United States Security Strategy for the East-Asia Pacific Region,* warns that Beijing's neighbors "may feel a need to respond to China's growing military power."[58] Goh Chok Tong, Singapore's prime minister, also has warned that "in Asia, China's rising power and arms build-up has stirred anxiety."[59] Desmond Ball, an analyst at Australian National University's Strategic and Defense Studies Center, concurs. He believes that "for many countries, China is emerging as the greatest security concern in the region. . . . Its military buildup is the fastest in the region and bears a major proportion of the responsibility for the buildups elsewhere in the region."[60] There is evidence to support this view.

As might be expected, Taiwanese officials are especially nervous about Beijing's military buildup. After learning about the PRC's acquisition of advanced Russian warplanes, Albert Lin, Taiwan's spokesman in

Washington, D.C., exclaimed that "somehow, somewhere, we have to get new aircraft."[61] Beijing's 1995 and 1996 military exercises and "missile tests" led Taiwanese officials to call for a military buildup on the island. Claiming that Beijing was "altering their strategic deployment [and] posing an extremely large threat to Taiwan and the Asia-Pacific region," Lee Teng-hui, Taiwan's president, called for the island to "accelerate the building of a second-generation armed force."[62] Lee also hinted that Beijing's provocative actions might lead Taiwan to reconsider its posture toward the development of nuclear weapons.

Taiwan is not the only government that is nervous about the PRC. Other regional actors, including Malaysia, Thailand, and Indonesia, also have opted to put more muscle into their military arsenals. In fact, some analysts have described the regional buildup as an impending international crisis.

Summary

The end of the Cold War has contributed both to China's military modernization and the East Asian arms race. These developments represent challenges to Taiwan's security.

Some studies suggest that a correlation exists between arms races and the onset of war.[63] Asia's heavily armed governments might attempt to settle some of the region's unresolved territorial disputes with force. Authorities in Taipei view the prospect of such a conflict with alarm:

> At present, some potentially unstable factors do exist in Northeast Asia, such as on the Korean peninsula, and in Southeast Asia as in Indochina and the South China Sea [sic]. The sudden eruption of violence in any of these areas would inevitably pose a broad range of threats to the ROC's security and interests.[64]

In short, an Asian arms race—fueled in part by the end of the Cold War—represents a threat to Taiwan's security.

Taiwan's security also is undermined by the PRC's military buildup. Although Beijing's growing military power may not be directed against the ROC, it nevertheless undermines Taipei's defensive capabilities vis-à-vis Beijing. Taiwanese officials are especially nervous about the resumption of Sino-Russian military cooperation and its implications for the island's security. Beijing's modern Su-27s are more than a match for Taiwan's fleet of F-5E, F-104, and IDF aircraft. Furthermore, the inflight refueling technology obtained from Moscow will enable Beijing to expand its reach to Taiwan. Hei You-long, a noted Taiwanese weaponry expert, explains:

> Before Peking acquires the [inflight refueling] technology, only some 1,000 of China's 6,000 military aircraft could pose an immediate threat to

Taiwan. But with the aerial refueling technology, which is able to increase the flight distance by five to ten times, the combat aircraft now deployed in Sichuan and Sinjiang can also pose an immediate threat to the security of Taiwan.[65]

The collapse of the Soviet Union also could jeopardize Taiwan's security in other ways. During the height of the Sino-Soviet split, the PLA was charged with the responsibility of tying down an estimated forty-six Soviet divisions—somewhere between 750,000 and 1 million troops—as well as mobile, multiple-warhead SS-20 intermediate-range ballistic missiles and supersonic Backfire bombers that were deployed along the Sino-Soviet border. Taiwanese authorities fear that the reduction of the Soviet threat has enabled the PRC to free up these forces and deploy them elsewhere. Hau Pei-tsun, Taiwan's former premier, explains:

> When the Soviet Union still existed, Communist China had to deploy a large number of troops along its 6,000-mile-long border with Russia. With the Soviet Union gone, Communist China can now redeploy more troops in its southeastern coastal provinces opposite Taiwan. *The Communist threat to Taiwan has increased, not decreased, in the post–Cold War era* [emphasis added].[66]

Sun Chen, Taiwan's defense minister, concurs with Hau's assessment. Sun claims that Beijing already has redeployed China's northern border forces to southeastern coastal provinces:

> Intelligence reports also indicate that since the collapse of the former Soviet Union and the reduction of [the] threat from the North, the Chinese communists have moved a large number of their forces to strengthen battlefield management in southeastern coastal provinces. They have built railways and highways, repaired harbors, and installed military facilities in civilian seaports and airports to serve combat planes and warships at a moment's notice. The Chinese communists have also built a strategic airport on Woody Island in the Paracels. All these show their ability for oceanic power expansion is growing and that *their threat against Taiwan is rising* [emphasis added].[67]

In sum, Taiwanese officials contend that "the world has not become a safer place since the so-called Cold War ended."[68]

Notes

1. Nayan Chanda, "Fear of the Dragon," *Far Eastern Economic Review,* April 13, 1995, p. 25.
2. U.S. General Accounting Office (hereafter GAO), *National Security: Impact of China's Military Modernization in the Pacific Region* (Washington, D.C.: GAO, June 1995), p. 16.

3. Ibid., p. 4.
4. Chanda, "Fear of the Dragon."
5. See "Taiwan Alarmed by Beijing's Military Buildup," *South China Morning Post,* March 17, 1994, in *Lexis/Nexis.*
6. See Chong-Pin Lin, "China on the Move," *Current,* June 1994, p. 35.
7. Stockholm International Peace Research Institute (hereafter SIPRI), *SIPRI Yearbook 1994* (New York: Oxford University Press, 1994), p. 441.
8. PRC officials also claim that "the so-called assertion of China's hidden national defense spending is groundless . . . they are deceiving themselves as well as others." See "Article Refutes 'Theory' of 'Military Threat,'" *Renmin Ribao* (Beijing), July 28, 1995, in *FBIS, China,* August 14, 1995, p. 44.
9. Lin, "China on the Move," p. 35.
10. See SIPRI, *SIPRI Yearbook,* p. 443.
11. See testimony of Robert M. Gates, director, Central Intelligence Agency, in *Potential Threats to American Security in the Post–Cold War Era,* U.S. Congress, House, Hearings Before the Defense Policy Panel of the Committee on Armed Services, 102nd Congress, 1st Session, December 10, 11, and 13, 1991 (Washington, D.C.: U.S. Government Printing Office, 1992), p. 9.
12. See "Questions and Answers for Mr. Woolsey from Senator Glenn," in *Proliferation Threats of the 1990s,* U.S. Congress, Senate, Hearing Before the Committee on Governmental Affairs, 103rd Congress, 1st Session, February 24, 1993 (Washington, D.C.: U.S. Government Printing Office, 1993), p. 150. Also see Han Nai-kuo, "Russia Promoting Military Sales to Mainland China," *CNA* (Taipei), October 12, 1993.
13. Thomas L. Friedman, "China Warns U.S. on Taiwan Jet Deal," *New York Times,* September 4, 1992, p. A3.
14. See Robert G. Sutter and Shirley Kan, "China as a Security Concern in Asia: Perceptions, Assessment and U.S. Options," *Congressional Research Service Report* (No. 95-46S, December 22, 1994) as reprinted in Congressional Research Service, *What Should Be the Policy of the United States Toward the People's Republic of China* (Washington, D.C.: U.S. Government Printing Office, 1994), pp. 222–223. Also see Chanda, "Fear of the Dragon," p. 23.
15. Jim Mann and David Holley, "China Builds Military; Neighbors Uneasy," *Los Angeles Times,* September 13, 1992, p. A26.
16. Testimony of Ronald Montaperto, senior fellow, Institute for National Strategic Studies, National Defense University, in Hearings Before Senate Foreign Relations Committee's Subcommittee on East Asian and Pacific Affairs, *The Chinese Military: Its Role and Growth,* October 11, 1995, in *Federal Document Clearing House,* in *Lexis/Nexis.*
17. Mann and Holley, "China Builds Military," p. A26.
18. See SIPRI, *SIPRI Yearbook,* p. 442.
19. Barbara Starr, "MiG Buy May Lead to Chinese Copies," *Jane's Defence Weekly,* October 10, 1992, p. 18.
20. Ross Munro, "Awakening Dragon," *Policy Review,* Fall 1992, p. 13.
21. Peter Seidlitz, "Russians Lead the Beijing Arms Race," *South China Morning Post* (Hong Kong), July 18, 1993, p. 8.
22. For a discussion of capability analysis, see Amos A. Jordan, William J. Taylor, Jr., and Lawrence J. Korb, *American National Security: Policy and Process* (Baltimore, Maryland: Johns Hopkins University Press, 1989), pp. 26–27.
23. Kenneth Waltz, *Theory of International Politics* (New York: McGraw Hill, 1979), p. 192.
24. For more information, see prepared statement of James A. Lilley, former

ambassador to China, in *Future of United States–China Policy,* U.S. Congress, House, Joint Hearings Before the Subcommittees on Economic Policy, Trade and Environment; International Security, International Organizations and Human Rights; and Asia and the Pacific of the Committee on Foreign Affairs, 103rd Congress, 1st Session (Washington, D.C.: U.S. Government Printing Office, 1993), p. 111.

25. John Caldwell, *China's Conventional Military Capabilities, 1994–2004: An Assessment* (Washington, D.C.: Center for Strategic and International Studies, 1994), p. 8.

26. For more information, see Jim Mann, "China Seeks Russian Weapons in Effort to Modernize Military," *Los Angeles Times,* July 13, 1992, p. 3.

27. See Testimony of Richard D. Fisher, senior research fellow, Asian Studies Center, Heritage Foundation, in *The Chinese Military: Its Role and Growth,* in *Lexis/Nexis.*

28. For more information, see "Russia Sells PRC Fighter Plans," *China Post* (Domestic Edition), February 4, 1996, p. 1.

29. John W. R. Taylor, "Gallery of Soviet Aerospace Weapons," *Air Force Magazine,* March 1990, p. 75.

30. See ibid. The Su-27's range could be extended with inflight refueling, another of China's acquisition priorities.

31. See Testimony of Richard D. Fisher in *The Chinese Military: Its Role and Growth,* in *Lexis/Nexis.*

32. See David A. Fulghum and Paul Proctor, "Chinese Coveting Offensive Triad," *Aviation Week & Space Technology,* September 21, 1992, p. 21.

33. See GAO, *National Security: Impact of China's Military Modernization in the Pacific Region,* pp. 20–21.

34. See Sutter and Kan, "China as a Security Concern in Asia."

35. See ibid.; and Testimony of Richard D. Fisher in *The Chinese Military: Its Role and Growth,* in *Lexis/Nexis.*

36. Taeho Kim, "China's Military Buildup in a Changing Security Climate in Northeast Asia," in Richard H. Yang (ed.), *China's Military: The PLA in 1992/93* (Boulder, Colorado: Westview Press, 1993), p. 126.

37. See GAO, *National Security: Impact of China's Military Modernization in the Pacific Region,* p. 23.

38. See Caldwell, *China's Conventional Military Capabilities, 1994–2004,* p. 6.

39. See GAO, *National Security: Impact of China's Military Modernization in the Pacific Region,* p. 24.

40. See Lin, "China on the Move."

41. For more information, see "Nuclear Tests 'Show Haste to Upgrade,'" *South China Morning Post* (Weekly Edition), August 26, 1995, p. A6.

42. See GAO, *National Security: Impact of China's Military Modernization in the Pacific Region,* p. 25.

43. Michael Gordon, "U.S. to China: Be More Open on Arms Plan," *New York Times,* October 19, 1994, p. A14.

44. Quoted from Karl W. Eikenberry, "Does China Threaten Asia-Pacific Regional Stability," *Parameters: The U.S. Army War College Quarterly* 25, No. 1, Spring 1995, p. 91.

45. Robert J. Skebo, Gregory K. S. Man, and George H. Stevens, "China's Military Capabilities: Problems and Prospects," in *China's Economic Dilemmas in the 1990s: The Problems of Reforms, Modernization and Interdependence,* Vol. 2, Study Papers Submitted to the Joint Economic Committee, Congress of the United States, (Washington, D.C.: U.S. Government Printing Office, April 1991), p. 664.

46. June Teufel Dreyer, *China's Political System: Modernization and Tradition* (New York: Paragon House, 1993), p. 252.

47. Ibid.

48. See Jack H. Harris, "Enduring Chinese Dimensions in Peking's Military Policy and Doctrine," *Issues and Studies* 15, No. 7, July 1979, p. 86.

49. For more information, see Harlan W. Jencks, "China's Defense Buildup: A Threat to the Region?" in Yang, *China's Military: The PLA in 1992/93*, pp. 97–98.

50. Skebo, Man and Stevens, "Chinese Military Capabilities: Problems and Prospects," p. 664.

51. See Christe Su, "ROC Military Says Mainland Shift Perils Taiwan," *Free China Journal,* March 3, 1995, p. 2. Also see Julian Baum, "Idling Threat," *Far Eastern Economic Review,* April 13, 1995, p. 29.

52. See Willy Wo-Lap Lam, "Taiwan Gamble Pays Off for Jiang," *South China Morning Post* (Weekly Edition), August 5, 1995, p. 7.

53. See Nigel Holloway, "Jolt from the Blue," *Far Eastern Economic Review,* August 3, 1995, pp. 22–23.

54. Ibid.

55. See Testimony of D. Richard Fisher, *The Chinese Military: Its Role and Growth,* in *Lexis/Nexis.*

56. According to official U.S. government estimates, "Asia was the only region that showed an increase in its share of arms transfer agreements from 1985–1988 to 1989–1992" (increasing to 29.5 percent from 23.3 percent). For more information, see *U.S. Congress, Congressional Research Service, Conventional Arms Transfers to the Third World, 1985–1992,* Richard F. Grimmett (ed.), *CRS Report for Congress* (Washington, D.C.: U.S. Government Printing Office, July 19, 1993), p. 26.

57. William Branigin, "Beijing Buildup Has Asia Worried," *China Post* (International Airmail Edition), April 5, 1993, p. 2.

58. The study warns that "China's military posture and development have a great impact on the expectations and behavior of other states in the region. Although China's leaders insist their military buildup is defensive and commensurate with China's overall economic growth, others in the region cannot be certain of China's intentions, particularly in this period of leadership transition. China's military modernization effort is in an early stage, and its long-term goals are unclear. Moreover, it has territorial disputes with several neighboring states. Absent a better understanding of China's plans, capabilities, and intentions, other Asian nations may feel a need to respond to China's growing military power. For more information, see U.S. Department of Defense, Office of International Security Affairs, *United States Security Strategy for the East Asia–Pacific Region* (Washington, D.C.: The Pentagon, February 1995), p. 15.

59. See Merray Hiebert, "Treading Softly," *Far Eastern Economic Review,* August 3, 1995, p. 20.

60. See Branigin, "Beijing Buildup Has Asia Worried," p. 2.

61. Susumu Awanohara, "Election Dynamics: Candidate Bush to Review Aircraft Sale to Taiwan," *Far Eastern Economic Review,* August 20, 1992, p. 20.

62. Dennis Engbarth, "Taiwan Leader Calls for Rapid Military Build-up," *South China Morning Post,* October 6, 1995, p. 1.

63. For example, see Michael Wallace, "Armaments and Escalation," *International Studies Quarterly* 26, No. 1, March 1982, pp. 37–56.

64. "Answers to Written Questions from Mr. Robert Karniol of *Jane's Defence Weekly* by Sun Chen, Minister of National Defense, Republic of China." Transcript provided courtesy of Moses Lu, Assistant Information Office, Taipei Economic and Cultural Representative Office, Chicago, Illinois.

65. "Peking Seen More Threatening to Taiwan," *CNA* (Taipei), August 25, 1992, in *Lexis/Nexis*.
66. *Central News Agency* (Taipei), March 28, 1992, in *Lexis/Nexis*.
67. See Dennis Hickey, "Special Report: Interview with Sun Chen, Taiwan's Defense Minister," *Asian Defense Journal,* February 1994, pp. 30–35.
68. See "CNA Reports Minister Chien's Colorado Address," *CNA* (Taipei), June 19, 1993, in *FBIS, China,* June 21, 1993, p. 86.

10

U.S. Foreign Policy in the 1990s

Taiwan is largely dependent upon the United States for its security. Although Washington abrogated its formal defense treaty with Taipei, the prospect of U.S. military intervention has long played a key role in deterring PRC aggression. However, recent changes in the international system could undermine U.S. support.

This chapter discusses U.S. foreign policy during the post–Cold War era. It examines the growth in isolationist sentiment and analyzes the U.S. military drawdown in the Asia Pacific region. The chapter also discusses Washington's new emphasis on economic matters in international affairs. In conclusion, the author explains how these developments could complicate the U.S.-ROC security dyad.

U.S. Foreign Policy and the End of the Cold War

In the late 1940s, events in Eastern Europe, Asia, and elsewhere led the United States to adopt a global policy to contain the spread of Soviet influence. Containment defined U.S. foreign policy for roughly four decades. The United States built new institutions, alliances, and strategies to meet the demands of the Cold War. Although U.S. public opinion differed occasionally over the means of containment, few questioned its need.

With the collapse of the Soviet Union, the United States finds itself in a world that has fundamentally changed. Many Cold War assumptions, institutions, and policies are no longer relevant. In fact, some believe that the end of the era of superpower rivalry has left the United States without a predominant foreign policy focus.

The Resurgence of Isolationism

With the end of the Cold War, U.S. leaders can no longer use containment as a pretext to justify U.S. involvement in world affairs. The United States is experiencing a clash between those who advocate a more circumscribed role in international affairs and those who seek to maintain a primarily interventionist foreign policy.

Patrick J. Buchanan, well-known journalist and Republican candidate for the presidency in 1992 and 1996, contends that the United States should focus on domestic affairs rather than wasting money on the problems of foreign nations:

> With the Cold War over, America must look homeward. We must repair the damage done to our society and nation. . . . America cannot afford to be bailing out every bankrupt regime on Earth and pulling everybody's bacon out of the fire.[1]

Others argue that most of the U.S. security obligations in East Asia and elsewhere are obsolete relics of the Cold War. Rather than press for increased "burden sharing," Ted Carpenter, director of foreign policy studies at the Cato Institute, contends that "Washington's goal should be one of burden shedding."[2]

A growing number of U.S. citizens agree with the views expressed by Buchanan, Carpenter, and others who think that the level of internationalism exhibited by the United States during the Cold War is no longer necessary nor economically viable. They believe that the end of the Cold War should be treated the same as the end of any other major conflict: the war is won, bring the troops home. Harvey Sicherman explains: "History shows that, when a war ends, the psychology of peace turns a nation inward. The demise of the Cold War is proving no exception."[3] Public opinion polls support Sicherman's hypothesis. Table 10.1 outlines the growth in isolationist sentiment.

Table 10.1 Trend Toward Isolationism (percentage of respondents)

	1972	1992
United States should mind own business		
Agree	35	44
Disagree	56	53
No opinion	9	3
Total	100	100
United States should focus on domestic issues		
Agree	73	82
Disagree	20	17
No opinion	7	1
Total	100	100

Source: Leslie McAneny, "Huge Majority Backs Shift from International to Domestic Agenda," *Gallup Poll Monthly,* No. 316, January 1992, p. 12.

Studies suggest that, when the U.S. public turns inward, the U.S. Congress soon follows:

> Congress has reliably checked presidential initiatives during times of national introversion, when isolationist sentiment prevailed. By legislation and inaction, congressional leaders have limited White House international options.[4]

The end of the Cold War is proving to be no exception to this rule. For example, lawmakers are attempting to dismantle principal institutions in the foreign policy establishment. Some favor moving the U.S. Information Agency, the Agency for International Development, and the Arms Control and Disarmament Agency into the Department of State. Others advocate eliminating the Department of Commerce, curtailing loans and guarantees to Mexico, cutting funds to help Russia dismantle its nuclear weapons, and slashing funding for international organizations.[5] President Clinton has described these recommendations as "the most isolationist proposals to come before Congress in 50 years."[6]

Summary

As the 1990s continue to unfold, a growing number of the U.S. public believes that the United States no longer needs to involve itself in global affairs. In part, this surge in inward-looking sentiment may be traced to the perception that because the United States is no longer threatened by the Soviet Union, it can afford to scale back its involvement overseas. However, other considerations also may be fueling the drive toward isolationism.

President Clinton has warned that "there is a struggle going on between those of us who want to carry on the tradition of American leadership and those who would advocate a new American isolationism."[7] At times, however, it is difficult to tell which side the president supports. Indeed, some administration officials have suggested that the United States ought to retreat from its leadership role in international affairs.

In May 1993, a senior State Department official announced that the White House is "setting limits on U.S. engagement around the world" and that "the U.S. no longer has the inclination to use military force or the resources to pay for it."[8] He explained that "things have changed with the Cold War's end, including a new priority focus on the domestic economy and a preoccupation with justifying every dollar spent."[9] Although Secretary of State Warren Christopher attempted to back away from the statement, he also has argued that the United States must "jealously guard" its power and that the country "would only act unilaterally if its national interests were threatened, as with an invasion."[10]

The administration also might be helping the isolationist movement in other ways. Ironically, the president's awkward handling of foreign policy crises may have succeeded only in fueling the popular movement toward isolationism in the United States.[11] Some contend that the administration's "misguided policies" are contributing to an "isolationist backlash":

> The "new age" vocation of the Clinton Administration has already produced an isolationist backlash among the American people. A series of clumsy humanitarian interventions in Somalia, Bosnia, Rwanda and Haiti has come close to discrediting all intervention; a naive multilateralism has come close to discrediting U.S. involvement in international institutions.[12]

Finally, public opinion polls reveal that a majority of the U.S. public disapproves of President Clinton's handling of international affairs and only a fraction of the population believes that he has a coherent foreign policy. The president's "flip-flops," which have ranged from the Korean nuclear crisis to the Haitian refugee question, have confused the public.[13] When polled, "the main criticism that the public has is that he doesn't seem to have a plan. . . . [The United States is] destined to lurch from crisis to crisis where average Americans never quite digest what the issues are."[14] As Douglas Paal, president of the Asia Pacific Policy Center, observed, "the problem of U.S. foreign policy in Asia has far more to do with the quality of American leadership than with the quantity of money."[15]

U.S. Military Drawdown

During a recent visit to East Asia, former British prime minister Margaret Thatcher observed, "In Asia, there are no multilateral defense institutions . . . stability will, therefore, depend both on a balance of power between great countries, and most importantly on a continued American presence."[16] Many U.S. officials agree with Thatcher's assessment. In fact, a 1995 U.S. Department of Defense study emphasizes that "a U.S. military forward presence in the Asia-Pacific region is an essential element of regional security."[17]

Despite such statements from Washington, it is clear that the United States is reducing its presence in East Asia and the Western Pacific. A 1995 study commissioned by the General Accounting Office outlined a number of key events that have reinforced the perceptions in Asia of a reduced U.S. commitment to the region. These events include:

- President's Nixon's 1969 Guam Doctrine, which states that the United States will look to Asian nations to be primarily responsible for their own defense

- The subsequent U.S. pullout from Vietnam and Indochina
- President Carter's decision (later reversed) to withdraw U.S. ground forces from South Korea
- U.S. requests for Japan and South Korea to assume a greater role in their own defense
- The closure of U.S. bases in the Philippines
- U.S. reluctance to commit forces to peacekeeping operations in Cambodia
- Post–Cold War cuts in U.S. defense spending and military capabilities worldwide
- The 1992 U.S. East Asian Strategic Initiative, which called for a phased reduction in U.S. forces in the Pacific[18]

With respect to the final point, it is noteworthy that the United States maintained roughly 125,000 troops in the East Asia Pacific region in 1985 (see Table 10.2). By 1994, however, troop levels had dropped 20 percent.

Table 10.2 U.S. Troop Strength

	Worldwide	Europe	East Asia Pacific
1985	2,200,000	358,000	125,000
1990	2,000,000	291,000	119,000
1994	1,600,000	142,000	101,000

Source: U.S. Department of Defense, as reported in Jim Mann, "U.S. Troop Strength Is Questioned," *Los Angeles Times,* October 14, 1994, p. 25A, in *Lexis/Nexis.*

Some governments interpret the U.S. military drawdown as a sign of weakness. Indeed, one PRC report speculated that "although the end of the Cold War has left the United States as the only superpower, its real power and position has very clearly been weakened."[19] Another PRC publication gloated that "the U.S. strength is not equal to its ambition to seek sole global hegemony."[20] There is evidence to support this view.

In addition to troop cutbacks, questions have been raised concerning the general state of U.S. military preparedness. In 1994, Secretary of Defense William J. Perry conceded that the United States could not meet the strategic objective of "win-hold-win" as outlined in the Clinton administration's "bottom-up review."[21] In other words, the United States would not be able to win one major conflict, hold off an enemy in a second war, and then ultimately defeat the second enemy.

Some predict that the U.S. military position will continue to erode: "We are buying no new tanks and very few fighter aircraft. Shipbuilding is way down. We're running out of things to cut."22 Current plans call for even deeper cuts in the U.S. defense budget. As outlined in Table 10.3, the U.S. Department of Defense's budget will continue to drop throughout the 1990s.

Table 10.3   U.S. Department of Defense Budget: Fiscal Years 1990–1997

	1990	1991	1992	1993	1994	1995	1996	1997
Current 1995 dollars	292.9	276.2	281.9	267.4	251.4	252.6	245.9	242.8
Percent real growth	–2.2	–10.1	0.0	–8.1	–8.5	–1.9	–5.3	–4.1

Source: William J. Perry, secretary of defense, *Annual Report to the President and the Congress* (Washington, D.C.: U.S. Government Printing Office, February 1995), p. B-2.

More than troop reductions and budget cuts are undermining U.S. military preparedness. Some believe that the Clinton administration's penchant for "peacekeeping" missions compounds these problems. They worry that deployments in Haiti, Eastern Europe, and elsewhere could leave the United States ill-prepared and ill-equipped to deal with a major crisis. Elliot Cohen, professor of strategic studies at Johns Hopkins University's School of Advanced International Studies, explains:

> We're picking up long-term commitments in various places. That causes a real strain. The basic rule of thumb is that, for every soldier deployed somewhere, you've got two others either going or coming back and another one or two who have to support the people deployed.23

Finally, there remains a possibility that domestic political pressures may compel some governments to request that the United States reduce troop deployments in the region. With the end of the Cold War, an increasing number of Japanese and Koreans believe that the "inconveniences" associated with protection under the U.S. security umbrella outweigh the benefits.24 As most U.S. forces in the region are stationed in Japan or South Korea (roughly 47,000 and 37,000, respectively), this development would greatly complicate the Western Pacific security equation.

Economic Tensions

With the end of the Cold War, the economic dimensions of U.S. foreign policy have assumed greater importance. Warren Christopher has stated that "we must elevate American economic security as a primary goal of our foreign policy."25 The U.S. public supports the new emphasis on economic affairs. In fact, public opinion polls reveal that "the preoccupation with the economy began to happen before the end of the Cold War . . . in the 1980s."[26]

Taiwan is the sixth largest trading partner of the United States. For roughly two decades, however, the island has enjoyed an enormous trade surplus with the United States. During the 1980s and early 1990s, Taipei was either the second or third largest contributor to Washington's spiraling trade deficit.[27]

In recent years, Taiwan has taken steps to reduce its trade surplus with the United States. It has lowered tariffs on agricultural items, opened its markets to U.S. liquor and tobacco products, and made concessions in response to U.S. demands for liberalization of its service sector. The appreciation of the NT dollar and the relocation of Taiwan's low-tech industries to the PRC also have helped reduce the trade imbalance. Consequently, Taiwan's trade surplus has dropped significantly (Table 10.4), and Taiwan now ranks as the fifth largest contributor to the U.S. trade deficit (Table 10.5).

Table 10.4   U.S. Trade Deficit with Taiwan, 1988–1994 (U.S.$ in millions)

	1988	1989	1990	1991	1992	1993	1994
Deficit with Taiwan	12,015	12,978	11,175	9,841	9,346	8,934	9,597

Source: U.S. Department of Commerce, International Trade Administration, *U.S. Foreign Trade Highlights, 1994* (Washington, D.C.: U.S. Government Printing Office, September 1995), p. 33.

Table 10.5   Top Ten Deficit Countries in U.S. Trade, 1994 (U.S.$ in millions)

Rank	Country	Amount
1	Japan	65,668
2	China	29,505
3	Canada	13,967
4	Germany	12,515
5	Taiwan	9,597
6	Italy	7,620
7	Malaysia	7,013
8	Thailand	5,441
9	Venezuela	4,332
10	Nigeria	3,921

Source: U.S. Department of Commerce, International Trade Administration, *U.S. Foreign Trade Highlights, 1994* (Washington, D.C.: U.S. Government Printing Office, September 1995), p. 33.

Although Taiwan's trade surplus has declined, it continues to be a major economic headache for the United States. The island's remaining import restrictions, currency manipulation, banking system, and lack of intellectual copyright protection are emerging as major issues of contention. U.S. officials also complain that "high tariffs remain on a number of products of U.S. export interest."[28]

Implications for Taiwan

As described, a wave of neoisolationist sentiment is gaining strength in the United States. At the same time, the United States is reducing its military presence in the Asia Pacific region and placing a greater emphasis on economic concerns. What implications do these developments hold for Taiwan?

With the end of the Cold War, the U.S. public is not as concerned about developments overseas. As Andrew Kohut, director of the Times-Mirror Center for the People and the Press, observed, this indifference extends to events in all regions of the world, including Asia:

> More than ever before, I think that the American public is indifferent to the specifics of what is going on in the world, in large part because the lack of a Communist threat has lessened the urgency with which Americans follow what is happening in the Balkans or what is happening in Africa or Asia.[29]

Asian defense specialists believe that this ambivalence is contributing to "the significantly reduced confidence of most regional countries in the U.S. commitment to intervene in future regional crises."[30]

With respect to Taiwan, public opinion polls reveal that an overwhelming majority of U.S. citizens now oppose sending military forces to help protect the island from a mainland invasion. In fact, a 1995 Harris poll found that only 22 percent of the U.S. public believed the United States should help defend Taiwan.[31] Taiwanese polls also indicate that, although most of the island's residents believe that the United States should help to defend Taiwan if attacked, only 39 percent believe that the United States will actually do so.[32] ROC officials believe that Taiwan must be prepared to defend itself without U.S. assistance. As one Kuomintang lawmaker observed, "the U.S. cares and supports us but it will not pay any price to protect our safety."[33]

Taiwanese officials also view the U.S. military drawdown in East Asia and the Western Pacific with apprehension. Some fear that "the U.S. military is gradually withdrawing from the Asia-Pacific region and the area is increasingly unstable."[34] President Lee Teng-hui also has warned that "with the end of the Cold War, the United States is gradually pulling its military presence out of Asia. A new emerging vacuum is creating major problems in Asia."[35]

Members of Taiwan's chief opposition party, the DPP, share the government's concern. They are especially troubled by the recent "flip-flops" in U.S. policy and an apparent unwillingness to counter the PRC's growing military capabilities:

> The role of the U.S., the former "Globocop," has been in a state of flux since the conclusion of the Cold War, with current U.S. foreign policy flip-flopping between globalism and regionalism. In response to the new Asian order, the U.S. is unwilling to expand its military development beyond maintaining forces in South Korea and Japan. The U.S. government understands well that the current U.S. military force in Asia is insufficient to resolve any Chinese military expansion or internal unrest.[36]

Finally, there is a strong possibility that the United States may adopt a tougher approach to trade problems with Asian countries in the future. Representative Doug Bereuter (Republican–Nebraska) echoed the sentiment of numerous U.S. lawmakers when he suggested that the end of the Cold War provides the United States with "a historic opportunity for an adjustment in the cost and benefits of our relationships with Japan, South Korea, Taiwan and even China, all of whom maintain serious barriers to our exports."[37] Taiwanese officials fear that persistent tensions in economic relations could ultimately jeopardize Taiwan's close relationship with the United States. Authorities acknowledge that differences over trade issues might "not only cause local exporters to lose their U.S. markets, but also adversely affect ROC-U.S. relations."[38] As the ROC is largely dependent upon the United States for its defensive needs, this development could complicate the island's security situation.

Notes

1. See Patrick J. Buchanan, "An America-First Foreign Policy," *Human Events,* May 2, 1992, pp. 6–7.

2. See prepared statement of Ted G. Carpenter, director, Foreign Policy Studies, Cato Institute, in *Funding Implications of the United States' Worldwide Presence,* U.S. Congress, House, Hearing Before the Task Force on Defense, Foreign Policy, and Space of the Committee on the Budget, 102d Congress, 1st Session, December 5, 1991, p. 41.

3. See Harvey Sicherman, "Winning the Peace in the Post–Cold War World," *Orbis* 37, No. 4, Fall 1993, p. 501.

4. Gerald Felix Warburg, *Conflict and Consensus: The Struggle Between Congress and the President over Foreign Policymaking* (New York: Harper & Row, 1989), p. 21.

5. For more information, see Theodore C. Sorensen, "U.S. Leadership Role Is in Doubt," *China Post* (International Airmail Edition), July 4, 1995, p. 2.

6. See Nigel Holloway, "Deficit Diplomacy," *Far Eastern Economic Review,* July 6, 1995, p. 23.

7. Walter R. Means, "The U.S. Role: Isolation? Pre-emptive Strikes," *China Post* (International Airmail Edition), March 6, 1995, p. 2.

8. See Johanna Neuman, "U.S. Status as Superpower 'Undiminished,'" *USA Today,* May 27, 1993, p. 8A.

9. Carol Giacomo, "Foreign Policy Mired in Confusion," *China Post* (International Airmail Edition), May 28, 1993, p. 2.

10. Ibid.

11. For more information, see Tom Raum, "Foreign Setbacks Fuel Isolationism," *China Post* (International Airmail Edition), October 14, 1993, p. 2.

12. Peter Rodman, "Points of Order," *National Review,* May 1, 1995, p. 36.

13. For a chronicle of President Clinton's foreign policy "flip-flops" toward China, see Lawrence T. DiRita, "Read My Flips: Clinton's Foreign Policy Reversals in His Own Words," *F.Y.I., The Heritage Foundation,* June 20, 1994, p. 5.

14. Testimony of Daniel Yankelovich, chairman, DYG, Inc. in *American Public Attitudes Toward Foreign Policy,* Hearing Before the Committee on Foreign Affairs, 103rd Congress, 2nd Session, July 27, 1994 (Washington, D.C.: U.S. Government Printing Office, 1994), p. 25.

15. Holloway, "Deficit Diplomacy," p. 23.

16. "U.S. in Asia Crucial to Stability, Says Thatcher," *Hong Kong Standard,* January 18, 1996, on the World Wide Web at *http://www.hkstandard.com/.*

17. U.S. Department of Defense, Office of International Security, *United States Security Strategy for the East Asia–Pacific Region* (Washington, D.C.: The Pentagon, February 1995), p. 23.

18. See U.S. Congress, General Accounting Office, *Impact of China's Military Modernization in the Pacific Region* (Washington, D.C.: U.S. General Accounting Office, June 1995), p. 37.

19. Quoted from Martin L. Lasater, "Bill Clinton and the Security of the ROC," *Issues and Studies* 29, No. 1, January 1993, p. 54.

20. Jim Mann, "Shift Seen in Administration's Asia Policies," *Los Angeles Times,* July 24, 1994, p. A4, in *Lexis/Nexis.*

21. See Jim Mann, "U.S. Troop Strength Is Questioned," *Los Angeles Times,* October 14, 1994, p. 25A, in *Lexis/Nexis.*

22. Ibid.

23. Ibid.

24. For more information, see Robert Burns, "Perry Encounters Doubts About Reliance on U.S.," *China Post* (International Airmail Edition), November 6, 1995, p. 2.

25. See Statement of Hon. Warren M. Christopher of California, nominee for secretary of state, in *Nomination of Warren M. Christopher to Be Secretary of State,* Hearing Before the Committee on Foreign Affairs, 103rd Congress, 1st Session, January 13 and 14, 1993 (Washington, D.C.: U.S. Government Printing Office, 1993), p. 19.

26. See testimony of Daniel Yankelovich in *American Public Attitudes Toward Foreign Policy,* p. 23.

27. For more information, see U.S. Department of Commerce, International Trade Administration, *U.S. Foreign Trade Highlights, 1991* (Washington, D.C.: U.S. Department of Commerce, May 1992).

28. See U.S. Trade Representative, *The 1995 National Trade Estimate Report on Foreign Trade Barriers* (Washington, D.C.: U.S. Government Printing Office, 1995), p. 290.

29. See testimony of Andrew Kohut, director, Times-Mirror Center for the People and the Press, in *American Public Attitudes Toward Foreign Policy,* p. 9.

30. Richard Halloran, "The Krulak Doctrine," *Far Eastern Economic Review,* September 28, 1995, p. 32.

31. When asked, "Should America fight to defend Taiwan?" 22 percent responded positively, 71 percent negatively, and 7 percent were not sure. Humphrey Taylor, "Americans Perceive Taiwan as a Separate and Independent Country from China; Majority Support U.S. Government Allowing the President of Taiwan to Visit U.S. Alma Mater," *The Harris Poll 1995*, No. 50, August 8, 1995, p. 5.

32. See Susan Yu, "Survey Finds Fears of War Amid Will to Defend Island," *Free China Journal*, August 18, 1995, p. 1.

33. Yeh Ching, "ROC Has to Rely on Itself: Survey," *China Post* (International Airmail Edition), August 15, 1995, p. 4.

34. Peter Seidlitz, "Russians Lead the Beijing Arms Race," *South China Morning Post*, July 18, 1993, p. 8.

35. See "President Li Teng-hui Holds News Conference," *China Broadcasting Corporation News Network* (Taipei), May 20, 1993, in *FBIS, China*, May 21, 1993, p. 70.

36. See Democratic Progressive Party, *Give Taiwan a Chance* (Taipei: Democratic Progressive Party, 1995), p. 2. Advance copy provided courtesy of Tom Hughes, DPP Department of Foreign Affairs.

37. Nigel Holloway, "No Retreat," *Far Eastern Economic Review*, September 28, 1995, p. 31.

38. Deborah Shen, "Groups Set Up to Avert Sanctions," *China Post* (International Airmail Edition), March 26, 1993, p. 1.

11

Conclusions

The preceding chapters provide an overview of Taiwan's security environment. They also explain how recent transformations in the international system are generating both opportunities and challenges for Taipei. This chapter suggests that, on balance, the end of the Cold War and a conjunction of long-term trends are combining to enhance the island's security. In this respect, recent modifications in the global system augur well for Taiwan's security. However, real threats to Taiwan remain. Especially worrisome are domestic political developments occurring within mainland China. These could offset some of the gains generated by systemic changes and hold important implications for Washington, Taipei, and the international community.

Taiwan's Security and the End of the Cold War

How has the end of the Cold War affected Taiwan's security environment? Although recent changes in global politics represent both dangers and opportunities for Taipei, it is likely that the challenges generated by systemic transformation are overstated.

The United States and Taiwan

As described in Chapter 10, the United States is sorting out its role in the post–Cold War world. But it is an exaggeration to suggest that the end of the era of superpower rivalry leaves the United States without a foreign policy focus in the Asia Pacific region. During the early twentieth century, the United States attempted to contain Japanese imperialism. Following World War II, U.S. policy shifted to prevent the spread of Soviet influence. In fact, as a U.S. Department of Defense study observed, U.S. policy in the Western Pacific has been "remarkably consistent over the past two centuries: peace and security; commercial access to the region; freedom of navigation; *and the prevention of the rise of any hegemonic power or coalition* [emphasis added]."[1]

The U.S. military drawdown in the Asia Pacific region is worrisome. But U.S. officials dispute claims that the United States is withdrawing from the region. Winston Lord, assistant secretary of state for East Asian and Pacific affairs, has testified before Congress that the Clinton administration is calling for little change in forces deployed in Asia and that "defense cuts have been at the expense of European bases and bases here at home."[2] Furthermore, Secretary of Defense William J. Perry has pledged that the United States is "committed to maintaining its current level of approximately 100,000 troops in Asia."[3] Taiwanese officials also acknowledge that they "are confident that the U.S. will not go so far as to withdraw forces from the region on a large scale."[4]

Public opinion polls reveal that isolationist sentiment is rising in the United States and that many people are indifferent to the specifics of what is going on in the world. But polls also show that a solid majority of the population still shares a "settled conviction that the United States has strong leadership responsibilities in the world."[5] The neoisolationist movement represents only a small, albeit vocal, segment of the populace.

With regard to Taiwan specifically, U.S. public opinion polls do indicate that a majority would oppose sending troops to help Taiwan. At the same time, however, more than 60 percent of the population believes that the island is either an ally or friend (Table 11.1) of the United States. Furthermore, as You Ying-lung, the DPP Campaign Policy Committee director, observed, "the figure of Americans supporting Washington sending troops to defend Taiwan is fairly high at a time when no sign of immediate war is at hand."[6] It is likely that this support would rise sharply if a U.S. president called on the military to rescue the island.[7]

Table 11.1 How the U.S. Public Views Taiwan (percentages of respondents)

Close ally	Friendly	Not friendly	Enemy	Not sure
14	50	22	5	8

Source: The Harris Poll 1995, No. 60, "Canada, Britain and Australia Top the List of Countries Which Americans Think of as Allies and Friends," October 2, 1995.

The Taiwan Relations Act does not specifically guarantee a U.S. response to an attack directed against Taiwan (the law provides the United States only with an *option* to defend Taiwan). Officials emphasize, however, that the law does not rule out U.S. military action. As cross-Strait relations deteriorated in early 1996, U.S. authorities drew parallels between U.S. actions in Korea in 1950 and in Taiwan in 1996. They stressed that the

United States originally did not include South Korea within its defensive perimeter, but nevertheless, U.S. troops were sent to repel North Korean aggression. Washington also dispatched two carrier battle groups to patrol the waters around Taiwan, and it warned Beijing that any attack directed against the island would not be tolerated and "could" lead to a U.S. military response.[8]

Finally, it is unlikely that economic tensions with Taipei will lead the United States to reduce its security commitment. Although the island is only a fraction of the size of the PRC, U.S. investment in Taiwan is higher than investment in mainland China, and U.S. exports to Taipei are double those to Beijing. Moreover, tensions over trade issues are decreasing. In 1993, Taiwan was moved from the U.S. Trade Representative's most severe Special 301 "priority foreign countries" list to the less stringent "priority watch" list. The following year, it was moved to the least serious "watch" list. After the passage of two key laws protecting intellectual property rights, most observers expect Taiwan to be removed entirely from the U.S. government's list in 1996 or 1997.[9]

PRC Military Capabilities

Chapter 9 suggested that the PRC's military buildup could represent a challenge to Taiwan's security. But China's leaders claim that it is motivated by a desire to correct glaring deficiencies in the People's Liberation Army. There is evidence to support this view.

Less than half of the PRC's submarine fleet is operational. In fact, as Paul Godwin, an authority on China's military, observed, "most of the Chinese Navy consists of junk."[10] Furthermore, as a majority of the PLA Air Force still flies 1960s era warplanes, Joseph Nye, U.S. assistant secretary of defense for international security affairs, has testified before Congress that the PLA is "not going to have an air force that's competitive for a decade. And I would think we're talking about a number of decades."[11]

It will take China several years to prepare production lines and start manufacturing Su-27 fighters. By that time, Taiwan will have enough F-16 and Mirage aircraft to handle the Russian warplanes. It also appears that most of the profits generated by the PLA's burgeoning network of 20,000 commercial enterprises, which range from hotels and discos to farms and real estate firms, is not being used to upgrade China's backward weapons systems. Rather, profits are being employed to raise the living standards of ordinary soldiers and provide officers with foreign automobiles and other luxuries.[12]

Most analysts agree that any invasion of Taiwan would be a massive military operation. Martin Lasater, a noted authority on Taiwan's security, explains:

During World War II, the U.S. estimated that it would take 300,000 American troops to defeat 32,000 Japanese ground forces then occupying Taiwan—a ten to one ratio. Assuming a very low three to one numerical advantage needed by the PLA to successfully invade Taiwan today, a minimum of 800,000–900,000 troops would be required to defeat Taiwan's standing army of 270,000 soldiers and 30,000 marines. The PLA figure would grow to astronomical levels if the ROC army reserves are added to its defense, which of course they would be.[13]

The international response to an attack—particularly the reaction of the United States—would raise costs further. Given such a scenario, it is hardly surprising that most security experts believe that decisionmakers in Beijing will calculate that the expected costs and risks (negative utilities) of attacking Taiwan outweigh the expected benefits (positive utilities). But would a determined or irrational China have the ability to take Taiwan?

Of course, China could traumatize Taiwan with missile attacks and/or a naval blockade. But launching a successful invasion of the island would be very risky. Su Jing-chang, a research fellow at Taiwan's prestigious Institute for National Policy Research, contends that the ROC is well positioned to defend itself against such an attack:

> Taiwan's military can't compare with the size of the PLA. But if you consider the special circumstances of island defense, our armed forces are basically sufficient to face the threat of a PLA assault. Levels of technology are more critical in modern warfare than numbers and the limited space of action around Taiwan will block the PLA from concentrating all their force on us.[14]

An Australian defense study concurs. The report observes that "expert assessments are that China would have poor prospects of successfully invading and occupying Taiwan in the next two years [1996 and 1997]. These prospects would diminish further in 1998 when Taiwan takes delivery of its F-16 and Mirage aircraft."[15] General John Shalikashvili, chairman of the U.S. military's Joint Chiefs of Staff, is even more confident. In February 1996, the general revealed that the U.S. military does "not believe they [the PRC] have the capability to conduct amphibious operations of the nature that would be necessary to invade Taiwan."[16]

A blockade would also prove to be a difficult and expensive undertaking. Having stockpiled a six-month oil reserve and invested heavily in nuclear energy, the island is capable of "holding out for about one year," according to military authorities.[17] Furthermore, Taiwan's new naval vessels, warplanes, and helicopters represent a significant boost to its antisubmarine warfare capabilities. Finally, it is difficult to envision how a blockade could fail to escalate quickly into conflict—one could hardly expect Taiwan to sit by as the PRC attempted to strangle it. In the event of a blockade, analysts believe Taiwan would use its "air force against mainland shipping and port targets, as well as the mining of PRC ports such as Shanghai."[18] In fact, high-ranking military officials have suggested that a blockade directed solely against Wuchiu, one of the ROC's smallest offshore islets, could lead the military "to call in air support to break it, which could risk escalation into a wider conflict."[19]

In sum, it appears that China's military power and its threat to Taiwan are exaggerated. However, a word of caution is in order. Although PRC military action against Taiwan is unlikely, it is not entirely outside the realm of possibility. Tai-ming Cheung, a noted Hong Kong–based military analyst, explains:

> It [an attack] all depends on the price the Chinese are willing to pay. If you look at it from a purely military perspective, and especially from a Western military perspective, the Chinese are not capable of mounting a major military operation to invade Taiwan. But Western intelligence agencies have always been caught by surprise. For example, they didn't anticipate the Chinese attacking Vietnam or coming into Korea.[20]

The Asian Arms Race

Chapter 9 also suggested that an Asian arms race could jeopardize peace and stability in the Asia Pacific region. Thus far, however, the arms race appears to be manageable. As Derek da Cunha, a Singaporean military analyst, observed, "so far, [it's] a friendly arms race."[21] Many believe that the increased defense spending in the region may be traced to a need to modernize outdated and obsolete Vietnam era military equipment. While acknowledging that some governments are purchasing expensive arms, Japanese defense specialists claim that "it is still not on the level of a full-blown arms race."[22]

Taiwanese Independence Movement

Perhaps most alarming for Taipei is the drive for Taiwanese independence—a movement emboldened by the end of the Cold War. Ralph N. Clough, an authority on Taiwanese politics, has described the independence movement as "a potentially explosive time bomb."[23] Whether the PRC would respond to a formal declaration of Taiwanese independence with an invasion, a naval blockade, or some other form of military pressure is unclear. However, General Zhang Wannian, vice chair of China's Central Military Commission, has vowed that, should the island declare itself independent, "we definitely will use force."[24]

Ironically, it would appear that one of the greatest threats to Taiwan's security in the post–Cold War world is Taiwan itself. But is sentiment for independence actually growing? Following the 1994 Qiandao Lake tour boat murders, support for independence reportedly jumped to an all-time high of 27 percent.[25] But public opinion polls also reveal that a vast majority of the Taiwanese population do not support de jure separation from mainland China. Furthermore, Taiwanese officials insist that many polls are inaccurate and that, as a consequence, support for independence is often exaggerated. More sophisticated polling techniques reveal that less than 10 percent of the Taiwanese population could be characterized as hard-core supporters of independence (Table 11.2).

Table 11.2 Public Opinion on the Future Development of Cross-Strait Relations (percentage of respondents)

Response	February 1994	April 1994	July 1994	October 1994	February 1995	June 1995	September 1995
Unification as soon as possible	4.2	2.5	3.5	3.7	3.2	3.4	3.3
Status quo leading to unification	23.4	18.3	17.2	18.9	21.4	23.1	24.2
Status quo, then decide on unification or independence	32.3	43.1	42.2	36.6	34.9	32.4	42.8
Status quo indefinitely	12.5	12.8	9.9	12.7	21.2	13.8	12.2
Status quo leading to independence	8.1	8.3	8.4	7.1	7.4	6.7	8.0
Independence as soon as possible	4.4	4.0	3.2	4.6	2.4	6.4	3.7
Don't know	15.8	11.0	15.6	16.3	9.6	14.2	3.9

Source: Election Study Center, National Chengchi University, Burke Marketing Research, Ltd., Taipei and China Credit Information Service. Poll provided to author courtesy of Su Chi, vice chairman, Mainland Affairs Council, Republic of China.

It also is noteworthy that the Democratic Progressive Party, the island's chief opposition party, seems to be backing away from its hard-line pro-independence stance.[26] In 1995, Shih Ming-teh, DPP chairman, said that the party would not declare Taiwan an independent state if it gained power because such a declaration would be unnecessary. As one party official explained, "Shih Ming-teh's remarks followed a certain logic. The DPP holds that Taiwan is already an independent state."[27] Such statements anger hard-core separatists—some of whom accuse the DPP of "abandoning its ideals."[28] But as Taiwan's voters now appear to be rejecting independence activists at the polls, the shift might more accurately be interpreted as an astute political maneuver.

Summary

Threats generated by the end of the Cold War are overstated. Despite some evidence to the contrary, the new international environment is helping enhance Taiwan's security. Strains in U.S.-PRC relations—tensions elevated in part by the end of the Cold War and the accompanying demise of the so-called strategic triangle—are helping Taipei strengthen its ties with Washington. Moreover, Western governments increasingly view arms sales to Taiwan as a means by which key corporations can make it through what is certain to be a painful transition away from a Cold War economy. These weapons boost the island's defensive capabilities, and thereby deter PRC aggression. Furthermore, the ROC's growing economic clout and democratization have prompted some governments to upgrade relations with Taiwan; several have elevated contacts with Taipei to a level just short of official recognition. These diplomatic successes enhance the ROC's international standing, bolster the position that it is a political entity, and undermine the PRC's claims of sovereignty over the island.

Taiwan's Security and Domestic Political Developments in the People's Republic of China

If Taiwan's security is enhanced by recent transformations in the international system, why is it so nervous? Why is the island described as one of the most dangerous places in the world?[29]

In international relations, it is possible to study phenomena from a variety of perspectives. Scholars refer to these viewpoints as the levels of analysis. Thus, one may study the global system, a nation-state, or an individual decisionmaker when attempting to explain state behavior.[30]

This study has focused primarily upon recent changes at the systemic or global level and their impact on Taiwan's security. On balance, these transformations have enhanced the island's security. However, changes occurring at another level of analysis—namely, domestic political developments occurring within China—could offset some of these gains. Samuel Ho, an analyst at Taiwan's Institute for International Relations, explains:

> It's very possible that, given the passing of the Cold War, Taiwan's international security is enhanced. But on the other hand, the interacting units, meaning the domestic politics in the PRC, may very well threaten Taiwan's security.[31]

The following discussion shows how domestic political trends within China—particularly the succession crisis and the rise of nationalism—jeopardize the island's safety.

China's Leadership Crisis

Due to the secretive nature of mainland China's government, analysts often must rely upon unconfirmed reports for information about high-level decisionmaking. But most available evidence suggests that Beijing is in the throes of a leadership crisis. Deng Xiaoping, China's elderly patriarch, no longer holds any official position and has not appeared in public for two years. His health is a matter of intense speculation.

Deng's frail condition complicates Taiwan's security environment. Until Beijing resolves the thorny succession issue (a process that could persist years after Deng's demise), China's leaders will be engaged in a power struggle. In this contest, no one can afford to appear "soft" on Taiwan. As Nancy Bernkopf Tucker, an authority on China's domestic politics, observed, "in the midst of a power struggle, it's hard to be seen as soft on anyone."[32]

During an interview with the author in early 1996, Fredrick Chien, Taiwan's foreign minister, suggested that Beijing's leadership crisis played a major role in the deterioration in cross-Strait relations during 1995 and 1996:

> I want to apologize first because as a Chinese I should not say these things. ... But I think the fact that Mr. Deng has been critically ill for so long and is not leading, that is a very critical point—the one reason—contributing to the "disquietness" within mainland China and contributing to the tension between the two sides and between the U.S. and the PRC. So, the earlier Deng departs, in my humble opinion, the better.[33]

Chien believes that only after the leadership crisis is resolved will Beijing be able to adopt a more realistic position toward Taiwan. The foreign minister also cautions, however, that a "showdown" could endanger the island:

> You have to have a showdown in the end. And in the end, it could be the hardliners who would win. Then, we all suffer. Then again, it could be those who are more pragmatic who will win. Then, we will fare much better.[34]

In short, the succession crisis in Beijing jeopardizes Taipei's safety, and there is no guarantee that its resolution will enhance the island's security.

Nationalism

Since 1989, the Socialist bloc has experienced a series of unparalleled crises and major reversals. Despite public displays of confidence and bravado, events in Eastern Europe and the Soviet Union have left China's hard-line leadership feeling more insecure at home and abroad.

In the aftermath of the 1989 Tiananmen Square incident, it was widely anticipated that the hard-line regime in Beijing would last no longer than one or two years. Officials in the U.S. Department of State warned that the PRC would experience "instability as Deng and other leaders struggle to sustain economic reform and openness to the outside world."[35] Taro Nakayama, then Japan's foreign minister, predicted that "the wave of historic changes cascading over Eastern Europe will also sweep the Asia-Pacific region, especially Communist North Korea and China."[36] Chang Shallyen, Taiwan's vice minister, opined that "this kind of situation [in China] cannot last any longer than two to three years—there will be fundamental change."[37]

As the 1990s progress, it is becoming increasingly obvious that the negative forecasts predicted by so many are not coming to pass. Indeed, the PRC government has proved to be remarkably resilient.

Beijing has employed a number of strategies to ensure the Chinese Communist Party's continued rule of mainland China.[38] Many of China's leaders share the belief that their survival may depend ultimately upon continued economic growth. Therefore, the government has undertaken economic measures making China one of the world's fastest-growing economies. Beijing also has taken steps to ensure the PLA's continued loyalty, and it has tightened security in China's restive border regions, namely, Xinjiang, Tibet, and Inner Mongolia. Finally, the regime has moved to replace the bankrupt ideology of Marxist-Leninist-Maoist thought with Chinese nationalism.

As part of its effort to hold on to power, the Communist government is taking refuge in nationalism. Officials are using appeals to national pride to hold the country together and to legitimize their continued rule. James Lilley, former U.S. ambassador to China, outlines Beijing's reasoning:

> Communism doesn't work anymore. What can we use? The answer is nationalism and a powerful military. Standing up to the world. Greater China is the wave of the future, they tell their people.[39]

Beijing's appeals to patriotism could jeopardize Taiwan's security. Some officials now call for China's unification with Taiwan at any cost. Not surprisingly, many of the most blood-curdling war cries are coming from the "hawks" within the top echelons of the PLA. As one diplomat explained, "the military has no interest in war, but they have an interest in a permanent state of instability in the region . . . it's good for budgets, and for ensuring their irrefutable place in the power structure."[40]

Summary

Systemic variables play an important role in state behavior. A world with two dominant states—superpowers—differs in many ways from a multipolar world or a world with only one superpower. But systemic variables are not the only determinants of a state's behavior. Phenomena occurring at other levels of analysis also influence outcomes. In Taiwan's case, the PRC's leadership crisis and the sense of nationalism that is sweeping China could have a devastating impact on the island's security. At a minimum, they complicate Taiwan's security equation and make it difficult for the two sides to discuss sensitive issues.[41]

Implications for U.S. Policy

If systemic changes are enhancing Taiwan's security while domestic political developments within the PRC are jeopardizing the island's security, how will Taiwan's security situation evolve in coming decades? Will the probability of military confrontation across the Taiwan Strait increase or decrease? What are the implications for U.S. policy? These are difficult questions to address. In fact, forecasts about Taiwan's future security environment vary significantly.

Some believe that the chances for military conflict between the two Chinas are negligible. During his 1991 visit to Taiwan, former president Gerald R. Ford was asked how the United States might respond if the PRC attacked Taiwan. Ford replied, "that day [for an attack] is over."[42] Howard Baker, former White House chief of staff, also believes that "the likelihood of an invasion of Taiwan is very, very small, virtually impossible."[43]

Even during the midst of the 1996 Taiwan Strait crisis, U.S. officials discounted the possibility of a Chinese invasion. As William Perry, U.S. secretary of defense, explained, "I do not expect China to be attacking Taiwan. I do not think there is a long-term problem in that regard, simply because the fundamentals argue so strongly against it."[44] Former president George Bush concurred. Bush said, "I am confident there will be no war. . . . It's not in China's interest to take Taiwan by force."[45]

Others have suggested that China's threat to Taiwan is very real and that the probabilities for hostilities will rise during the 1990s. In 1994, Thomas W. Robinson, president of the American Asian Research Enterprise, predicted that "Taiwan will, in all probability, become a major security issue sometime in the 1990s, more likely in the last few years of the decade than in the next several."[46] Martin Lasater, president of the Pacific Council and research associate at Pennsylvania State University, also believes that "Peking's threat to Taiwan in the 1990s will be somewhat higher than in the 1980s, despite the greater interaction across the Taiwan Strait."[47]

Still others believe the PRC is unlikely to threaten Taiwan during the 1990s. Paul H. Kreisberg, a senior research associate at the East-West Center, suggests that Beijing "is unlikely to use force to challenge its neighbors or the U.S. in the 1990s. . . . Chinese economic development will be a strong disincentive for it to use force to change the political status quo."[48] Niu Hsien-chung, a Taiwanese military strategist, agrees. He believes that "the Communist Chinese military will not attack Taiwan before the year 2000. . . . Beijing will be preoccupied with resolving the thorny problems related to retrocession of Hong Kong and Macau until the turn of the century."[49] At the same time, however, Niu warns that "Taiwan will be at an increased risk of attack during the years 2001 to 2010."[50]

It is to be expected that analyses about Taiwan's future security situation will vary significantly. Indeed, the further ahead an analyst is required to look, the greater the degree of uncertainty, miscalculation, and error.[51] More often than not, the most that a long-term forecast can do is alert one to the various possibilities and their likely impact. The discussion below examines several ways Taiwan's future could develop in coming decades and the implications for U.S. policy.

Peaceful and Negotiated Unification with China

Both sides of the Taiwan Strait agree that there is only one China and that Taiwan is a part of China. As discussed in previous chapters, however, they do not agree on the terms for national unification.

Should Taipei and Beijing overcome this impasse and negotiate unification, Washington may adjust its policies accordingly. Arms sales to the island might be reduced, and the TRA could be revised or revoked.[52] The Taiwan question—a lingering issue of contention in Sino-U.S. relations—would cease to exist. One might expect an improvement in U.S.-PRC relations. After all, from the PRC's viewpoint, it is the U.S. government, not the authorities on Taiwan, that stands in the way of a peaceful unification of China. Authorities in the PRC have long insisted that U.S. support for Taiwan—particularly the steady supply of U.S. arms—encourages the Kuomintang to reject Beijing's unification overtures.

In his 1996 inaugural address, Lee Teng-hui made a bold proposal to travel to mainland China on a "journey of peace." As it stands, however, there is little chance for peaceful unification. Indeed, while a cross-Strait summit and direct exchanges are distinct possibilities, it would be extremely unrealistic to expect a sudden "breakthrough" in Taiwan-mainland relations leading to unification.

China's socialist system holds little appeal for Taiwan. But more than economic systems separates the two sides of the Taiwan Strait. While an explosion in trade and investment is moving the Taiwanese and Chinese economies closer together, mounting social and political differences are pushing the two societies further apart. An increasing number of Taiwanese—particularly the younger generation and/or those who have visited China—view the mainland as poor, dirty, and backward.[53] They also are dismayed and disheartened by the spiraling social problems plaguing

Chinese society. In sum, few Taiwanese favor unification, and it is unlikely that support for unification, will grow in coming decades.

De Jure Independence from China

Since the end of the Cold War, the separatist movement in Taiwan has grown in popular support. But China will not tolerate the establishment of an independent Republic of Taiwan. In fact, Taiwan's independence is now identified as one of the four major threats confronting China.[54]

As the cross-Strait crises of 1995 and 1996 demonstrated, Taiwan's "China problem" will not go away. Following the 1989 Tiananmen Square incident, some glibly prophesied that the PRC's days were numbered. But these individuals were mistaken. Moreover, it would be a mistake to assume that a successor government or a new generation of Chinese leaders will forsake all claims to Taiwan.

The Taiwan question has become an irredentist issue in Chinese politics. As Roderick MacFarquhar, professor of Chinese politics at Harvard University, observed, "No leadership could allow Taiwan to do what it wants, and if it wanted independence accept that, because they would be so weak and this has been an issue so long, they would not be able to take that political risk, even if no one in China gave a damn."[55]

At the same time, China's leaders fear that Taiwan's independence could trigger a spiral of events culminating in turmoil, dissolution, and collapse. During an interview with the author, retired general Chiang Wego explained why PRC officials would consider it their "duty" to attack a breakaway Taiwan:

> Since they [the PRC] think they are the central government, how could they let any part of the PRC be independent? If Taiwan can be independent, Tibet can be independent, Xinjiang can be independent, Inner Mongolia can be independent—the whole country could fall apart.[56]

Public opinion polls reveal that a majority of Taiwanese believe that Beijing will attack if the island declares itself independent.[57] U.S. analysts agree that if Taiwan attempts "to move from de facto [independence] to de jure [independence], then the chances of a provocative PRC response are very high."[58] As such, Taiwanese independence could hold potentially disastrous consequences for the United States, which might have to fight to protect Taiwan. After all, the TRA's provisions of support for the ROC appear to apply equally to an independent Republic of Taiwan.[59]

Would the United States go to war to protect Taiwan? It is likely that a U.S. response to that question would depend upon the events that led up to an attack:

If an invasion were unprovoked, a U.S. military response would be more likely. If provoked by a Taiwan declaration of independence or political instability in the island, U.S. action would probably be somewhat less likely.[60]

In other words, conflict with China over Taiwanese independence is not a certainty. At a minimum, however, the issue would present Washington with "a problem that deserves a lot of attention."[61] The United States would have to be prepared to defend Taiwan indefinitely against PRC attack or be prepared to accept the PRC's conquest of the island.

Maintaining the Status Quo

When commenting on the state of ROC-PRC relations, Thomas Gold once observed that "the status quo is not static."[62] Recent years have witnessed an explosion in linkages across the Taiwan Strait. Contacts unthinkable only a few years ago have become common occurrences. It is estimated that several million Taiwanese compatriots have traveled to the mainland since travel restrictions were eased in the late 1980s, and Taiwanese trade and investment in the PRC has soared.[63] Moreover, a formal channel for ROC-PRC communication—albeit an indirect one—has been established.

These developments ultimately could lead the two Chinese governments into a more stable and harmonious relationship. But these changes in cross-Strait relations should not be exaggerated. It would be unrealistic to suggest that China and Taiwan are moving toward unification. Indeed, as most Taiwanese oppose both de jure independence and unification, it would seem that the majority favor a continuation of the status quo.[64] Interestingly, cross-Strait tensions in 1996 bolstered this sentiment. Public opinion polls found that support for both unification and independence suffered during the crisis, whereas support for the status quo increased markedly.[65]

For almost fifty years, Taiwan has enjoyed de facto independence from China. On the face of it, there is no compelling reason why this arrangement should not be sustainable for the next fifty years. So long as the United States complies with the provisions of the TRA—providing Taiwan with a sufficient self-defense capability—and Taipei maintains its claim to be the Republic of China, the probabilities for armed conflict across the Taiwan Strait should remain low.

Implications for U.S. Policy

The maintenance of the status quo—the continued separation of two rival Chinese states—appears most likely during the short- to medium-term future. But when looking at Taiwan's long-term security prospects, the outlook becomes murky. Indeed, most Taiwanese express uncertainty when asked about the island's long-term future.[66] The question remains open as to how much longer the people on Taiwan—East Asia's noisiest democracy—will tolerate an existence stranded somewhere in the twilight zone of international politics. But as any move from de facto to de jure independence would likely trigger a military response from China—an act that would undermine peace and stability in the Asia Pacific region and thereby threaten vital U.S. interests—it is *not* in the U.S. interest to promote, assist, or otherwise encourage Taiwanese independence.

Present U.S. security strategy calls for maintaining a strong, constructive relationship with both mainland China and Taiwan. It is likely that a solid, productive relationship with both Chinese governments will continue to serve U.S. interests in coming years. U.S. security policy toward Taiwan should be developed accordingly.

With regard to Taiwan's long-range security situation, the following recommendations seem paramount.

- The United States should maintain the present policy toward Taiwan's security. The TRA provides the United States with an *option* to defend Taiwan, but a U.S. response is not guaranteed. This situation enables Washington to establish a linkage between U.S. policy and the policies and actions of other states, and it contains an element of uncertainty that may lead both militarists in Beijing and separatists in Taipei to act with restraint. As executive branch officials now concede that the TRA takes precedence over all communiqués, there is no need to amend, alter, or otherwise revise the TRA or the communiqués.
- In the event of another cross-Strait crisis, the United States should resist calls that it make clear its intentions lest Beijing "miscalculate" and attack. Rather than revise the TRA, the White House should be encouraged to use the law. The delivery of arms could be expedited or weapons systems previously denied to Taiwan might be approved. In fact, there is a wide spectrum of options available, ranging from economic sanctions to direct U.S. military assistance.
- In keeping with the terms of the TRA, the United States should continue to provide Taiwan with such weapons as may be necessary for its security and an adequate defensive capability. These arms help deter a PRC attack by keeping military action prohibitively costly. When assessing Taiwan's defensive needs, U.S. officials should consider the defense buildups undertaken by the island's neighbors.
- The United States should maintain the present policy toward the future of Taiwan. As the United States has not committed itself to any particular solution to the Taiwan issue (except that it be peaceful), it may adapt easily to practically any eventuality. At the same time, the present policy enables the United States to avoid becoming entangled in cross-Strait nego-

tiations or playing a role as guarantor of any future agreement. The United States also should avoid statements supporting "unification," "plebiscites," and "self-determination," as they serve only to inflame passions in mainland China and/or Taiwan.

- Although reductions in force levels may be inevitable, the United States should continue to maintain a forward military presence in the Western Pacific region to help deter aggression. Furthermore, military planners should study ways in which the United States might be able to assist Taiwan should such a need ever arise.

- Despite Beijing's opposition, the United States should actively support Taiwan's inclusion in international governmental organizations (IGOs). As Beijing has acquiesced—albeit reluctantly—to Taipei's admission to some institutions (APEC and ADB), it will tolerate Taiwan's membership in other organizations. As one of the world's largest trading nations and the owner of more than U.S.$80 billion in foreign reserves, Taiwan could play a constructive role in the World Bank, the International Monetary Fund, and many other IGOs. At the same time, inclusion in IGOs helps dampen sentiment for de jure independence from China.[67]

- The United States should not reestablish official ties with Taiwan, but it should continue the review of U.S.-Taiwan relations initiated by the Clinton administration. Recent changes—including permission for Taipei to change the name of its representative office in the United States—are a step in the right direction. But other subtle changes are also in order. In other words, Taiwan—the most democratic society in Chinese history—should be treated with a modicum of respect. Humiliating Taiwanese government authorities will only encourage Taiwan's separatist movement.

- Although the United States should not attempt to mediate the unification issue, Taipei and Beijing should be encouraged to talk to each other. To this end, they need to expand negotiations so that they can better understand each other and find common ground to build on. This is the only sensible approach to the thorny Taiwanese identity issue, and public opinion polls reveal that such talks enjoy widespread support in Taiwan.

- The United States should seek out ways to somehow persuade the Chinese leadership to adopt a more mature approach toward Taiwan. After all, this vibrant democracy is not going to agree to unification under China's present terms, and bullying Taiwan only fuels the island's separatist movement.

Conclusion

Although the end of the Cold War and a conjunction of long-term trends are combining to enhance Taiwan's security, nothing can *guarantee* the island's security—no state is perfectly capable of fully satisfying its national security needs. Of course, occasional crises in cross-Strait relations may be expected, and some might prove severe. Unfortunately, such problems are unavoidable. But so long as Taiwan resists calls for de jure separation from China and maintains a military force sufficient to deter the PRC, the probabilities for conflict across the Taiwan Strait should remain at a manageable level.

With regard to Taiwan's long-term security prospects, it is likely that circumstances occasionally may dictate some subtle adjustments in U.S. relations with Taiwan. However, the United States should not revise its overall position toward Taiwan's security—it should continue to comply with the provisions of the TRA and make available to Taiwan such arms as may be necessary to enable the island to maintain a sufficient self-defense capability. Furthermore, despite changes in the international system, the United States should not revise its policy on Taiwan's future—it should continue to resist calls that it become involved in issues relating to Chinese "unification" or Taiwanese "self-determination." The current policy toward Taiwan's security and future, albeit vague and ambiguous, will continue to serve U.S. interests in the post–Cold War era.

Notes

1. See U.S. Department of Defense, Office of International Security Affairs, *United States Security Strategy for the East-Asia Pacific Region* (Washington, D.C.: The Pentagon, February 1995), p. 5.

2. See Peter Grier, "U.S. Defense Goals Reflect Rising Importance of Asia," *Christian Science Monitor,* November 17, 1993, p. 13.

3. William J. Perry, secretary of defense, *Annual Report to the President and the Congress* (Washington, D.C.: U.S. Government Printing Office, February 1995), p. 29.

4. See Dennis Van Vranken Hickey, "Special Report: Interview with Sun Chen, Taiwan's Defense Minister," *Asian Defense Journal,* February 1994, pp. 30–35.

5. See Statement of Andrew Kohut, director, Times-Mirror Center for the People and the Press, in *American Public Attitudes Toward Foreign Policy,* U.S. Congress, House, Hearing Before the Committee on Foreign Affairs, 103rd Congress, 2nd Session, July 27, 1994 (Washington, D.C.: U.S. Government Printing Office, 1994), p. 7.

6. Yeh Ching, "ROC Has to Rely on Itself: Survey," *China Post* (International Airmail Edition), August 15, 1995, p. 4.

7. There is a historical tendency of the public to go along with most foreign policy initiatives. For example, although only 7 percent of the U.S. public favored an invasion of Cambodia in early 1970, 50 percent favored it after President Richard Nixon announced the "incursion." For more information, see Charles W. Kegley, Jr., and Eugene R. Wittkopf, *American Foreign Policy: Pattern and Process,* 3rd ed., (New York: St. Martin's Press, 1987), p. 307.

8. Bill Wang, "U.S. Will Not Tolerate Attack on Taiwan," *CNA* (Taipei), March 19, 1996.

9. See Debbie Kuo, "ROC May Get Off the 'List,'" *China Post* (Domestic Edition), February 5, 1996, p. 1.

10. See Simon Beck, "Taiwan 'Safe from Invasion,'" *South China Morning Post,* September 15, 1995, p. 13, in *Lexis/Nexis*.

11. Testimony of Joseph Nye, U.S. assistant secretary of defense for international security affairs, in *Growth and Role of the Chinese Military,* Hearing of the East Asian and Pacific Affairs Subcommittee, October 11, 1995, Federal News Service, 1995, p. 23.

12. See "Giving the PLA the Business," *Asian Wall Street Journal,* May 31, 1994, p. 8.

13. Martin Lasater, *U.S. Interests in the New Taiwan* (Boulder, Colorado: Westview Press, 1993), p. 154.

14. See Dennis Engbarth, "The Price of Invasion," *South China Morning Post,* August 24, 1995, p. 19, in *Lexis/Nexis*.

15. This report was leaked to the press in 1996. For more information, see "Invasion Unlikely Says Secret Australian Report," *Hong Kong Standard,* January 26, 1996, on the World Wide Web at *http://www.hkstandard.com/*.

16. "China Can't Take Taiwan by Force, Says Top U.S. General," *Hong Kong Standard,* February 16, 1996, on the World Wide Web at *http://www.hkstandard.com/*.

17. "Peking Might Be Eyeing an Invasion of Taiwan, with World's Attention Focused on Middle East," *Free China Journal,* November 19, 1990, p. 2.

18. Lasater, *U.S. Interests in the New Taiwan*, p. 148.

19. See "ROC to Counter If Islet Attacked," *China Post* (International Airmail Edition), February 28, 1996, p. 4.

20. Ron Tempest, "How Far Will Beijing Go to Rein in Taiwan?" *China Post* (International Airmail Edition), February 23, 1996, p. 4.

21. See Clayton Jones, "Search for Security in the Pacific," *Christian Science Monitor,* November 17, 1993, p. 12.

22. See Robert Birsel, "Prosperous Asia Buying More Arms," *China Post* (International Airmail Edition), January 22, 1996, p. 2.

23. "A New Timebomb," *CNA* (Taipei), August 29, 1992, in *Lexis/Nexis*.

24. Susan V. Lawrence with Tim Zimmerman, "A Political Test of When Guns Matter," *U.S. News & World Report,* October 30, 1995, p. 47.

25. See Alice Hung, "27% Support Independence," *China Post* (International Airmail Edition), April 18, 1994, p. 1.

26. Shih Ming-teh, the DPP's new chairman and an advocate of Taiwanese independence, has asserted that he will not abruptly declare Taiwan's independence if elected president. Shih claims, "If I become the head of state, I will not make such an announcement without taking into consideration the wishes of all the people in Taiwan." As the vast majority of Taiwanese oppose independence, such a declaration would be a remote possibility. See "Shih Ming-teh Elected Head of DPP," *China Post* (International Airmail Edition), May 2, 1994, p. 1.

27. "DPP Repeats Independence Stand," *China Post* (International Airmail Edition), September 16, 1995, p. 4.

28. "See "New Alliance to Seek Independence," *China News,* February 6, 1996, p. 1.

29. See Victor Lai and Danielle Yang, "Taiwan Strait World's Riskiest Area: Paper," *China Post* (International Airmail Edition), January 2, 1996, p. 1.

30. J. David Singer, the scholar often credited with introducing the idea of levels of analysis, discussed only two broad levels: the international system and the nation-state. In later studies, analysts have identified more levels. For more infor-

mation, see James N. Rosenau, *The Scientific Study of Foreign Policy* (London: Frances Pinter, 1980).

31. Author's interview with Samuel Ho, Institute of International Relations, Taipei, Taiwan, February 8, 1996.

32. George Gedda, "With the Cold War Over, U.S.-Beijing Ties Begin to Suffer," *China Post* (International Airmail Edition), July 17, 1995, p. 2.

33. Author's interview with Fredrick Chien, foreign minister, Republic of China, Taipei, Taiwan, February 8, 1996.

34. Ibid.

35. "Widespread Abuses Seen Since Tiananmen Massacre" (Text: Solomon Testimony Before House Panel), *East Asia/Pacific Wireless File #036* (Shanghai, PRC: Press and Cultural Section, Consulate General of the United States, February 22, 1990), EPF 404, p. 1.

36. See "Democracy Wave to Hit Asia, Nakayama Says," *Japan Times*, December 12, 1989, p. 3.

37. Author's interview with Chang Shallyen, vice minister for foreign affairs, Republic of China, Taipei, Taiwan, February 15, 1990.

38. For a complete discussion, see Dennis Van Vranken Hickey, "The Crises of Communism and the Prospects for Change in the People's Republic of China," *Asian Affairs* 19, No. 4, Winter 1993, pp. 195–205.

39. Testimony of James Lilley, former ambassador to China, in *Future of United States–China Policy,* U.S. Congress, House, Joint Hearings Before the Subcommittees on Economic Policy, Trade and Environment; International Security, International Organizations and Human Rights; and Asia and the Pacific of the Committee on Foreign Affairs, 103rd Congress, 1st Session, May 20, 1993 (Washington, D.C.: U.S. Government Printing Office, 1993), p. 47.

40. See Nayan Chanda, "The New Nationalism," *Far Eastern Economic Review,* November 9, 1995, p. 23.

41. Lee Teng-hui, Taiwan's president, has stated that "if Jiang survives [the power struggle], it may be a very good time for talking. Before that, it will be difficult." See Susan Yu, "Lee Links High-Level Talks to Mainland Tilt for Power," *Free China Journal,* May 17, 1996, p. 1.

42. "Former President Ford Exchanges Views with Lee Teng-hui on Global Affairs," *China Post* (International Airmail Edition), June 10, 1991, p. 1.

43. "U.S. Committed to Taiwan's Freedom: Howard Baker," *Free China Journal,* November 12, 1990, p. 2.

44. See Han Nai-kuo, "U.S. Defense Secretary Perry Negates Chances of Mainland Attack on Taiwan," *CNA* (Taipei), February 28, 1996.

45. "Bush Says There Will Be No War," *Hong Kong Standard,* March 22, 1996, on the World Wide Web at *http://www.hkstandard.com/*.

46. Thomas W. Robinson, "Post–Cold War Security in the Asia-Pacific Region," in Zhiling Lin and Thomas W. Robinson (eds.), *The Chinese and Their Future* (Washington, D.C.: AEI Press, 1994), p. 403.

47. Martin Lasater, "Taiwan's Security in the 1990s," *Asian Outlook* 25, No. 6, September–October 1990, p. 1.

48. See Testimony of Paul H. Kreisberg, senior research associate, East-West Center, in *Regional Threats and Defense Options for the 1990s,* U.S. Congress, House, Hearings Before the Defense Policy Panel and the Department of Energy Defense Nuclear Facilities Panel of the Committee on Armed Services, 102nd Congress, 2nd Session, March 10, 1993 (Washington, D.C.: U.S. Government Printing Office, 1993), p. 383.

49. Debbie Kuo, "Expert Rules Out Beijing Military Attack Before 2000," *CNA* (Taipei), March 26, 1994, in *Lexis/Nexis*.

50. Ibid.

51. See Paul Hawkins, "The Analytics of Country Reports and Checklists," in Ronald L. Solberg (ed.), *Country Risk-Analysis: A Handbook* (New York: Routledge, 1991), p. 29.

52. Interestingly, PRC officials have stated that Taiwan could maintain its own military after unification. It is not clear, however, why Taiwan would need its own military or whether it could continue to purchase foreign arms.

53. Surveys have revealed that visitors are appalled by the mainland's social problems and backward living conditions, and often return with lower expectations for political reconciliation between Taipei and Beijing. For more information, see Julian Baum, "Nice Place to Visit . . ," *Far Eastern Economic Review*, October 18, 1990, p. 32.

54. See "Beijing 'War Plan' in Bid to Isolate Taiwan," *South China Morning Post* (Weekly Edition), September 10–11, 1994, p. 1. The three other "major threats" to China are (1) U.S. and Western attempts to contain China, (2) the challenge posed by the rapid economic growth of other Asia Pacific nations, and (3) instability in countries and areas of critical importance to China such as North Korea.

55. See Testimony of Roderick MacFarquhar in *The Future of Communist Systems in Asia*, U.S. Congress, House, Hearing Before the Subcommittee on Asian and Pacific Affairs of the Committee on Foreign Affairs, 102nd Congress, 1st Session, November 22, 1991 (Washington, D.C.: U.S. Government Printing Office, 1992), p. 55.

56. Author's interview with General (ret.) Wego W. K. Chiang, Taipei, Taiwan, May 17, 1994.

57. See "Most People Believe Pro-Independence Move to Provoke Peking Invasion," *CNA*, October 21, 1991, in *Lexis/Nexis*.

58. See Testimony of Professor Harry Harding, senior fellow, Foreign Policy Department, Brookings Institution, in *The Future of U.S. Foreign Policy (Part I): Regional Issues*, U.S. Congress, House, Hearings Before the Committee on Foreign Affairs, 103rd Congress, 1st Session, February 2, 3, 17, 23, 24, and March 18, 1993 (Washington, D.C.: U.S. Government Printing Office, 1993), p. 135.

59. According to Section 15 of the TRA, the provisions of the law apply to "the governing authorities on Taiwan recognized by the United States as the Republic of China prior to January 1, 1979, and *any successor governing authorities* (including political subdivisions, agencies and instrumentalities thereof)."

60. John Copper, "ROC Must Stay Alert," *Free China Journal*, October 15, 1990, p. 5.

61. Kenneth Lieberthal, professor of Chinese studies, Michigan University, made this observation. For more information, see Han Hai-kuo, "U.S. Urged to Resolve 'Taiwan Question,'" *CNA* (Taipei), May 11, 1994, in *Lexis/Nexis*.

62. Thomas B. Gold, "The Status Quo Is Not Static: Mainland-Taiwan Relations," *Asian Survey* 27, No. 3, March 1987, p. 315.

63. According to unofficial estimates, Taiwan's investment in the PRC now stands at more than U.S.$15 billion. For more information, see "Investment in Mainland Declines 20%," *China News*, May 27, 1994, p. 12.

64. As described, a majority (78.8 percent) of Taiwan's residents oppose unification under Beijing's "one-country, two-systems" scheme. At the same time, a plurality (45.6 percent) oppose a formal declaration of independence from China. Paradoxically, few (11.4 percent) claim to support the status quo. See Sofia Wu, "Beijing's Intentions Toward Taiwan Doubted: Poll," *CNA*, November 29, 1993, in

Lexis/Nexis; and Dennis Engbarth, "Lake Deaths Boost Bid for Breakaway," *South China Morning Post,* April 18, 1994, p. 8.

65. See "Beijing's Threats Cut Both Ways in Taiwan," *China Post* (Domestic Edition), February 2, 1996, p. 20.

66. Forty-two percent believe that the status quo between Taiwan and China will be maintained during the coming five years, 14.3 percent believe that would be the case ten years from now, and only 7.9 percent believe that would be case in thirty years. For more information, see Dennis Engbarth, "Lake Deaths Boost Bid for Breakaway."

67. Independence activists argue that an independent Republic of Taiwan, as opposed to the Republic of China, could more easily gain admission to IGOs and reintegrate into the global community. Public opinion polls reveal that approximately 40 percent of the island's residents believe that support for independence will grow if Beijing continues to block Taiwan's drive to rejoin the international community. See Bear Lee, "Most People Want Equal Footing with Mainland," *CNA* (Taipei), August 3, 1994, in *Lexis/Nexis.*

SELECT BIBLIOGRAPHY

Books

Abshire, David M., and Allen, Richard V., eds. *National Security: Political, Military and Economic Strategies in the Decade Ahead.* New York: Praeger, 1963.

Allison, Graham, and Treverton, Gregory F., eds. *Rethinking America's Security: Beyond Cold War to New World Order.* New York: W. W. Norton and Company, 1992.

Atlantic Council of the United States and National Committee on United States–China Relations. *United States and China Relations at a Crossroads.* Washington, D.C.: Atlantic Council of the United States, 1993.

Bader, William B., and Bergner, Jeffrey T. *The Taiwan Relations Act: A Decade of Implementation.* Indianapolis, Indiana: Hudson Institute, 1989.

Bailey, Thomas A. *A Diplomatic History of the American People.* Englewood Cliffs, New Jersey: Prentice-Hall, 1974.

Baldwin, Robert E. *The Political Economy of U.S.-Taiwan Trade.* Ann Arbor: University of Michigan Press, 1995.

Barnett, A. Doak. *U.S. Arms Sales: The China-Taiwan Tangle.* Washington, D.C.: The Brookings Institution, 1982.

Betts, Richard, ed. *Conflict After the Cold War: Arguments on Causes of War and Peace.* New York: Macmillan Publishing, 1994.

Borg, Dorothy, and Heinrichs, Waldo, eds. *Uncertain Years: Chinese-American Relations, 1947–1950.* New York: Columbia University Press, 1980.

Brzezinski, Zbigniew. *Power and Principle.* New York: Farrar, Straus and Giroux, 1983.

Bueler, William M. *U.S. China Policy and the Problem of Taiwan.* Boulder: Colorado Associated University Press, 1971.

Buzan, Barry. *People, States and Fear: The National Security Problem in International Relations.* Chapel Hill: University of North Carolina Press, 1983.

———. *People, States and Fear: An Agenda for International Security Studies in the Post–Cold War Era,* 2d edition. Boulder, Colorado: Lynne Rienner Publishers, 1991.

Caldwell, John. *China's Conventional Military Capabilities, 1994–2004: An Assessment.* Washington, D.C.: Center for Strategic and International Studies, 1994.

Chang, Jaw-ling Joanne. *United States–China Normalization: An Evaluation of Foreign Policy Decision Making.* Baltimore: University of Maryland School of Law OPRSCAS, 1986 (Copublished with Monograph Series in World Affairs, University of Denver, Colorado).

Chang, King-yuh. *ROC-U.S. Relations Under the Taiwan Relations Act: Practice*

and Prospects. Taipei: Institute of International Relations, National Chengchi University, 1988.
Chang, Parris H., and Lasater, Martin L., eds. *If China Crosses the Taiwan Strait: The International Response.* Lanham, Maryland: University Press of America, Inc., 1993.
Chen, Min. *Understanding the Process of Doing Business in China, Taiwan and Hong Kong: A Guide for International Executives.* Lewiston, New York: Edward Mellen Press, 1993.
Cheng, Chu-yuan. *Behind the Tiananmen Massacre: Social, Political and Economic Ferment in China.* Boulder, Colorado: Westview Press, 1990.
Cheng, Tun-jen, and Haggard, Stephan, eds. *Political Change in Taiwan.* Boulder, Colorado: Lynne Rienner Publishers, 1992.
Chiao, Chiao Hsieh. *Strategy for Survival.* London: Sherwood Press, 1985.
China in Crisis: The Role of the Military. Alexandria, Virginia: Jane's Defence Data, 1989.
Chiu, Hungdah, ed. *China and the Taiwan Issue.* New York: Praeger, 1979.
Clark, Cal. *Taiwan's Development: Implications for Contending Political Economy Paradigms.* New York: Greenwood Press, 1989.
Claude, Innis L. *Power and International Relations.* New York: Random House, 1962.
Clough, Ralph N. *Island China.* Cambridge, Massachusetts: Harvard University Press, 1978.
———. *Reaching Across the Taiwan Strait: People-to-People Diplomacy.* Boulder, Colorado: Westview Press, 1993.
Cohen, Marc J. *Taiwan at the Crossroads: Human Rights, Political Development and Social Change on the Beautiful Island.* Washington, D.C.: Asia Resource Center, 1988.
Cohen, Warren. *America's Response to China: A History of Sino-American Relations,* 3d edition. New York: Columbia University Press, 1990.
Congressional Quarterly. *China Policy Since 1945.* Washington D.C.: Congressional Quarterly, Inc., 1980.
Copper, John F. *A Quiet Revolution: Political Development in the Republic of China.* Lanham, Maryland: University Press, 1988.
———. *Taiwan: Nation-State or Province?* Boulder, Colorado: Westview Press, 1990.
———. *China Diplomacy: The Washington-Taipei-Beijing Triangle.* Boulder, Colorado: Westview Press, 1992.
———. *Taiwan: Nation-State or Province?* 2d edition. Boulder, Colorado: Westview Press, 1995.
Copper, John F., and Papp, Daniel S., eds. *Communist Nations' Military Assistance.* Boulder, Colorado: Westview Press, 1983.
Dellios, Rosita. *Modern Chinese Defence Strategy.* New York: St. Martin's Press, 1990.
Dibb, Paul. *Toward a New Balance of Power in Asia.* New York: Oxford University Press, 1995.
Downen, Robert L. *Of Grave Concern: U.S.-Taiwan Relations on the Threshold of the 1980s.* Washington, D.C.: Georgetown University, Center for Strategic and International Studies, 1981.
Dreyer, June Teufel. *Chinese Defense and Foreign Policy.* New York: Paragon House, 1989.
———, ed. *Asian-Pacific Regional Security.* Washington, D.C.: Washington Institute Press, 1990.

———. *China's Political System: Modernization and Tradition.* New York: Paragon House, 1993.
Dulles, Foster Rhea. *American Policy Toward Communist China: 1949–1969.* New York: Thomas Crowell Company, 1972.
Eisenhower, Dwight D. *Mandate for Change.* New York: Signet Books, 1963.
Engholm, Christopher. *Doing Business in Asia's Booming "China Triangle."* Englewood Cliffs, New Jersey: Prentice Hall, 1994.
Fairbank, John King. *The United States and China.* Cambridge, Massachusetts: Harvard University Press, 1980
Feigenbaum, Evan A. *Change in Taiwan and Potential Adversity in the Strait.* Santa Monica, California: RAND, 1995.
Feldman, Harvey, ed. *Constitutional Reform and the Future of the Republic of China.* Armonk, New York: M. E. Sharpe, 1991.
Feldman, Harvey, and Kim, Ilpyong J. *Taiwan in a Time of Transition.* New York: Paragon House, 1988.
Finkelstein, David Michael. *Washington's Taiwan Dilemma, 1949–1950: From Abandonment to Salvation.* Fairfax, Virginia: George Mason University Press, 1993.
Fu, Jen-ken. *Taiwan and the Geopolitics of the Asian-American Dilemma.* New York: Praeger, 1992.
Garver, John W. *China's Decision for Rapprochement with the United States.* Boulder, Colorado: Westview Press, 1982.
George, Alexander L. *Presidential Decisionmaking in Foreign Policy.* Boulder, Colorado: Westview Press, 1980.
George, Alexander L., and Smoke, Richard. *Deterrence in American Foreign Policy.* New York: Columbia University Press, 1974.
Gold, Thomas. *State and Society in the Taiwan Miracle.* Armonk, New York.: M. E. Sharpe, 1986.
Goldstein, Steven M. *Minidragons: Fragile Economic Miracles in the Pacific.* Boulder, Colorado: Westview Press, 1991.
Goodman, David, and Segal, Gerald, eds. *China at Forty: Mid-Life Crisis?* New York: Oxford University Press, 1989.
———, eds. *China in the 1990's: Crisis Management and Beyond.* Oxford: Clarendon Press, 1991.
Grasso, June M. *Truman's Two-China Policy.* Armonk, New York: M. E. Sharpe, 1987.
Grayson, Benson Lee, ed. *The American Image of China.* New York: Frederick Ungar, 1979.
Gregor, A. James. *The China Connection: U.S. Policy and the People's Republic of China.* Stanford, California: Hoover Institution Press, 1986.
———. *Arming the Dragon.* Berkeley: University of California Press, 1989.
Haig, Alexander M., Jr. *Caveat: Realism, Reagan and Foreign Policy.* New York: Macmillan Publishing, 1984.
Harding, Harry. *A Fragile Relationship: The United States and China Since 1972.* Washington, D.C.: The Brookings Institution, 1992.
Harrel, Steven, and Huang, Chun-chieh, eds. *Cultural Change in Postwar Taiwan.* Boulder, Colorado: Westview Press, 1994.
Harris, Stuart, and Cotton, James. *The End of the Cold War in Northeast Asia.* Boulder, Colorado: Lynne Rienner Publishers, 1991.
Hickey, Dennis V. *United States–Taiwan Security Ties: From Cold War to Beyond Containment.* Westport, Connecticut: Praeger, 1994.

Hsiung, James C., and Chai, Winberg, ed. *Asia and U.S. Foreign Policy*. New York: Praeger, 1981.
Hsu, Immanuel C. Y. *The Rise of Modern China*. New York: Oxford University Press, 1975.
———. *China Without Mao*. New York: Oxford University Press, 1982.
Huntington, Samuel P. *The Third Wave: Democratization in the Late 20th Century*. Norman: University of Oklahoma Press, 1991.
Institute for Contemporary Studies, ed. *U.S.-Taiwan Relations: Economic and Strategic Dimensions*. San Francisco: ICS Press, 1985.
International Institute for Strategic Studies. *The Military Balance: 1994–1995*. London: Brassey's, 1994.
Joffe, Ellis. *The Chinese Army After Mao*. Cambridge, Massachusetts: Harvard University Press, 1987.
Johnson, Gale, and Hou, Chi-ming. *Agricultural Policy and U.S.-Taiwan Trade*. Washington, D.C.: AEI Press, 1993.
Jordan, Amos A., Taylor, William J., and Korb, Lawrence J. *American National Security: Policy and Process*. Baltimore, Maryland: Johns Hopkins University Press, 1989.
Joseph, William A., ed. *China Briefing. 1991*. Boulder, Colorado: Westview Press, 1992.
Kegley, Charles W., and Wittkopf, Eugene R. *American Foreign Policy: Pattern and Process*. New York: St. Martin's Press, 1987.
Kim, Samuel, ed. *China and the World: Chinese Foreign Relations in the Post–Cold War Era*. Boulder, Colorado: Westview Press, 1994.
Kissinger, Henry. *The White House Years*. Boston: Little, Brown and Company, 1979.
Klintworth, Gary. *New Taiwan, New China: Taiwan's Changing Role in the Asia-Pacific Region*. New York: St. Martin's Press, 1995.
———, ed. *Taiwan in the Asia-Pacific in the 1990s*. Canberra: Australian National University Printery, 1994.
Knorr, Klause, and Verba, Sidney, eds. *The International System*. Princeton, New Jersey: Princeton University Press, 1961.
Koenig, Louis W., Hsiung, James C., and Chang, King-yuh, eds. *Congress, the Presidency and the Taiwan Relations Act*. New York: Praeger, 1985.
Kuan, John C. *A Review of U.S.-ROC Relations, 1949–1978*. Taipei: Asia and World Institute, 1980.
———, ed. *Symposium on ROC-U.S. Relations*. Taipei: Asia and World Institute, 1981.
Kusnitz, Leonard A. *Public Opinion and Foreign Policy: America's China Policy, 1949–1979*. Westport, Connecticut: Greenwood Press, 1984.
Lai, Tse-han, Myers, Ramon H., and Wei, Wou. *A Tragic Beginning: The Taiwan Uprising of February 28, 1947*. Stanford, California: Stanford University Press, 1991.
Lasater, Martin. *The Security of Taiwan: Unraveling the Dilemma*. Washington, D.C.: Center for Strategic and International Studies, 1982.
———. *The Taiwan Issue in Sino-American Strategic Relations*. Boulder, Colorado: Westview Press, 1984.
———. *Beijing's Blockade Threat to Taiwan*. Washington, D.C.: Heritage Foundation, 1985.
———. *Policy in Evolution: The U.S. Role in China's Reunification*. Boulder, Colorado: Westview Press, 1988.
———. *A Step Toward Democracy: The December 1989 Elections in Taiwan, Republic of China*. Washington, D.C.: AEI Press, 1990.

———. *U.S. Interests in the New Taiwan.* Boulder, Colorado: Westview Press, 1993.
———. *Changing of the Guard: President Clinton and the Security of Taiwan.* Boulder, Colorado: Westview Press, 1995.
Lee, Lai To. *The Reunification of China: PRC-Taiwan Relations in Flux.* New York: Praeger, 1991.
Li, Victor, ed. *The Future of Taiwan: A Difference of Opinion.* Armonk, New York: M. E. Sharpe, 1980.
Liao, Wen-chung. *China's Blue Waters Strategy in the 21st Century: From the First Islands Chain Toward the Second Islands Chain.* Taipei: Chinese Council of Advanced Policy Studies, 1995.
Lilley, James R., and Willkie II, Wendell L., eds. *Beyond MFN: Trade with China and American Interests.* Washington, D.C.: AEI Press, 1994.
Lin, Bih-jaw, and Myers, James T., eds. *Contemporary China and the Changing International Community.* Columbia: University of South Carolina Press, 1994.
Lin, Zhinling, and Robinson, Thomas R., eds. *The Chinese and Their Future.* Washington, D.C.: AEI Press, 1994.
Long, Simon. *Taiwan: China's Last Frontier.* New York: St. Martin's Press, 1991.
McLaurin, Ronald D., and Moon, Chung-in. *The United States and the Defense of the Pacific.* Boulder, Colorado: Westview Press, 1990.
Mendel, Douglas. *The Politics of Formosan Nationalism.* Berkeley: University of California Press, 1970.
Medvedev, Roy. *China and the Super Powers.* New York: Basil Blackwell, 1986.
Metraux, Daniel. *Taiwan's Political and Economic Growth in the Late Twentieth-Century.* New York: Edwin Mellen Press, 1991.
Miller, Merle. *Plain Speaking: An Oral Biography of Harry S. Truman.* New York: Berkeley Publishing Corporation, 1974.
Moody, Peter R. *Political Change on Taiwan: A Study of Ruling Party Adaptability.* New York: Praeger, 1992.
Moore, Barrington. *Social Origins of Dictatorship and Democracy.* Boston: Beacon Press, 1966.
Mosher, Steven W., ed. *The United States and the Republic of China: Democratic Friends, Economic Partners and Strategic Allies.* New Brunswick, New Jersey: Transaction Press, 1990.
Murray, Douglas J., and Viotti, Paul R. *The Defense Policies of Nations: A Comparative Study,* 3d edition. Baltimore, Maryland: Johns Hopkins University Press, 1994.
Myers, Ramon H., ed. *A Unique Relationship: The United States and the Republic of China Under the Taiwan Relations Act.* Stanford, California: Hoover Institution Press, 1989.
———. *Two Societies in Opposition: The Republic of China and the People's Republic of China After Forty Years.* Stanford, California: Hoover Institution Press, 1991.
Nixon, Richard M. *RN: The Memoirs of Richard Nixon.* New York: Warner Books, 1979.
———. *The Real War.* New York: Warner Books, 1980.
Nordlinger, Eric. *Isolationism Reconfigured: American Foreign Policy for a New Century.* Princeton, New Jersey: Princeton University Press, 1995.
Oxnam, Robert B., ed. *Dragon and Eagle—United States–China Relations: Past and Future.* New York: Basic Books, 1978.
Peng, Ming-min. *A Taste of Freedom: Memoirs of a Formosan Independence Leader.* New York: Holt, Rinehart and Winston, 1972.

Radvanyi, Janos, ed. *The Pacific in the 1990's: Economic and Strategic Change.* Lanham, Maryland: University Press, 1990.
Ranis, Gustav. *Taiwan: From Developing to Mature Economy.* Boulder, Colorado: Westview Press, 1992.
Rielly, John E., ed. *American Public Opinion and U.S. Foreign Policy, 1995.* Chicago, Illinois: Chicago Council on Foreign Relations, 1995.
Research Institute for Peace and Security. *Asian Security, 1994–95.* Washington, D.C.: Brassey's, 1994.
Robinson, Thomas. *China's Potential Military Threat to Asian-Pacific Security in the 1990s, AARE Report.* Washington, D.C.: American Asian Research Enterprises, September 1994.
———, ed. *Democracy and Development in East Asia: Taiwan, South Korea and the Philippines.* Lanham, Maryland: University Press, 1990.
Romm, Joseph J. *Defining National Security: The Nonmilitary Aspects.* New York: Council on Foreign Relations Press, 1993.
Rosenau, James N. *The Scientific Study of Foreign Policy.* London: Frances Pinter, 1980.
Schaller, Michael. *The United States & China in the Twentieth Century.* Oxford: Oxford University Press, 1979.
Segal, Gerald. *Defending China.* New York: Oxford University Press, 1985.
———, ed. *Chinese Politics and Foreign Policy.* New York: Paul International for the Royal Institute of International Affairs, 1990.
Selochan, Viberto. *Armed Forces in Asia and the Pacific.* Boulder, Colorado: Westview Press, 1991.
Sharpe, Richard. *Jane's Fighting Ships, 1991–92.* Alexandria, Virginia: Jane's Information Group, 1991.
Shaw, Yu-ming. *ROC-U.S. Relations: A Decade After the "Shanghai Communiqué."* Taipei: The Asia and World Institute, 1983.
Shepherd, John R. *Statecraft and Political Economy on the Taiwan Frontier, 1600–1800.* Stanford, California: Stanford University Press, 1993.
Simon, Denis Fred, and Kau, Michael Y. M., eds. *Taiwan: Beyond the Economic Miracle.* Armonk, New York: M. E. Sharpe, 1992.
Snow, Edgar. *Red Star over China.* New York: Random House, 1938.
Solberg, Ronald L. *Country Risk-Analysis: A Handbook.* New York: Routledge, 1991.
Stockholm International Peace Research Institute. *SIPRI Yearbook 1994: World Armaments and Disarmament.* New York: Oxford University Press, 1994.
Sutter, Robert G., and Johnson, William R., eds. *Taiwan in World Affairs.* Boulder, Colorado: Westview Press, 1994.
Tan, Qingshan. *The Making of U.S. China Policy: From Normalization to Post–Cold War Era.* Boulder, Colorado: Lynne Rienner Publishers, 1992.
Thibault, George Edward, ed. *The Art and Practice of Military Strategy.* Washington, D.C.: National Defense University, 1984.
Tien, Hung-mao. *Mainland China, Taiwan and U.S. Policy.* Cambridge, Massachusetts: Oelgeschlager, Gun and Hain Publishers, Inc., 1983.
———. *The Great Transition: Political and Social Change in the Republic of China.* Stanford, California: Hoover Institution Press, 1989.
Tierney, John, ed. *About Face: The China Decision and Its Consequences.* New Rochelle, New York: Arlington House, 1979.
Tow, William T., ed. *Building Sino-American Relations: An Analysis for the 1990's.* New York: Paragon House, 1991.
Tsai, Wen-hui. *Toward Greater Democracy: An Analysis of the Republic of China on*

Taiwan's Major Elections in the 1990s. Baltimore: School of Law, University of Maryland, 1994.
Tsang, Steve, ed. *In the Shadow of China: Political Development in Taiwan Since 1949*. Honolulu: University of Hawaii Press, 1993.
Vasey, Lloyd R. *China's Growing Military Power and Implications for East Asia*. Washington, D.C.: Pacific Forum, CSIS, August 1993.
Wachman, Alan. *Taiwan: National Identity and Democratization*. Armonk, New York: M. E. Sharpe, 1994.
Waltz, Kenneth. *Theory of International Politics*. New York: McGraw Hill, 1979.
Wang, Kuo-chang. *United Nations Voting on Chinese Representation: An Analysis of General Assembly Roll-Calls, 1950–71*. Taipei: Academia Sinica, 1984.
Wang, Yu San. *Foreign Policy of the Republic of China on Taiwan: An Unorthodox Approach*. New York: Praeger, 1990.
Warburg, Gerald Felix. *Conflict and Consensus: The Struggle Between Congress and the President over Foreign Policymaking*. New York: Harper and Row, 1989.
William, Jack F., ed. *The Taiwan Issue*. New York: Praeger, 1979.
Winckler, Edwin, and Greenhalgh, Susan M. *Contending Approaches to the Political Economy of Taiwan*. Armonk, New York: M. E. Sharpe, 1988.
Wolf, Charles, Jr., Yeh, K.C., Bamezai, Anil, Henry, Donald P., and Kennedy, Michael. *Long-Term Economic and Military Trends 1994–2015: The United States and Asia*. Santa Monica, California: RAND Institute, 1995.
Wolfers, Arnold. *Discord and Collaboration*. Baltimore, Maryland: Johns Hopkins University Press, 1962.
Wortzel, Larry M., ed. *China's Military Modernization: International Implications*. Westport, Connecticut: Greenwood Press, 1988.
Wu, Hsin-hsing. *Bridging the Strait: Taiwan, China and the Prospects for Reunification*. New York: Oxford University Press, 1994.
Wu, Jaushieh Joseph. *Taiwan's Democratization: Forces Behind the New Momentum*. New York: Oxford University Press, 1995.
Wu, Yu-shan. *Comparative Economic Transformations: Mainland China, Hungary, the Soviet Union and Taiwan*. Stanford, California: Stanford University Press, 1994.
Wylie, J. C. *Military Strategy: A General Theory of Power and Control*. New Brunswick, New Jersey: Rutgers University Press, 1976.
Xiangze, Jiang. *The United States and China*. Chicago: University of Chicago Press, 1988.
Yager, Joseph A. *Nuclear Nonproliferation Strategy in Asia*. McLean, Virginia: Center for National Security Negotiations, 1988.
Yang, Richard H., ed. *China's Military: The PLA in 1992/93*. Boulder, Colorado: Westview Press, 1993.
Yu, George, ed. *China in Transition: Economic, Political and Social Developments*. Lanham, Maryland: University Press of America, 1993.
Zhan, Jun. *Ending the Chinese Civil War: Power, Commerce and Conciliation Between Beijing and Taipei*. New York: St. Martin's Press, 1993.

Articles

"ADJ News Analysis: Will China Attack Taiwan After March 1996?" *Asian Defense Journal* (February 1996): 120–121.
Auw, David. "The Growing Military Ties Between Peking and Washington." *Issues & Studies* 20, no. 7 (July 1984): 1–4.

Awanohara, Susumu. "Group Therapy." *Far Eastern Economic Review* (April 15, 1993): 11.
Baum, Julian. "A Case of Nerves: Chinese Military Manoeuvres Cause Alarm." *Far Eastern Economic Review* (July 20, 1995): 26.
———. "Chinese Hurdle." *Far Eastern Economic Review* (November 14, 1991): 30.
———. "Dire Straits: Beijing Frets over a More Independent Taiwan." *Far Eastern Economic Review* (July 21, 1994): 19–20.
———. "Don't Tread on Me: China's Bullying Brings Out Steel in Taiwanese." *Far Eastern Economic Review* (September 14, 1995): 22–23.
———. "Fear of Falling: Prophet of Chinese Invasion Makes Many Nervous." *Far Eastern Economic Review* (October 13, 1994): 24.
———. "Frankly Speaking: Pragmatism Increasingly Determines China Policy." *Far Eastern Economic Review* (June 15, 1995): 24.
———. "He's No China Doll: Presidential Challenger Favors Independence." *Far Eastern Economic Review* (August 31, 1995): 17–18.
———. "Idling Threat." *Far Eastern Economic Review* (April 13, 1995): 29.
———. "In Search of Recognition." *Far Eastern Economic Review* (July 18, 1991): 26.
———. "Jiang Talks Strait." *Far Eastern Economic Review* (February 16, 1995): 14–15.
———. "Lee's Challenge." *Far Eastern Economic Review* (September 14, 1995): 20–21.
———. "New Party Line: Breakaway Group Sets Its Agenda." *Far Eastern Economic Review* (August 26, 1993): 19.
———. "Officers and Nursemaids: Controversy Continues over Military's Role on Campus." *Far Eastern Economic Review* (February 3, 1994): 26.
———. "Prepare to Surface." *Far Eastern Economic Review* (February 4, 1993): 10–11.
———. "Pressure Cooker." *Far Eastern Economic Review* (August 24, 1995): 16–17.
———. "Red Alert: Taipei Seeks Better Arms to Bolster Defense." *Far Eastern Economic Review* (September 14, 1995): 23–26.
———. "Revolt from Within: President Faces Threat from Inside the KMT." *Far Eastern Economic Review* (April 27, 1995): 24.
———. "Split in the Ranks: Issue of Taiwan Independence Haunts the KMT." *Far Eastern Economic Review* (December 24–31, 1992): 25.
———. "Strategic Slip: Opposition Under Fire for Calls to Demilitarize Islands." *Far Eastern Economic Review* (November 17, 1994): 17.
———. "Talking Back to Back: Taipei Responds Tentatively to Beijing." *Far Eastern Economic Review* (April 20, 1995): 26.
———. "Up and Running." *Far Eastern Economic Review* (September 7, 1995): 14–15.
———. "Winged: Locally Made Jet Fighter Fails to Convince Critics." *Far Eastern Economic Review* (January 12, 1995): 21.
"Boosting Firepower: Cash-Rich Southeast Asia Goes on an Arms-Buying Binge." *Asiaweek* (November 13, 1992): 28–31.
Borrus, Amy. "Peace Reigns, but Asia Is Stockpiling Arms." *Business Week* (October 5, 1992): 61.
Buchanan, Patrick J. "An American-First Foreign Policy." *Human Events* (May 2, 1992): 6–7.
Carpenter, William M., and Gibert, Stephen P. "The Republic of China: A Strategic Appraisal for the Decade Ahead." *Issues & Studies* 27, no. 12 (December 1981): 12–32.

Chanda, Nayan. "Fear of the Dragon." *Far Eastern Economic Review* (April 13, 1995): 25.
———. "Storm Warning." *Far Eastern Economic Review* (December 1, 1994): 14–15.
———. "The New Nationalism." *Far Eastern Economic Review* (November 9, 1995): 23.
———. "Treacherous Shoals." *Far Eastern Economic Review* (August 13, 1992): 14–17.
———. "Winds of Change." *Far Eastern Economic Review* (June 22, 1995): 16.
Chang, King-yuh. "Partnership in Transition: A Review of Recent Taipei-Washington Relations." *Asian Survey* 21, no. 6 (June 1981): 603–621.
Chao, Linda, and Myers, Ramon H. "The First Chinese Democracy." *Asian Survey* 34, no. 3 (March 1994): 213–230.
Chen, Lung-chu, and Reisman, W. M. "Who Owns Taiwan: A Search for International Title." *Yale Law Journal* 81, no. 4 (March 1972): 642–671.
Chen, Guoqing. "China Threat Rings Hollow." *Defense News* 8, no. 19 (May 17–23, 1993): 19–20.
Cheng, Arthur. "The IDF Close Up." *Sinorama* 16, no. 4 (April 1991): 24–29.
Cheng, Chu-yuan. "Economic Development in Taiwan and Mainland China: A Comparison of Strategies and Performance." *Asian Affairs* 10, no. 1 (Spring 1983): 60–86.
Cheung, Tai Ming. "Back to the Front: Deng Seeks to Depoliticize the PLA." *Far Eastern Economic Review* (October 29, 1992): 15–16.
———. "China's Buying Spree: Russia Gears Up to Upgrade Peking's Weaponry." *Far Eastern Economic Review* (July 8, 1993): 24–26.
———. "Lacking Depth." *Far Eastern Economic Review* (February 4, 1993): 11.
———. "Nuke Begets Nuke." *Far Eastern Economic Review* (June 4, 1992): 22–23.
———. "Quick Response: Military Planners Focus on External Threats." *Far Eastern Economic Review* (January 14, 1993): 19–22.
———. "Serve the People." *Far Eastern Economic Review* (October 14, 1993): 64–66.
———. "Still Gung-ho." *Far Eastern Economic Review* (May 18, 1989): 23.
———. "Talk Soft, Carry Stick." *Far Eastern Economic Review* (October 18, 1990): 37.
"China Goes Ballistic." *Economist* (July 29, 1995): 23.
Ching, Frank. "An About-Turn by Taiwan." *Far Eastern Economic Review* (August 4, 1994): 30.
———. "China Tightens the Noose." *Far Eastern Economic Review* (August 18, 1994): 31.
———. "China's Military Spurs Concern." *Far Eastern Economic Review* (May 11, 1995): 40.
———. "Taiwanese Exiles in U.S. Return to a Transformed Homeland." *Far Eastern Economic Review* (June 17, 1993): 34.
———. "Taiwan's Ruling Party Needs to Redefine Its Future Course." *Far Eastern Economic Review* (October 7, 1993): 32.
Chiu, Hungdah. "Prospects for the Unification of China: An Analysis of the Views of the Republic of China on Taiwan." *Asian Survey* 23, no. 10 (October 1983): 1081–1094.
———. "The Future of U.S.-Taiwan Relations." *Asian Affairs* 9, no. 1 (September–October 1981): 20–30.
Chou, David S. "The International Status of the Republic of China." *Issues and Studies* 20, no. 5 (May 1984): 10–21.
———. "The Role of the U.S. President and Congress in American Foreign Policy-

Making, with Special Reference to the Making and Implementation of the Taiwan Relations Act." *Issues and Studies* 20, no. 3 (March 1984): 41–66.

Christopher, Warren. "America's Leadership, America's Opportunity." *Foreign Policy*, no. 98 (Spring 1995): 6–27.

Clark, Cal. "Dynamics of Development in Taiwan: Reconceptualizing State and Market in National Competitiveness." *American Journal of Chinese Studies* 2, no. 1 (April 1994): 9–29.

Cooper, Pat, and Opall, Barbara. "Taiwan, U.S. Disconnect on Provision of C3 Links." *Defense News* 9, no. 29 (July 25–31, 1994): 28.

Copper, John F. "Taiwan's Legal Status: A Multilevel Perspective." *Journal of Northeast Asian Studies* 1, no. 4 (December 1982): 57–69.

———. "Will Peking Blockade the ROC?" *Asian Outlook* 26, no. 2 (January–February, 1991): 9–11.

Cossa, Ralph A. "The PRC's National Security Objectives in the Post–Cold War Era and the Role of the PLA." *Issues and Studies* 30, no. 9 (September 1994): 1–28.

Dalchoong, Kim. "Sino-American Normalization and Taiwan's Security and Strategic Issues." *Journal of Asiatic Studies* 23, no. 1 (1980): 1–16.

Dantes, Edmond. "Security Developments in Northeast Asia." *Asian Defense Review* (October 1992): 10–18.

———. "Taiwan's Military Build-Up—Move to Contain China?" *Asian Defense Review* (February 1993): 15–23.

De Brianti, Giovanni. "Dutch, Germans May End Taiwan Arms Ban." *Defense News* 7, no. 48 (November 30–December 6, 1992): 1–20.

Deng, Xiaoping. "Deng Xiaoping on One Country, Two Systems." *Beijing Review* 29, no. 5 (February 3, 1986): 25–26.

———. "More on One Country, Two Systems." *Beijing Review* 30, no. 14 (April 6, 1987): 21–22.

Ding, Arthur S. "On Peking's National Defense Budget." *Issues and Studies* 30, no. 4 (April 1994): 110–111.

———. "The PRC's Military Modernization and a Security Mechanism for the Asia-Pacific." *Issues and Studies* 31, no. 8 (August 1995): 1–18.

Doyle, Michael. W. "Kant, Liberal Legacies and Foreign Affairs." *Philosophy and Public Affairs* 12, no. 3 (Summer 1983): 205–235.

Dreyer, June Teufel. "Role of the Military on the Mainland and the Threat to the Republic of China." Unpublished manuscript, 1991, 23 pp.

———. "Taiwan's December 1991 Election." *World Affairs* 155, no. 2 (Fall 1992): 67–70.

Eberstadt, Nicholas. "Taiwan and South Korea: The 'Democratization' of Outlier States." *World Affairs* 155, no. 2 (Fall 1992): 80–89.

Eikenberry, Karl W. "Does China Threaten Asia-Pacific Regional Stability?" *Parameters: The U.S. Army War College Quarterly* 25, no. 1 (Spring 1995): 82–103.

Emerson, J. Terry. "What Determines U.S. Relations with China: The Taiwan Relations Act or the August 17, Communiqué with Beijing." *Asian Studies Center Backgrounder,* no. 72 (November 30, 1987): 1–12.

Emerson, Tony, Hoffman, Jeff, Huus, Kari, and Mabry, Marcus. "Would Beijing Dare Invade?" *Newsweek* (International Edition–Asia) (December 23, 1991): 16.

Fulghum, David A. "China Pursuing Two-Fighter Plan." *Aviation Week & Space Technology* (March 27, 1995): 44–45.

Fulghum, David A., and Proctor, Paul. "Chinese Coveting Offensive Triad." *Aviation Week & Space Technology* (September 21, 1992): 20–21.
Gold, Thomas. "The Status Quo Is Not Static: Mainland-Taiwan Relations." *Asian Survey* 27, no. 3 (March 1987): 300–315.
Goldstein, Carl. "An Independent Taiwan Is Not in the Cards." *Far Eastern Economic Review* (May 14, 1987): 28–30.
———. "The Military Weans Itself from Dependency on U.S." *Far Eastern Economic Review* (May 8, 1986): 26–29.
———. "The Winds of Change: KMT to Lift Martial Law and Allow Opposition Parties." *Far Eastern Economic Review* (October 30, 1986): 28–29.
Halloran, Richard. "The Krulak Doctrine: U.S. Marine Commandant Wants a Pacific Focus." *Far Eastern Economic Review* (September 28, 1995): 32.
Harris, Jack H. "Enduring Chinese Dimensions in Peking's Military Policy and Doctrine." *Issues and Studies* 15, no. 7 (July 1979): 77–88.
Harrison, Selig. "Interview/Hu Yaobang: Peking Lashes Out at Washington-Taipei Links." *Far Eastern Economic Review* (July 24, 1986): 26–27.
Hickey, Dennis V. "America's Military Relations with the People's Republic of China: The Need for Reassessment." *Journal of Northeast Asian Studies* 7, no. 3 (Fall 1988): 29–33.
———. "America's Two Point Policy and the Future of Taiwan." *Asian Survey* 28, no. 8 (August 1988): 881–896.
———. "American Technological Assistance, Technology Transfers and Taiwan's Drive for Defense Self-Sufficiency." *Journal of Northeast Asian Studies* 8, no. 3 (Fall 1989): 44–61.
———. "China's Threat to Taiwan." *Pacific Review* 5, no. 3 (1992): 250–258.
———. "Coming in from the Cold: Taiwan's Return to International Organizations." *Issues and Studies* 30, no. 10 (October 1994): 94–105.
———. "Interview with Sun Chen, Taiwan's Defense Minister." *Asian Defense Journal* (February 1994): 30–35.
———. "New Directions in China's Arms for Export Policy: An Analysis of China's Military Ties with Iran." *Asian Affairs: An American Review* 17, no. 1 (Spring 1990): 15–30.
———. "The Crises of Communism and the Prospects for Change in the People's Republic of China." *Asian Affairs: An American Review* 19, no. 4 (Winter 1993): 195–205.
———. "United States Policy and the International Status of Taiwan." *Journal of East Asian Affairs* 7, no. 2 (Summer/Fall 1993): 563–586.
———. "U.S. Arms Sales to Taiwan: Institutionalized Ambiguity." *Asian Survey* 26, no. 12 (December 1986): 1324–1336.
———. "U.S. Policy and Taiwan's Reintegration into the Global Community." *Journal of Northeast Asian Studies* 11, no. 1 (Spring 1992): 18–32.
Hickey, Dennis V., and Harmel, Christopher C. "U.S. Policy and China's Military Ties with the Russian Republics." *Asian Affairs* 20, no. 4 (Winter 1994): 241–254.
Hiebert, Murry. "Treading Softly." *Far Eastern Economic Review* (August 3, 1995): 16–20.
Ho, Szu-yin. "Walking the Tightrope: The ROC's Democratization, Diplomacy, Mainland Policy." *Issues and Studies* 28, no. 3 (March 1992): 1–20.
Holloway, Nigel. "Deficit Diplomacy: U.S. Budget Cuts Could Hurt in Asia." *Far Eastern Economic Review* (July 6, 1995): 23–24.
———. "Jolt from the Blue: U.S. Prodded to Firm Up Its Policy on Spratlys." *Far Eastern Economic Review* (August 3, 1995): 22–23.

———. "New Deal: Republican Congress Will Challenge Asia Policy." *Far Eastern Economic Review* (November 24, 1994): 20–21.

———. "No Retreat: Lawmakers See Continuing U.S. Influence in Asia." *Far Eastern Economic Review* (September 28, 1995): 30–32.

Holloway, Nigel, Baum, Julian, and Kaye, Lincoln. "Shanghaied by Taiwan." *Far Eastern Economic Review* (June 1, 1995): 15–16.

Holloway, Nigel, and Zyla, Melana K. "Collision Course." *Far Eastern Economic Review* (January 19, 1995): 14–15.

Huntington, Samuel P. "Political Development and Political Decay." *World Politics* 17, no. 3 (April 1965): 386–430.

Hsiao, Frank S. T., and Sullivan, Lawrence. "The Chinese Communist Party and the Status of Taiwan, 1928–1943." *Pacific Affairs* 52, no. 3 (Fall 1979): 446–467.

Hsieh, Shu-fen. "A Day in the Life of a Destroyer Captain." *Sinorama* 16, no. 9 (September 1991): 94–97.

———. "Missile Speedboats—Accurate, Swift and Deadly." *Sinorama* 16, no. 9 (September 1991): 98–99.

———. "Overcoming Adversity on the Seas—the Navy Plans for the Future." *Sinorama* 16, no. 9 (September 1991): 82–93.

———. "Top Gun Locks Sights on a MiG." *Sinorama* 16, no. 4 (April 1991): 30–35.

———. "Who Rules the Skies over Taiwan?" *Sinorama* 16, no. 4 (April 1991): 6–23.

Huan, Guo-cang. "Taiwan: A View from Beijing." *Foreign Affairs* 63, no. 5 (Summer 1985): 1064–1080.

Hughes, David. "Taiwan to Acquire Patriot Derivative." *Aviation Week & Space Technology* (March 1, 1993): 61.

Huus, Karl. "Back to Normal: U.S.-China Trade War Looms Closer." *Far Eastern Economic Review* (January 19, 1995): 52.

Jencks, Harlan W. "The PRC's Military and Security Policy in the Post–Cold War Era." *Issues and Studies* 30, no. 11 (November 1994): 65–103.

Kaye, Lincoln. "Atomic Intentions." *Far Eastern Economic Review* (May 3, 1990): 9.

———. "One-Way Street." *Far Eastern Economic Review* (November 11, 1993): 12–13.

———. "Trading Rights: Beijing Exacts a High Price for Copyright Accord." *Far Eastern Economic Review* (March 9, 1995): 16.

Lasater, Martin L. "Bill Clinton and the Security of the Republic of China." *Issues and Studies* 29, no. 1 (January 1993): 39–58.

———. "Taiwan's Security in the 1990's." *Asian Outlook* 25, no. 6 (September–October 1990): 1–9.

———. "The Dilemma of U.S. Arms Sales to Beijing." *Asian Studies Center Backgrounder*, no. 23 (March 8, 1985): 1–5.

———. "The Limits to U.S.-China Strategic Cooperation." *Asian Studies Center Backgrounder*, no. 12 (April 20, 1984): 1–14.

———. "U.S.-ROC-PRC Relations in an Era of Systemic Change." Paper presented at 4th Annual Tamkang University–University of Illinois Conference on U.S.-ROC Relations (November 1992): 1–23.

Lawrence, Susan V., and Zimmerman, Tim. "A Political Test of When Guns Matter." *U.S. News and World Report* (October 30, 1995): 47–48.

Lee, Win-chin. "The Birth of a Salesman: China as an Arms Supplier." *Journal of Northeast Asian Studies* 6, no. 4 (Winter 1987–88): 32–46.

Lewis, Paul. "Taiwan May Create Special Budget for New Arms." *Defense News* (October 12–18, 1992): 56.

Li, Jiaquan. "Mainland and Taiwan: Formula for China's Reunification." *Beijing Review* 25, no. 5 (February 3, 1986): 18–24.
Lin, Cheng-yi. "Taiwan's Security Strategies in the Post–Cold War Era." *Issues and Studies* 31, no. 4 (April 1995): 78–97.
Lin, Chong-pin. "Introduction." *World Affairs* 155, no. 2 (Fall 1992): 51–52.
———. "China on the Move: Revamping China's Military." *Current* (June 1994): 35–38.
———. "The Extramilitary Roles of the People's Liberation Army in Modernization: Limits of Professionalism." *Security Studies* 1, no. 4 (Summer 1994): 659–689.
Lipset, Seymour Martin. "Some Social Requisites of Democracy: Economic Development and Political Legitimacy." *American Political Science Review* 53 (1959): 69–105.
Liu, Melinda. "Accounting for the N-Factor." *Far Eastern Economic Review* (December 17, 1976): 32.
———. "Taiwan's Power Game." *Far Eastern Economic Review* (December 17, 1976): 33.
Lo, Amy. "Pragmatic Diplomacy, Creative Economics." *Free China Review* 41, no. 5 (May 1991): 4–9.
Lok, Joris Janssen. "U.S. Benefits from European MLU." *Jane's Defence Weekly* 18, no. 20 (November 14, 1992): 8.
"Make or Break for GD." *Jane's Defence Weekly* 18, no. 9, (August 29, 1992): 36–37.
Malik, J. Mohan. "Chinese Debate on Military Strategy: Trends and Portents." *Journal of Northeast Asian Studies* 9, no. 2 (Summer 1990): 3–31.
Maynes, Charles. "America Without the Cold War." *Foreign Policy* 78, no. 1 (Spring 1990): 3–25.
McAneny, Leslie. "Huge Majority Backs Shift from International to Domestic Agenda." *The Gallup Poll Monthly*, no. 316 (January 1992): 12–13.
Mecham, Michael. "China Updates Its Military, but Business Comes First." *Aviation Week & Space Technology* (March 15, 1993): 57–59.
Moore, Jonathon. "Securing the Skies." *Far Eastern Economic Review* (December 22, 1988): 26.
Muller. David G. "A Chinese Blockade of Taiwan." *Proceedings* 110, no. 9 (September 1994): 51–55.
Munro, Ross H. "Awakening Dragon: The Real Danger in Asia Is from China." *Policy Review* (Fall 1992): 10–16.
Myers, Ramon. "The Contest Between Two Chinese States." *Asian Survey* 23, no. 4 (April 1983): 537–552.
Niou, Emerson M. S. "An Analysis of the Republic of China's Security Issues." *Issues and Studies* 28, no. 1 (January 1992): 82–95.
Nixon, Richard M. "Asia After Vietnam." *Foreign Affairs* 41, no. 1 (October 1967): 111–125.
"No Sale of Advanced Aircraft to Taiwan." *Department of State Bulletin*, no. 2059 (February 1982): 191.
Oksenberg, Michael. "A Decade of Sino-American Relations." *Foreign Affairs* 61, no. 1 (Fall 1982): 175–195.
Opall, Barbara. "Taiwan Balks at U.S. Deal for Patriot." *Defense News* 8, no. 34 (August 30–September 5, 1993): 1–28.
———. "Taiwan Whittles Forces, Boosts Arms." *Defense News* 8, no. 35 (September 6–12, 1993): 16–28.
Prager, Karsten. "Bulls in the China Shop." *Time* (June 5, 1995): 35.

"Proclamation Defining Terms for Japanese Surrender." *Department of State Bulletin* 13, no. 318 (July 29, 1945): 137.

"Proposed F–16 Sale Draws Strong Protest." *Beijing Review* (September 14–20, 1992): 7–10.

Proctor, Paul. "First IDF Delivered as Taiwan Spools Up for Full Production." *Aviation Week & Space Technology* (April 27, 1992): 38–44.

Quester, George H. "Taiwan and Nuclear Proliferation." *Orbis* 18, no. 1 (Spring 1974): 140–150.

Reeve, Simon. "Thanks, but No Thanks." *Far Eastern Economic Review* (July 27, 1995): 19.

Reisman, Michael. "Who Owns Taiwan?" *New Republic* (April 1972): 21–23.

Rodman, Peter W. "Points of Order." *National Review* (May 1, 1995): 36–88.

Ross, Robert. "American China Policy and the Security of Asia." *NBR Analysis* 1, no. 3 (December 1990): 24–32.

Rustow, Dankwart A. "Transition to Democracy: Toward a Democratic Model." *Comparative Politics* 22, no. 2 (April 1990): 156–244.

Schlesinger, Arthur, Jr. "Back to the Womb? Isolationism's Renewed Threat." *Foreign Affairs* 74, no. 4 (July/August 1995): 2–8.

Sicherman, Harvey. "Winning the Peace in the Post–Cold War World." *Orbis* 37, no. 4 (Fall 1993): 501–503.

Silverberg, David. "Emerging Nations Hunger for Precision Weapons." *Defense News* (February 8–14, 1993): 9.

Solomone, Stacy. "The PLA's Commercial Activities in the Economy: Effects and Consequences." *Issues and Studies* 31, no. 3 (March 1995): 20–43.

Soong, James Chul-yul. "Political Development in the Republic of China on Taiwan, 1985–1992: An Insider's View." *World Affairs* 155, no. 2 (Fall 1992): 62–66.

Starr, Barbara. "F–16 Sale Justified by 'Discrepancy.'" *Jane's Defence Weekly* 18, no. 11 (September 12, 1992): 5.

———. "MiG Buy May Lead to Chinese Copies." *Jane's Defence Weekly* 18, no. 15 (October 10, 1992): 18.

Starr, Barbara, and Boatman, John. "USA Reconsiders F–16 Sale Ban." *Jane's Defence Weekly* 18, no. 16 (August 8, 1992): 5.

"Taiwan Battles Glitches, Expects IDF to Fly with Radar." *Defense News* 9, no. 28 (July 18–24, 1994): 26.

"Taiwan's Ching-kuo Fighter." *Jane's Defence Weekly* 11, no. 1. (January 7, 1989): 4.

"Taiwan Developing Medium-Range Missile?" *Asian Defense Journal* (February 1996): 120.

"Taiwan: Standing Alone." *Far Eastern Economic Review* (November 17, 1994): 13.

Taylor, Humphrey. "Americans Perceive Taiwan as Separate and Independent Country from China: Majority Support U.S. Government Allowing the President of Taiwan to Visit U.S. Alma Mater." *The Harris Poll, 1995*, no. 50 (August 8, 1995): 1–5.

———. "Canada, Britain and Australia Top the List of Countries Which Americans Think of as Friendly." *The Harris Poll, 1995*, no. 60 (October 2, 1995): 1–6.

"This Sale Is a Mirage." *Time* (July 13, 1992): 9.

Tien, Hung-Mao, and Shiau, Chyuan-jeng. "Taiwan's Democratization: A Summary." *World Affairs* 155, no. 2 (Fall 1992): 58–61.

"U.S. Arms Sales to Taiwan Top 4190m." *Jane's Defence Weekly* 10, no. 25 (December 24, 1988): 1584.

"U.S. Trade Facts." *Business America: The Magazine of International Trade* (May 1995): 17–18.

Walsh, James. "Cornell's Reunion Is China's Nightmare." *Time* (June 5, 1995): 34–35.
Waldron, Arthur. "Dragon Growling." *National Review* (July 31, 1995): 44–45.
Wallace, Michael. "Armaments and Escalation." *International Studies Quarterly* 26, no. 1 (March 1982): 37–56.
Wang, Chi-wu. "Military Preparedness and Security Needs: Perceptions from the Republic of China on Taiwan." *Asian Survey* 21, no. 6 (June 1981): 651–663.
Wei, Hung-chin. "Economics Comes Before Politics: Koo on Joining International Bodies." *Sinorama* 17, no. 1 (January 1992): 89–91.
———. "Opening Doors to International Organizations." *Sinorama* 17, no. 1 (January 1992): 80–88.
Weinberger, Caspar. "Taiwan's Rosy Future." *Forbes* (October 28, 1991): 33.
Whiting, Allen S. "Assertive Nationalism in Chinese Foreign Policy." *Asian Survey* 23, no. 8 (August 1983): 913–933.
Wright, Robert. "Trading Places." *New Republic* (December 4, 1995): 6–45.
Wu, Jaushieh Joseph. "The 1994 Elections in Taiwan: Continuity, Change, and the Prospect of Democracy." *Issues and Studies* 31, no. 3 (March 1995): 92–112.
Ye, Jianying. "Ye Jianying on Policy for Peaceful Reunification." *Beijing Review* 29, no. 5 (February 3, 1986): 24.
Yu, Bin. "Sino-Russian Military Relations." *Asian Survey* 33, no. 3 (March 1993): 302–316.
Yu, Peter Kien-hong. "Strategic Importance of the Republic of China on Taiwan." *Asian Outlook* 26, no. 2 (January–February 1991): 19–23.
———. "The JDW Interview: Dr. Li-an Chen, the Republic of China's Defense Minister, Says the Beijing Regime Still Wants to Take Over His Country." *Jane's Defence Weekly* 15, no. 1, (January 5, 1991): 32.
Yuan, Yvonne. "Building Better Relations." *Free China Review* 43, no. 2 (February 1993): 4–15.
Zhao, John Quansheng. "An Analysis of Unification: The PRC Perspective." *Asian Survey* 23, no. 10 (October 1983): 1094–1114.

U.S. Government Documents and Publications

Congressional Record, May 20, 1991.
———. July 21, 1994.
Public Papers of the Presidents of the United States: Harry S. Truman, 1949. Washington, D.C.: GPO, 1964.
———. Washington, D.C.: GPO, 1965.
U.S. Arms Control and Disarmament Agency. *World Military Expenditures and Arms Transfers, 1993–1994.* Washington, D.C.: U.S. Government Printing Office (hereafter GPO), 1995.
U.S. Congress. House. Committee on Foreign Affairs. *American Public Attitudes Toward Foreign Policy.* Hearing, 103rd Congress, 2nd Session, July 27, 1994.
———. Subcommittee on Economic Policy, Trade and Environment; International Security, International Organizations and Human Rights; and Asia and the Pacific of the Committee on Foreign Affairs. *China: Human Rights and MFN.* Hearing, 103rd Congress, 2nd Session, March 24, 1994.
———. Subcommittee of Committee on Appropriations. *Departments of Commerce, Justice, and State, the Judiciary and Related Agencies Appropriations for 1993.* Hearing, 102nd Congress, 2nd Session, March 10, 1992.

———. Task Force on Defense, Foreign Policy, and Space of the Committee on the Budget. *Funding Implications of the United States' Worldwide Presence.* Hearing, 102nd Congress, 1st Session, December 5, 1991.

———. Committee on Foreign Affairs. *The Future of U.S. Foreign Policy (Part I): Regional Issues.* Hearing, 103rd Congress, 1st Session, February 2, 3, 17, 23, 24, and March 18, 1993.

———. Subcommittee on Asian and Pacific Affairs of the Committee on Foreign Affairs. *The Future of Communist Systems in Asia.* Hearing, 102nd Congress, 1st Session, November 22, 1991.

———. Subcommittees on Economic Policy, Trade and Environment, International Security, International Organizations and Human Rights; and Asia and the Pacific of the Committee on Foreign Affairs. *Future of United States–China Policy.* Hearing, 103rd Congress, 1st Session, May 20, 1993.

———. Subcommittee on Trade of the Committee on Ways and Means. *H.R. 4590, United States–China Act of 1994.* Hearing, 103rd Congress, 2nd Session, July 28, 1994.

———. Committee on Foreign Affairs and Its Subcommittees on Human Rights and International Organizations and on Asian and Pacific Affairs. *Implementation of the Taiwan Relations Act.* Hearing, 99th Congress, 2nd Session, May 7, June 25, and August 1, 1986. Washington, D.C.: GPO, 1987.

———. Subcommittee on Asian and Pacific Affairs of the Committee on Foreign Affairs. *The National Affairs Council and Implications for Democracy.* Hearing, 101st Congress, 2nd Session, October 11, 1990.

———. Subcommittee on Asian and Pacific Affairs of the Committee on Foreign Affairs. *Political Developments in Taiwan.* Hearing, 98th Congress, 2nd Session, May 31, 1984. Washington D.C.: GPO, 1985.

———. Defense Policy Panel of the Committee on Armed Services. *Potential Threats to American Security in the Post–Cold War Era.* Hearing, 102nd Congress, 1st Session, December 10, 11, and 13, 1991.

———. The Defense and Policy Panel and the Committee on Armed Services. *Regional Threats and Defense Options for the 1990s.* Hearing. 102nd Congress, 2nd Session, March 10, 1993.

———. Subcommittee on Asian and Pacific Affairs of the Committee on Foreign Affairs. *The United States and the People's Republic of China: Issues for the 1980s.* Hearing, 96th Congress, 2nd Session, April 1, July 22, August 26, and September 23, 1980.

———. Subcommittee on Asian and Pacific Affairs of the Committee on Foreign Affairs. *Taiwan: The Upcoming National Assembly Elections.* Hearing, 102nd Congress, 1st Session, September 24, 1991. Washington D.C.: GPO, 1992.

U.S. Congress. Senate. Committee on Foreign Relations. *China and Taiwan.* Hearing, 97th Congress, 2nd Session, August 17, 1982. Washington D.C.: GPO, 1982.

———. Subcommittee on East Asian and Pacific Affairs, Foreign Relations Committee. *Growth and Role of the Chinese Military.* Hearing, 104th Congress, 1st Session, October 11, 12, 1995.

———. Committee on Foreign Relations. *The Future of Taiwan.* Hearing, 98th Congress, 1st Session, November 9, 1983.

———. Committee on Foreign Relations. *The Future of Taiwan.* Hearing, 98th Congress, 1st Session, November 9, 1983. Washington D.C: GPO, 1984.

———. Committee on Foreign Relations. *Nomination of Warren M. Christopher to Be Secretary of State.* Hearing, 103rd Congress, 1st Session, January 13 and 14, 1993.

———. Committee on Governmental Affairs. *Proliferation Threats of the 1990s.* Hearing, 103rd Congress, 1st Session, February 24, 1993.

———. Committee on Armed Service. *The President's Report on the U.S. Military Presence in East Asia.* Hearing, 101st Congress, 2nd Session, April 19, 1990.

———. Committee on Governmental Affairs. *Proliferation Threats of the 1990s.* Hearing, 103rd Congress, 1st Session, February 24, 1993.

———. Subcommittee on East Asian and Pacific Affairs of the Committee on Foreign Relations. *Sino-American Relations: Current Policy Issues.* Hearing, 102nd Congress, 1st Session, June 13, 25, and 27, 1991.

———. Committee on the Judiciary. *Taiwan Communiqué and Separation of Powers, Part One.* Report, June 1983. Washington D.C.: GPO, 1983.

———. Subcommittee on Separation of Powers of the Committee on the Judiciary. *Taiwan Communiqué and Separation of Powers, Part Two.* Hearing, 98th Congress, 1st Session, March 10, 1983. Washington D.C.: GPO, 1983.

———. Committee on Foreign Relations. *Trips to Taiwan, Hong Kong, Indonesia and Papua New Guinea.* Report, April 1992. Washington, D.C.: GPO, 1992.

———. Subcommittee on East Asian and Pacific Affairs. *U.S. Policy Toward China.* Hearing, 103rd Congress, 2nd Session, May 4, 1994.

U.S. Congress. House and Senate. Joint Economic Committee. *China's Economic Dilemmas in the 1990s: The Problems of Reforms, Modernization and Interdependence—Volumes 1 and 2.* Study Papers. Washington, D.C.: GPO, 1991.

U.S. Congress, Congressional Research Service. *Conventional Arms Transfers to the Third World, 1985–1992.* Washington, D.C.: GPO, 1993.

———. *Conventional Arms Transfers to the Third World, 1986–1993.* Washington, D.C.: GPO, 1994.

———. *China as a Security Concern in Asia: Perceptions, Assessment and U.S. Options.* Washington, D.C.: GPO, January 5, 1994.

———. *What Should Be the Policy of the United States Toward the People's Republic of China?* Washington, D.C.: GPO, 1994.

U.S. Congress. General Accounting Office. *Impact of China's Military Modernization in the Pacific Region.* Washington, D.C.: General Accounting Office, June 1995.

———. *National Security: Perspectives on Worldwide Threats and Implications for U.S. Forces.* Washington, D.C.: GPO, 1992.

U.S. Department of Commerce. International Trade Administration. *U.S. Foreign Trade Highlights, 1991.* Washington, D.C.: U.S. Department of Commerce, May 1992.

U.S. Department of Defense. Office of International Security. *United States Security Strategy for the East-Asia Pacific Region.* Washington, D.C.: The Pentagon, February 1995.

U.S. Department of State. "Conference of President Roosevelt, Generalissimo Chiang Kai-shek and Prime Minister Churchill in North Africa." *Department of State Bulletin* 9, no. 232 (December 4, 1943): 393.

———. "Proclamation Defining Terms for Japanese Surrender." *Department of State Bulletin* 13, no. 318 (July 29, 1945): 137–138.

———. "United States Policy Toward Formosa." *Department of State Bulletin* 22, no. 550 (January 16, 1950): 79–81.

———. "Taiwan Policy Review." *Department of State Dispatch* 5, no. 42 (October 17, 1994): 11.

———. *U.S. Department of State Foreign Relations of the United States 1950, Volume VI.* Washington D.C.: GPO, 1976.

———. *United States Relations with China.* Washington, D.C.: Department of State, Division of Publications, Office of Public Affairs, 1949.

U.S. International Trade Commission. *The Year in Trade, 1993: Operation of the*

Trade Agreements Program, 45th Report. Washington, D.C.: USITC Publications, June 1994.
U.S. Secretary of Defense. *Annual Report to the President and the Congress.* Washington, D.C.: GPO, February 1995.
U.S. Trade Representative. *The 1995 National Trade Estimate Report on Foreign Trade Barriers.* Washington, D.C.: GPO, 1995.

ROC Government Documents and Political Publications

Democratic Progressive Party. *Charter and Platform.* Taipei: Democratic Progressive Party Headquarters, 1994.
———. *Defense Policy Guidelines.* Taipei: Democratic Progressive Party, 1994.
———. *The Foreign Policy Stance of the Democratic Progressive Party.* Taipei: Democratic Progressive Party, June 20, 1993.
———. *Give Taiwan a Chance.* Taipei: Democratic Progressive Party, 1995.
Kwang Hwa Publishing Company, ed. *The Republic of China Is on the Move.* Taipei: Kwang Hwa Publishing Company, 1979.
ROC China Information Service. *Suppressing Communist-Banditry in China,* 2d edition. Shanghai: China United Press, 1934.
ROC Council for Economic Planning and Development. *Taiwan Statistical Data Book, 1992.* Taipei: Council for Economic Planning and Development, July 1992.
ROC Government Information Office. *A Study of a Possible Communist Attack on Taiwan.* Taipei: Government Information Office, 1992.
———. *Regional Security and Economic Cooperation: The Case for the Asian-Pacific Region.* Taipei: Government Information Office, October 1992.
———. *The Republic of China Yearbook, 1991–92.* Taipei: Kwang Hwa Publishing, 1991.
———. *The Republic of China Yearbook, 1993.* Taipei: Government Information Office, 1993.
———. *The Republic of China Yearbook, 1995.* Taipei: Government Information Office, 1995.
ROC Mainland Affairs Council. *Questions and Answers on the Guidelines for National Unification.* Taipei: Mainland Affairs Council, August 1993.
———. *Relations Across the Taiwan Straits.* Taipei: Mainland Affairs Council, July 1994.
———. *There Is No "Taiwan Question," There Is Only a "China Question."* Taipei: Mainland Affairs Council, September 16, 1993.
ROC Ministry of National Defense. *1992 National Defense Report, Republic of China.* Taipei: Li Ming Cultural Enterprise Co., 1992.
———. *1993–1994 National Defense Report.* Taipei: Li Ming Cultural Enterprise Co., 1994.

Interviews

Chang, Shallyen, director-general of Kuomintang Overseas Affairs Department and vice minister of foreign affairs, Republic of China. Interview by author, February 7, 1990. Tape recording, Taipei.

Chang, Shallyen, vice minister of foreign affairs, Republic of China. Interview by author, January 8, 1992. Tape recording, Taipei.
Chen, Stephen S. F., vice minister of foreign affairs, Republic of China. Interview by author, May 19, 1994. Tape recording, Taipei.
Chiang Wego, General (ret.), Republic of China. Interview by author, May 17, 1994. Tape recording, Taipei.
———. Interview by author, February 5, 1996. Tape recording, Taipei.
Chien, Fredrick, foreign minister, Republic of China. Interview by author, July 14, 1992. Tape recording, Taipei.
———. Interview by author, February 7, 1996. Tape recording, Taipei.
Fellows, Geoffrey, foreign affairs advisor, Democratic Progressive Party, Republic of China. Interview by author, May 16, 1994. Tape recording, Taipei.
Ho, Samuel, research associate, Institute of International Relations, National Chengchi University. Interview by author, February 8, 1996. Tape recording, Taipei.
Su Chi, vice chairman, Mainland Affairs Council, Republic of China. Interview by author, February 6, 1996. Tape recording, Taipei.
Wang, H. C., legislator, Committee of National Defense, Legislative Yuan, Republic of China. Interview by author, May 16, 1994. Tape recording, Taipei.
Yao, Jeff, counselor, Government Information Office, Republic of China, and director, *Free China Journal,* Taipei, Taiwan. Interview by author, January 8, 1992.
Yeh, Albert T. H., deputy director, Government Information Office, Republic of China. Interview by author, February 7, 1996. Tape recording, Taipei.

INDEX

Acheson, Dean, 142
ADB. *See* Asian Development Bank
ADHPMs. *See* Artillery-delivered high-precision munitions
AEC. *See* Atomic Energy Council
Aero Industry Development Center (AIDC), 22, 30
AIDC. *See* Aero Industry Development Center
Aircraft, 19, 20, 24(table), 39; AN-124 transport, 158; Backfire bomber, 165; electronic countermeasure pods, 78; engines, 78, 155, 158; E-2T early-warning, 20, 39, 71, 80, 89(n31), 158; F-5 series fighter, 22, 24(table), 38, 164; F-7 fighter, 158; F-16 series fighter, 20, 23, 24(table), 38, 71, 77–79, 85, 86, 158, 185, 186; F-104 series fighter, 22, 24(table), 38, 164; FX fighter, 83; Il transport, 155, 158; Indigenous Defense Fighter (IDF) (Chiang Ching-kuo fighter), 20, 22–23, 24(table), 38, 42, 87, 91(n69), 164; MiG-29 fighter, 20; MiG-31 fighter, 158; Mirage 2000-5 fighter, 20, 23, 24(table), 38, 79–80, 86–87, 89(n20), 185, 186; navigation system, 78; pilot training, 78–79; PRC, 20, 68, 155, 158–159; radar systems, 77, 78, 79, 80, 88(n9), 159; refueling, 155, 158, 164–165, 167(n30); Su-24 fighter, 20; Su-27 fighter, 20, 68, 155, 158, 164, 167(n30), 185; T-38 trainer, 20, 39, 78–79; Tu-22M bomber, 158–159. *See also* Helicopters
Air defense systems, 16, 39, 80, 88; Chang Wang (Strengthened Net), 19; Modified Air Defense System (MADS), 39, 80; Tien Wuang (Sky Net), 19. *See also* Missiles, Patriot
Air Force: PRC, 20, 158–159, 185; ROC, 19–20, 21(table), 23–24, 29, 38–39. *See also* Military equipment
AIT. *See* American Institute in Taiwan
American Asian Research Enterprise, 192
American Institute in Taiwan (AIT), 52(n33), 114
Amnesty International, 67
Amphibious forces, 18, 25, 26, 43, 158, 186
Antisubmarine forces, 18, 19, 38, 81, 82, 158, 186
ANZUS treaty (Australia, New Zealand, United States), 60
APEC. *See* Asia Pacific Economic Cooperation
Armed forces: PRC-ROC comparison, 21–22; ROC budget, 29; ROC command, 15; ROC personnel, 27–29, 30, 34(n84); ROC reserve, 15, 21. *See also* Air Force; Amphibious forces; Antisubmarine forces; Arms sales/purchases; Army; Marine Corps; Military equipment; Navy
Arms race: Asian, 2, 163–164, 168(nn 56, 58), 187
Arms sales/purchases, 2, 83–87, 105, 147, 168(n56). *See also* Military equipment; *individual countries*
Army: PRC, 159; ROC, 15–17, 21(table); ROC Armed Forces Police, 15, 16, 31(n6); ROC force levels, 17, 28–29, 38, 39. *See also* Military equipment

223

INDEX

Artillery-delivered high-precision munitions (ADHPMs), 88
Asian Development Bank (ADB), 121, 122, 197
Asia Open Forum (1995), 47
Asia Pacific Economic Cooperation (APEC), 122, 197
Asia Pacific Policy Center, 174
Asia Watch, 67
Association for Relations Across the Taiwan Straits (ARATS) (PRC), 48
Association of East Asian Relations (Japan), 120
Association of Parents of Students Abroad (ROC), 28
Atomic Energy Council (AEC) (ROC), 42, 52(n24)
Australia, 118(table), 163, 186

Baker, Howard, 192
Balaguer, John, 78
Ball, Desmond, 163
Barshefsky, Charlene, 64
Bentsen, Lloyd, 63, 86, 103
Bereuter, Doug, 179
Betts, Richard, 46
Biological weapons, 160
Blockade, 12, 18, 19, 186–187
Boutros-Ghali, Boutros, 122
Brzezinski, Zbigniew, 62, 69
Buchanan, Patrick, 172
Bush, George, 46, 120, 192; arms sales, 71, 86; human rights, 66, 71, 74(nn 39, 41)
Buzan, Barry, 8

Cairo Declaration (1943), 136, 137, 142
Cambodia, 175
Canada, 104, 118(table)
Cannons: M197 20mm, 81
Carpenter, Ted, 172
Carter, Jimmy, 175
Cato Institute, 172
CCNAA. *See* Coordinating Council for North American Affairs
CCP. *See* Chinese Communist Party
Center for Strategic and International Studies (U.S.), 24
Central Intelligence Agency (CIA). *See* United States
Central News Agency (ROC), 24

Chamber of Commerce (ROC), 27
Chang Hsien-yi, 42, 43, 52(n33)
Chang Hui-yuan, 53(n54)
Chang Shallyen, 40–41, 70–71, 107, 124, 191
Chemical weapons, 75(n50), 160
Cheng Ch'eng Kung, 136
Cheng Lin, 106
Chen Guoqing, 11
Chen Hsi-fan, 117
Chen Li-an, 84, 94(table)
Chen, Stephen S. F., 37–38, 53(n55)
Chen Yi, 137
Cheung, Tai-ming, 187
Chiang Ching-kuo, 22, 94, 95–97, 114, 139
Chiang Chung-ling, 80
Chiang Kai-shek, 26–27; democratization, 93, 96(table); economic development, 99, 102, 140; and PRC, 140, 149(n29); and UN, 114; U.S. recognition, 60, 137
Chiang Wego, 96, 105, 140, 194
Chien, Fredrick, 102, 122, 125; defense, 12, 47, 87; one-China policy, 116, 140; relations, 108, 126, 129(n15), 190
China. *See* People's Republic of China; Republic of China
China External Trade Development Council (ROC), 127
China Shipbuilding Corporation (ROC), 81
Chinese Civil War, 59–60, 142, 161
Chinese Communist Party (CCP), 106, 107, 115, 138, 140, 154, 191
Chinese Social Democratic Party, 94
Ching dynasty, 136
Chiu Yi-jen, 27
Chou En-lai, 140, 149(n29)
Chou Po-lun, 45
Christopher, Warren, 70, 173, 176
Chu Feng-chi, 26
Chung Shan Institute of Science and Technology (CSIST), 22, 42, 43, 45, 52(n24)
CIA (Central Intelligence Agency). *See* United States
Clinton, Bill, 71, 104, 120, 197; defense, 173, 174, 175, 176, 184; trade relations, 66, 68
Clough, Ralph N., 187

INDEX

Coast Guard (ROC), 20–21
Cohen, Elliot, 176
Cold War aftermath, 1, 28, 44, 146–147, 156, 172, 178
Collective security, 42, 46–47, 49, 54(n80), 126
Communication linkages, 9, 10, 41, 47, 120, 140, 193, 195, 201(n53). *See also* Substantive relations
Communiqués (U.S.-PRC), 150(nn 62, 63), 196; 1972 (Shanghai), 143, 144; 1978 (normalization), 143; 1979, 144; 1982, 84, 143, 144
Confucian tradition, 95, 102
Coordinating Council for North American Affairs (CCNAA) (U.S.), 71, 114, 120
Copper, John F., 50, 98
Cornell University, 11, 71, 125
Corruption, 25, 105, 145
Council for Advanced Policy Studies (ROC), 12
CSIST. *See* Chung Shan Institute of Science and Technology

da Cunha, Derek, 187
Dahl, Robert, 105
Dassault Aviation, 79, 86
Dassault, Serge, 79
Defense studies, 22, 155, 163, 173, 174, 175, 183, 186
Defense Treaty (U.S.-ROC) (1979), 39, 46, 62, 143
Democratic Progressive Party (DPP), 25, 94, 97(table), 105; defense, 22, 26, 28, 37, 178–179; independence, 26, 146, 147, 188, 199(n26); nuclear policy, 45, 48
Democratization, 2, 93–99, 103–105, 107, 139
Deng Xiaoping, 11, 48, 70, 190
Deterrence, 30, 37–38, 41, 43, 45, 50, 51(n19), 87
Ding Shou-chung, 86
Diplomatic relations, 2, 45, 85, 98, 104; dual recognition, 116, 140; history, 113–115; nations maintaining, 116, 117. *See also* Pragmatic diplomacy; Substantive relations
Dissidents, 93, 146
DPP. *See* Democratic Progressive Party
Dreyer, June Teufel, 161

Du Ling, 116
Dulles, John Foster, 143

East Asian Strategic Initiative (1992), 175
East China Sea, 18, 162
East-West Center (U.S.), 192
EC. *See* European Community
Economic development, 2, 8, 99–103; and democratization, 96–97; foreign relations, 85–86, 103–105, 114–115, 121–122, 126–127; PRC, 106, 192–193. *See also* Investment; Trade
Education, 136
Eisenhower, Dwight D., 26
Elections, 93–94, 107, 108(n4), 114; direct presidential, 94, 146, 157; PRC intimidation, 70, 157
Elites, 95–96
Entrepreneurship, 102
European Community (EC), 85
Exchanges, 9, 10, 41, 47, 140, 193, 195, 201(n53)
Exports: Taiwan, 102(table). *See also* Trade

Fairbank, John King, 60
Fang Chin-yen, 125–126
Fauroux, Roger, 120
Fishing: protection, 12, 17, 126
Ford, Gerald R., 192
Foreign exchange reserves, 85, 104, 105
Foreign Policy Research Institute (U.S.): Asia Program, 156
Formosa, 135, 136, 142; Republic of, 145
Formosan Association for Public Affairs, 147
Four Modernizations, 154
France, 85–86, 119(table), 120; arms sales to PRC, 83, 90(n51); arms sales to ROC, 17, 18, 20, 33(n65), 38, 79–80, 81–82, 86–87, 89(n20)
Freeman, Charles W., 12, 69

Gates, Robert, 154–155
GATT. *See* General Agreement on Tariffs and Trade
General Agreement on Tariffs and Trade (GATT), 65, 121, 127
General Dynamics Corporation, 77, 86

Germany, 38, 119(table)
Gilman, Benjamin, 70
Girardot, Dean, 86
Glenn, John, 46
GNP. *See* Gross national product
Godwin, Paul, 185
Goh Chok Tong, 163
Gold reserves, 85
Gold, Thomas, 195
Goure, Dan, 24
Government Information Office (ROC), 41, 43, 124
Grenada, 116
Gross national product (GNP), 85, 99, 100(table)
Grumman Aircraft Company, 80, 81, 89(n31)
Guam Doctrine (1969), 174
Guerrilla forces, 160–161
Guidelines for National Unification (ROC), 9, 47, 141
Gulf War, 155–156
Guns: Mk-15 Phalanx, 82

Haig, Alexander, 62
Hatano, Akira, 104
Hau Pei-tsun, 165
Havel, Vaclav, 120
Health care, 136
Hei You-long, 164
Helicopters, 18, 38, 39; AH-1W Cobra attack, 17, 81, 82; Mi17, 155; OH-58D Kiowa warrior scout, 17, 81, 82; PRC, 159; SH-2F Light Airborne Multipurpose System (LAMPS), 19, 81
Hills, Carla, 120
Ho, Samuel, 189
Hong Kong, 117, 118(table), 124, 139, 162
Hsu Hsin-liang, 26
Hu, Jason C., 124
Humanitarian intervention, 174
Human rights, 66–67, 74(n44), 84–85, 97. *See also* Tiananmen Square incident
Huntington, Samuel, 93

IAEA. *See* International Atomic Energy Agency
Ichiang Island, 27
IDF (Indigenous Defense Fighter). *See* Aircraft

IGOs. *See* International governmental organizations
IMF. *See* International Monetary Fund
Imports: PRC, 64–65; ROC, 102(table). *See also* Trade
Income: per capita, 85, 99, 101(table)
Independence, 2, 44, 45, 130(n46); domestic support, 26, 44(table), 188, 195, 197, 199(n26), 201(n64); 1895 declaration, 145; movement for, 125, 135–137, 139–141, 145–148, 187–188; opinion polls, 44, 188, 194, 195, 202(n67); PRC position, 11–12, 25–26, 34(n73), 125, 138–139, 148, 187, 194; U.S. position, 62, 141–145
Indigenous Defense Fighter (IDF). *See* Aircraft
Industry, 99, 100, 177
Infrastructure development, 85–86, 136, 165
Institute for International Relations (ROC), 189
Institute for National Policy Research (ROC), 186
Institute for National Strategic Studies (National Defense University) (U.S.), 155
Intellectual property rights, 65, 178, 185
Intelligence, 41
International Atomic Energy Agency (IAEA), 43, 52(n26)
International governmental organizations (IGOs), 121, 197, 202(n67). *See also* International organization membership
International Monetary Fund (IMF), 114, 121
International organization membership, 71, 124, 127; governmental (IGOs), 121, 197, 202(n67); nongovernmental (NGOs), 121, 122
International relations: state behavior, 189, 199(n30)
Invasion, 25, 26, 37–38
Investment, 27, 64, 138, 185; of ROC in PRC, 10, 14(n19), 107, 115, 195, 201(n63)
Isolationism: U.S., 171–174, 178

Japan, 44, 49, 104, 114, 120, 156, 187; Taiwan occupation, 136, 145–146

Jiang Zemin, 9, 138, 156
Jordan, Amos, 7

Kant, Immanuel, 107
Karinol, Robert, 159
Kinmen Island, 12, 16, 26, 27
Kissinger, Henry, 61
KMT. *See* Kuomintang
Kohut, Andrew, 178
Koo Chen-fu, 122
Koo Chung-lian, 23
Koo-Wang talks, 10
Korean War (1950–1953), 60–61, 137, 142, 162
Kreisberg, Paul H., 192
Kuan, John, 60
Ku Chong-lien, 87
Kuokkanen, Tarja, 104
Kuomintang (KMT), 93–94, 105, 178; democratization, 96, 97(table); post–World War II, 59, 60, 113, 137, 147
Kuo, Shirley, 122

Labor force, 99–100
LAMPS (Light Airborne Multipurpose System). *See* Helicopters
Land reform program, 102
Lantos, Tom, 72
Lasater, Martin, 185–186, 192
Laux, David, 85
Law on the Organization of Civic Groups (ROC), 94
Lee Cheng-chia, 114
Lee Teng-hui, 50, 115, 122, 141, 193; defense, 27, 40, 46, 47, 48, 164, 178; democratization, 96, 97, 98; presidential vote, 94; visits, 11, 71, 120, 125, 128
Legitimacy, 98, 103–104, 105
Lieberman, Joseph, 104
Lien Chan, 27, 50, 120, 123
Lilley, James R., 98, 125, 191
Lin, Albert, 163–164
Lin Biao, 140, 149(n29)
Lin Meng-kuei, 23
Lin Wen-li, 77
Lin Yang-kang, 94(table)
Li Peng, 11, 139
Lipset, Seymour Martin, 97–98
Liu Binyan, 106
Liu, David, 127
Liu Ho-chien, 19, 38

Liu Hui-hsiung, 45
Lockheed Corporation, 22, 24(table), 38, 77, 79
Loh, Christine, 107
Lord, Winston, 66, 184
Lung Ying-tai, 105

MacFarquhar, Roderick, 194
Mack, Andrew, 163
MADS (Modified Air Defense System). *See* Air defense systems
Mainland Affairs Council (ROC), 47, 72, 126, 141
Manchu dynasty, 136
Mao Zedong, 62, 138, 160
Marine Corps: PRC, 158; ROC, 18
Martial law, 22, 94, 95, 115
Matsu Island, 12, 16, 26, 27
Ma Ying-jeou, 47
McCurry, Michael, 144
Media, 93, 94, 105, 106
MFN. *See* Most-favored-nation status
Middle class, 97
Migration, 136
Military equipment: data links for, 24–25; ROC military production, 17, 20, 22–23, 87, 91(n69). *See also* Aircraft; Air defense systems; Artillery-delivered high-precision munitions; Cannons; Guns; Helicopters; Missiles; Submarines; Tanks; Torpedoes; Warships
Military maneuvers (PRC), 10, 70, 88, 162
Military Service Law, 27–28
Ming dynasty, 135–136
Missile defense systems. *See* Air defense systems
Missiles, 17, 38, 39, 77; ballistic, 80, 159, 165; Ching Feng (Green Bee) surface-to-surface, 42; Crotal ship-to-air, 82; Exocet ship-to-ship, 82; guidance technology, 155; Hai-feng shore-based, 18; Harpoon antiship, 71, 82; Hellfire antitank, 81; Hsiung Feng (Awe-Inspiring Air) antiship, 18, 32(n24), 38, 42; MICA air-to-air, 79; MIRV, 159; Mistral shoulder-fired, 17, 83; M-series, 69, 80, 162; Patriot, 17, 71, 155, 158; PRC, 80, 159, 162; S-300 surface-to-air, 155; SA-10 surface-to-air, 158;

228 INDEX

Sidewinder air-to-air, 20, 78, 81; Sparrow, 78; SS-20 ballistic, 165; Stinger, 17, 31(n9), 71; Tien Chien (Sky Arrow) surface-to-air, 91(n69); Tien Kung (Sky Bow) surface-to-air, 17, 42, 91(n69); TOW air-to-ground, 81. *See also* Air defense systems; Artillery-delivered high-precision munitions
Missile Technology Control Regime (MTCR), 68, 69, 75(n50)
Missile tests (PRC), 10, 26, 69, 70, 157
Missile threat (1996) (PRC), 12
Mong, Francis, 104
Montaperto, Ronald, 155
Moore, Barrington, 97
Morgenstern, Oskar, 41
Most-favored-nation (MFN) status, 66–67, 74(n41)
MTCR. *See* Missile Technology Control Regime
Munro, Ross, 156
Murray, Douglas, 7
Mutual Defense Treaty (U.S.-ROC) (1954), 39, 46, 62, 143

Nakayama, Taro, 191
National Association of Industry and Business (ROC), 27
National Defense Report (1992, 1993–1994) (ROC), 8, 13, 18, 123
National Federation of Industries (ROC), 27
Nationalism, 145–146; PRC, 190–191, 192
National security, 7–8, 123, 188, 199(n30)
Navy: PRC, 18, 157–158, 185; ROC, 17–19, 21(table), 23–24, 29, 31(n18), 38. *See also* Warships
NBC (National Broadcasting Corporation) (U.S.), 45
Netherlands, 119(table), 135–136
New Party, 26
NGOs. *See* Nongovernmental organizations
Niu Hsien-chung, 193
Nixon, Richard M., 61, 143, 174
Nonaggression pact, 42, 47–48, 49–50
Nongovernmental organizations (NGOs), 121, 122. *See also* International organization membership

North Korea, 44, 49, 185
Northrup Corporation, 22, 24(table), 38
NPT. *See* Nuclear Non-Proliferation Treaty
Nuclear Energy Research Institute (AEC) (ROC), 42, 52(n24)
Nuclear Non-Proliferation Treaty (NPT), 42, 43, 52(n26), 68, 75(n50)
Nuclear weapons, 11, 17, 42–46, 48–49, 53(nn 54, 55), 164; fuel reprocessing, 42; PRC, 61, 159; protests, 48–49
Nye, Joseph, 185

Oehler, Gordon, 46
Offshore islands (Penghu, Kinmen, Matsu), 16, 26–27, 34(n77), 61, 137, 162, 187
Okazaki, Hisahiko, 104
O'Leary, Hazel, 69
One-China policy: PRC position, 9, 11, 123, 138, 139; ROC position, 116–117, 123, 140, 141, 201(n64); U.S. position, 141–145, 147, 150(nn 62, 63). *See also* Unification
Opinion polls: democratization, 95–97; economic development, 106; independence, 44, 188, 194, 195, 202(n67); on PRC, 41, 63, 64(table); unification, 9, 195; U.S. Taiwan defense, 172, 178, 181(n31), 184, 198(n7)

Paal, Douglas, 174
Pacific Council (U.S.), 192
Paracel Islands, 143, 162, 165
Patriotism, 191
Peacekeeping, 176
Peace negotiations, 50, 107
Pell, Claiborne, 105
Pelosi, Nancy, 65
Peña, Federico, 120
Penghu Island, 16, 26, 27
Peng Ming-min, 26, 94(table)
People's Liberation Army (PLA), 12, 38, 67–69, 70, 154–162, 163–164, 165, 168(n58), 185–187; budget, 153–155, 166(n8); and CCP, 154, 191; commercial enterprises, 153, 185; and Gulf War, 155–156; service branches, 157–159; Sino-Soviet border, 165. *See also* Military equipment

People's Republic of China (PRC), 1, 113–114, 148, 194, 201(n54); arms purchases, 62, 63(table), 66, 68, 73(n22), 83, 90(n51), 155, 158; arms sales, 68; Central Military Commission, 187; democracy movement, 66, 74(n39); democratization of, 106–107; leadership succession, 11, 50, 190, 191; regional conflict, 161, 162, 165; regional power, 156–157; State Council, 67; threat of force on Taiwan, 8, 9, 10–12, 69, 70, 157, 162–163, 192–193. *See also* Military equipment; People's Liberation Army; ROC-PRC relations; Sino-Russian relations; Sino-Soviet relations; U.S.-PRC relations
People's War (PRC military doctrine), 160–162
Perry, William J., 160, 175, 184, 192
Philippines, 162, 175
PLA. *See* People's Liberation Army
PLAAF. *See* Air Force, PRC
PLAN. *See* Navy, PRC
Political parties, 93, 94, 97(table); multiparty state, 107. *See also individual parties*
Portugal, 119(table), 135
Postal service, 140
Potsdam Declaration (1945), 136, 142
Pragmatic diplomacy, 113, 115, 123–124, 125, 128; economic, 121–122, 126–127; PRC position, 128, 131(n60). *See also* Diplomatic relations; Substantive relations
Pratas Island, 12, 31(n18)
PRC. *See* People's Republic of China
Press, 93, 94, 106, 162
Private property, 138
Protectionism, 64–65, 127

Qiandao Lake boat murders, 44, 187–188
Quemoy Island. *See* Kinmen Island

Radar. *See* Aircraft
RAND Corporation, 68, 153, 154(table)
Raytheon Corporation, 78, 80
Reagan, Ronald, 62
Republic of China (ROC), 2, 8, 37–38, 123; arms purchases, 17, 18, 19, 20, 23–25, 29, 33(n65), 40(table), 71, 77–88, 91(n74), 193, 195, 196; Defense Ministry, 15, 16, 28, 39; defense reports, 8, 13, 18, 123; designations, 121–122, 124, 125; diplomatic/substantive recognition, 116–117, 118–119(tables), 120–121, 124–125; Interior Ministry, 28; Legislative Yuan, 93, 94, 98, 105; National Assembly, 94, 105, 108(n4); uprisings (1947, 1979), 137, 146. *See also* Armed forces; Economic development; Military equipment; Offshore islands; Political parties; ROC-PRC relations; Taiwan; U.S.-ROC relations
Republic of Taiwan, 146, 202(n67)
Resistance movements (ROC), 146
Richards, Ann, 86
Robinson, Thomas W., 192
ROC. *See* Republic of China
ROC-PRC relations, 1, 9, 10, 195–196, 202(n66); China representation, 113–115, 138–141; democratization and economic development, 106–107; exchanges/linkages, 9, 10, 41, 47, 140, 193, 195, 201(n53); investment, 10, 14(n19), 107, 115, 195, 201(n63); nuclear capability, 44, 45, 48; peace negotiations, 50, 107; ROC designation/international relations, 117, 121–125, 128, 131(n60); trade, 10, 115. *See also* Independence; Military maneuvers; Missile tests; Missile threat; Offshore islands; One-China policy; Substantive relations; Unification
ROC-Soviet relations, 61
Romm, Joseph, 7
Russia: arms sales, 2, 68, 155, 158, 163. *See also* Sino-Russian relations; Soviet Union
Rustow, Dankwart, 95

Sanctions, 69
Saudi Arabia, 117, 119(table), 129(n15)
SEATO. *See* South East Asia Treaty Organization
Security, 7–8, 123, 188, 199(n30). *See also* Armed forces; Collective security; Nuclear weapons
Separatist movements, 25, 146–147, 148, 194
Shalikashvili, John, 186
Shanghai communiqué (1972), 143, 144

Shaw Yu-ming, 43
Shih Ming-teh, 25, 27, 188, 199(n26)
Sicherman, Harvey, 172
Siew, Vincent, 127, 141
Simon, Paul, 103
Singapore, 118(table), 163
Sino-Japanese War (1895), 136
Sino-Russian relations, 164
Sino-Soviet relations, 60, 61, 162
Six-Year National Development Plan (ROC), 85
"Smart weapons," 88
South Africa, 116
South China Sea, 16, 17, 18, 26, 31(n18), 158, 162
South East Asian Treaty Organization (SEATO), 60
South Korea, 44, 49, 117, 129(n15), 184, 185
South Pacific Forum, 122
Sovereignty, 124, 137–140, 141, 150(n63). *See also* Unification
Soviet Union, 136, 162. *See also* ROC-Soviet relations; Russia; Sino-Soviet relations
Spain, 119(table), 135
Spratly Island, 31(n18), 143, 156, 162
Stuart, John Leighton, 59
Students, 28, 66
Submarines, 18, 19, 38, 87–88; Kilo-class, 68, 155, 157–158; Ming-class, 157; PRC, 18, 157–158, 159, 185; Xia-class, 159. *See also* Antisubmarine forces; Warships
Substantive relations, 104, 114, 115, 117–121, 126–127; nations maintaining, 118, 119(table), 120, 121. *See also* International organization membership; Pragmatic diplomacy
Su Chi, 72, 126
Su Jing-chang, 186
Sun Chen, 18, 26, 44, 47, 156, 165
Sun Yat-sen, 96; Center for Policy Studies, 155
Sun Zu, 160
Su Shaozhi, 107

Tachen Islands, 27
Taipei Economic and Cultural Representative Office, 71, 104, 110(n45), 118–119(tables), 120
Taipei Representative Office, 110(n45), 118(table)

Taiwan, 135–137, 146, 202(n67); "fever," 106. *See also* Republic of China
Taiwan Relations Act (TRA) (1979), 39–40, 51(n10), 97, 128(n5), 144, 150(n62), 184–185, 193, 194, 196, 198, 201(n59)
Taiwan Strait, 12, 17, 60, 137, 162
Tanks, 18, 39, 175; M48A-series, 17; M48H "Brave Tiger," 17; M60, 17; M60-A3, 17, 29, 71, 82, 83; PRC, 159; T-72, 155, 159
Taylor, William, 7
Technology transfer, 39
Teheran Conference (1945), 136
Television, 94, 105
Thailand, 118(table), 164
Thatcher, Margaret, 107, 174
Third World nations, 75, 104, 122, 127, 131(n56)
Thomson CSF (corporation), 79, 81
Tiananmen Square incident, 66, 84–85, 74(n39), 154
Tien, Hung-mao, 97
Torpedoes, 38, 82; Mk-46, 19, 71. *See also* Submarines; Warships
TRA. *See* Taiwan Relations Act
Trade: regional, 127, 130(n56); Taiwan rank in world, 100–101, 102(table); transshipments, 65. *See also* ROC-PRC relations; U.S.-ROC relations
Trade Council (U.S.-ROC), 85
Travel, 10, 71, 120, 140, 193, 195, 201(n53)
Treaty of Shimonoseki (1895), 136
Truman, Harry S, 60, 137, 141–142
Tsai Cheng-wen, 128
Tucker, Nancy Bernkopf, 190
Tungyin Island, 32(n24)
21st Century Foundation (ROC), 125
Two-Chinas policy, 139

Unification: opinion polls, 9, 188(table), 195; PRC position, 9, 10–11, 25–26, 47, 50, 63, 107, 123–124, 138–139, 140, 201(n52); ROC position, 9, 11–12, 47, 49, 99, 123–124, 141, 193, 195, 210(n64). *See also* One-China policy
United Kingdom, 119(table), 136
United Nations, 72, 98, 104, 113–114, 121, 122, 124, 130(n46), 143
United States, 136, 118(table), 197(n7);

INDEX

Arms Control and Disarmament Agency, 154(table), 173; arms sales to PRC, 62, 63(table), 66, 73(n22); arms sales to ROC, 17, 19, 20, 23–25, 29, 40(table), 71, 77–79, 80–81, 82–84, 86, 88, 91(n74), 193, 195, 196; Asian defense, 178; Central Intelligence Agency (CIA), 42–43, 52(n33), 63, 153, 154(table); collective security, 46–47, 60; Commerce Department, 173; Congress, 70, 72, 86, 88, 91(n74), 97–98, 114, 143, 173; Defense Department, 143, 144, 154(table), 183; defense spending, 175–176; defense studies, 163, 173, 174, 183; General Accounting Office, 153, 174; Information Agency, 173; isolationism, 171–175, 178, 184; PRC missile threat, 70; State Department, 67, 71–72, 76(n68), 142, 143, 173, 191; troop strength, 175, 184. *See also* U.S.-PRC relations; U.S.-ROC relations; U.S.-Soviet relations

U.S.-PRC relations, 2, 59–64, 69–72, 83–84; communiqués, 84, 143, 144, 150(nn 62, 63), 196; economic, 64–65; human rights, 66–67; normalization, 62, 73(n17), 114; Taiwan status, 84, 142, 143, 144, 145, 150(nn 62, 63); trade, 64–65, 74(n32); unification, 193; U.S. arms sales to Taiwan, 83–84; U.S. domestic reaction, 65, 66–67, 74(n39); U.S. naval defense of Taiwan, 185

U.S.-ROC relations, 2, 71–72, 76(n68), 97–98, 143; defense, 39, 46, 60, 62, 143, 178–179, 183–185, 192–197; economic, 85, 86, 102, 103(table), 185; Taiwan status, 62, 73(n17), 84, 114, 141–145, 150(nn 62, 63), 196; trade, 2, 176–178, 179, 185. *See also* Diplomatic relations; Substantive relations; Taiwan Relations Act

U.S.-Soviet relations, 61

Veteran Affairs Council, 30

Vietnam, 161, 162, 175
Viotti, Paul, 7

Wachman, Alan, 94
Waltz, Kenneth, 157
Wang Daohan, 48
Wang, H. C., 49
Warships, 18, 19, 38, 176; Dayun-class resupply, 157; Houjian missile patrol, 157; Houxin-class patrol, 147; Jiangwei-class frigate, 157; Knox-class destroyer, 19, 71; Knox-class frigate, 38, 82; Kuanghua-I, 38; LaFayette-class frigate, 18, 38, 81; Luhu-class destroyer, 157; minesweeper, 18, 19, 38; Perry-class frigate, 18; PRC, 157–158; Varyag aircraft carrier, 158
Weapons systems. *See* Military equipment
Westinghouse Electric Corporation, 78
Wolfers, Arnold, 7
Woody Island, 165
Woolsey, R. James, 44
World Bank, 114, 121
World Trade Organization (WTO), 65, 72
World War II, 136–137, 161
WTO. *See* World Trade Organization
Wu, Jaushieh Joseph, 93
Wuchiu Island, 12, 187
Wu Jiaxiang, 106
Wu Jinglian, 106
Wu Ta-you, 42
Wylie, J. C., 37

Yang, Andrew, 12, 155
Yan Jiaqi, 106
Yeh Chang-tung, 38
Yellow Sea, 18
Yen Chen-hsiung, 42
Yen Chia-kan, 96(table)
Yin Ching-feng, 25, 33(n65)
Youth, 106
You Ying-lung, 184

Zhang Wannian, 187
Zhongguo, 141

ABOUT THE BOOK

One of the most critical tasks facing Taiwan's government in the post–Cold War era is the need to reassess its security environment. In this context, Hickey discusses the island's security concerns, the structure and composition of its armed forces, and its defensive strategy. He also explores the opportunities and challenges for Taipei generated by recent transformations in the international system.

Hickey suggests that, on balance, the end of the Cold War and a conjunction of several long-term trends are combining to enhance Taiwan's security. He cautions, however, that domestic political developments within the People's Republic of China may offset some of the gains generated by systemic changes. These domestic considerations played a paramount role in the perilous deterioration of cross-Strait relations during 1995 and 1996.

Dennis Van Vranken Hickey is associate professor of political science at Southwest Missouri State University. He is author of *U.S.-Taiwan Security Ties: From the Cold War to Beyond Containment.*